Deadpool and Philosophy

Popular Culture and Philosophy® Series Editor: George A. Reisch

Volume 1 *Seinfeld and Philosophy: A Book about Everything and Nothing* (2000)

Volume 2 *The Simpsons and Philosophy: The D'oh! of Homer* (2001)

Volume 3 *The Matrix and Philosophy: Welcome to the Desert of the Real* (2002)

Volume 4 *Buffy the Vampire Slayer and Philosophy: Fear and Trembling in Sunnydale* (2003)

Volume 9 *Harry Potter and Philosophy: If Aristotle Ran Hogwarts* (2004)

Volume 12 *Star Wars and Philosophy: More Powerful than You Can Possibly Imagine* (2005)

Volume 13 *Superheroes and Philosophy: Truth, Justice, and the Socratic Way* (2005)

Volume 19 *Monty Python and Philosophy: Nudge Nudge, Think Think!* (2006)

Volume 30 *Pink Floyd and Philosophy: Careful with that Axiom, Eugene!* (2007)

Volume 35 *Star Trek and Philosophy: The Wrath of Kant* (2008)

Volume 36 *The Legend of Zelda and Philosophy: I Link Therefore I Am* (2008)

Volume 42 *Supervillains and Philosophy: Sometimes Evil Is Its Own Reward* (2009)

Volume 45 *World of Warcraft and Philosophy: Wrath of the Philosopher King* (2009) Edited by Luke Cuddy and John Nordlinger

Volume 46 *Mr. Monk and Philosophy: The Curious Case of the Defective Detective* (2010) Edited by D.E. Wittkower

Volume 48 *The Red Sox and Philosophy: Green Monster Meditations* (2010) Edited by Michael Macomber

Volume 49 *Zombies, Vampires, and Philosophy: New Life for the Undead* (2010) Edited by Richard Greene and K. Silem Mohammad

Volume 51 *Soccer and Philosophy: Beautiful Thoughts on the Beautiful Game* (2010) Edited by Ted Richards

Volume 52 *Manga and Philosophy: Fullmetal Metaphysician* (2010) Edited by Josef Steiff and Adam Barkman

Volume 53 *Martial Arts and Philosophy: Beating and Nothingness* (2010) Edited by Graham Priest and Damon Young

Volume 54 *The Onion and Philosophy: Fake News Story True, Alleges Indignant Area Professor* (2010) Edited by Sharon M. Kaye

Volume 55 *Doctor Who and Philosophy: Bigger on the Inside* (2010) Edited by Courtland Lewis and Paula Smithka

Volume 57 *Rush and Philosophy: Heart and Mind United* (2011) Edited by Jim Berti and Durrell Bowman

Volume 58 *Dexter and Philosophy: Mind over Spatter* (2011) Edited by Richard Greene, George A. Reisch, and Rachel Robison-Greene

Volume 60 *SpongeBob SquarePants and Philosophy: Soaking Up Secrets Under the Sea!* (2011) Edited by Joseph J. Foy

Volume 61 *Sherlock Holmes and Philosophy: The Footprints of a Gigantic Mind* (2011) Edited by Josef Steiff

Volume 63 *Philip K. Dick and Philosophy: Do Androids Have Kindred Spirits?* (2011) Edited by D.E. Wittkower

Volume 64 *The Rolling Stones and Philosophy: It's Just a Thought Away* (2012) Edited by Luke Dick and George A. Reisch

Volume 67 *Breaking Bad and Philosophy: Badder Living through Chemistry* (2012) Edited by David R. Koepsell and Robert Arp

Volume 68 *The Walking Dead and Philosophy: Zombie Apocalypse Now* (2012) Edited by Wayne Yuen

Volume 69 *Curb Your Enthusiasm and Philosophy: Awaken the Social Assassin Within* (2012) Edited by Mark Ralkowski

Volume 71 *The Catcher in the Rye and Philosophy: A Book for Bastards, Morons, and Madmen* (2012) Edited by Keith Dromm and Heather Salter

Volume 72 *Jeopardy! and Philosophy: What Is Knowledge in the Form of a Question?* (2012) Edited by Shaun P. Young

Volume 73 *The Wire and Philosophy: This America, Man* (2013) Edited by David Bzdak, Joanna Crosby, and Seth Vannatta

Volume 74 *Planet of the Apes and Philosophy: Great Apes Think Alike* (2013) Edited by John Huss

Volume 75 *Psych and Philosophy: Some Dark Juju-Magumbo* (2013) Edited by Robert Arp

Volume 79 *Frankenstein and Philosophy: The Shocking Truth* (2013) Edited by Nicolas Michaud

Volume 80 *Ender's Game and Philosophy: Genocide Is Child's Play* (2013) Edited by D.E. Wittkower and Lucinda Rush

Volume 81 *How I Met Your Mother and Philosophy: Being and Awesomeness* (2014) Edited by Lorenzo von Matterhorn

Volume 82 *Jurassic Park and Philosophy: The Truth Is Terrifying* (2014) Edited by Nicolas Michaud

Volume 83 *The Devil and Philosophy: The Nature of His Game* (2014) Edited by Robert Arp

Volume 84 *Leonard Cohen and Philosophy: Various Positions* (2014) Edited by Jason Holt

Volume 85 *Homeland and Philosophy: For Your Minds Only* (2014) Edited by Robert Arp

Volume 86 *Girls and Philosophy: This Book Isn't a Metaphor for Anything* (2014) Edited by Richard Greene and Rachel Robison-Greene

Volume 87 *Adventure Time and Philosophy: The Handbook for Heroes* (2015) Edited by Nicolas Michaud

Volume 88 *Justified and Philosophy: Shoot First, Think Later* (2015) Edited by Rod Carveth and Robert Arp

Volume 89 *Steve Jobs and Philosophy: For Those Who Think Different* (2015) Edited by Shawn E. Klein

Volume 90 *Dracula and Philosophy: Dying to Know* (2015) Edited by Nicolas Michaud and Janelle Pötzsch

Volume 91 *It's Always Sunny and Philosophy: The Gang Gets Analyzed* (2015) Edited by Roger Hunt and Robert Arp

Volume 92 *Orange Is the New Black and Philosophy: Last Exit from Litchfield* (2015) Edited by Richard Greene and Rachel Robison-Greene

Volume 93 *More Doctor Who and Philosophy: Regeneration Time* (2015) Edited by Courtland Lewis and Paula Smithka

Volume 94 *Divergent and Philosophy: The Factions of Life* (2016) Edited by Courtland Lewis

Volume 95 *Downton Abbey and Philosophy: Thinking in That Manor* (2016) Edited by Adam Barkman and Robert Arp

Volume 96 *Hannibal Lecter and Philosophy: The Heart of the Matter* (2016) Edited by Joseph Westfall

Volume 97 *The Ultimate Walking Dead and Philosophy: Hungry for More* (2016) Edited by Wayne Yuen

Volume 98 *The Princess Bride and Philosophy: Inconceivable!* (2016) Edited by Richard Greene and Rachel Robison-Greene

Volume 99 *Louis C.K. and Philosophy: You Don't Get to Be Bored* (2016) Edited by Mark Ralkowski

Volume 100 *Batman, Superman, and Philosophy: Badass or Boyscout?* (2016) Edited by Nicolas Michaud

Volume 101 *Discworld and Philosophy: Reality Is Not What It Seems* (2016) Edited by Nicolas Michaud

Volume 102 *Orphan Black and Philosophy: Grand Theft DNA* 2016) Edited by Richard Greene and Rachel Robison-Greene

Volume 103 *David Bowie and Philosophy: Rebel Rebel* (2016) Edited by Theodore G. Ammon

Volume 104 *Red Rising and Philosophy: Break the Chains!* (2016) Edited by Courtland Lewis and Kevin McCain

Volume 105 *The Ultimate Game of Thrones and Philosophy: You Think or Die* (2016) Edited by Eric J. Silverman and Robert Arp

Volume 106 *Peanuts and Philosophy: You're a Wise Man, Charlie Brown* (2017) Edited by Richard Greene and Rachel Robison-Greene

Volume 107 *Deadpool and Philosophy: My Common Sense Is Tingling* (2017) Edited by Nicolas Michaud

In Preparation:

The X-Files and Philosophy: The Truth Is in Here (2017) Edited by Robert Arp

Hamilton and Philosophy (2017) Edited by Aaron Rabinowitz and Robert Arp

Mr. Robot and Philosophy (2017) Edited by Richard Greene and Rachel Robison-Greene

The Man in the High Castle and Philosophy (2017) Edited by Bruce Krajewski and Joshua Heter

Jimi Hendrix and Philosophy (2017) Edited by Theodore G. Ammon

Twin Peaks and Philosophy (2017) Edited by Richard Greene and Rachel Robison-Greene

For full details of all Popular Culture and Philosophy® books, visit www.opencourtbooks.com.

Popular Culture and Philosophy®

Deadpool and Philosophy

My Common Sense Is Tingling

Edited by

NICOLAS MICHAUD AND
JACOB THOMAS MAY

OPEN COURT
Chicago

Volume 107 in the series, Popular Culture and Philosophy®, edited by George A. Reisch

To find out more about Open Court books, call toll-free 1-800-815-2280, or visit our website at www.opencourtbooks.com.

Open Court Publishing Company is a division of Carus Publishing Company, dba Cricket Media.

First printing 2017

Printed and bound in the United States of America.

Deadpool and Philosophy: My Common Sense Is Tingling

ISBN: 978-0-8126-9949-4.

Library of Congress Control Number: 2016959381

This book is also available as an e-book.

Contents

Jacob would like to dedicate this book to his Uncle Shane, who sparked his love of comics in the first place, to his wife Jessica—who kept it aflame with her own nerdiness, and his friend Nick who keeps on (wrongly) arguing with him about who would win made-up pointless comic battles (like Supes vs. Bats or Goku). May all of us never grow up . . . like ever.

Oh, and also to Deadpool and Ryan Reynolds—may neither of you ever realize that you haven't grown up yet.

Nick would like to dedicate this book to himself, because, let's be honest, who else ever will? (Well obviously Jake in the above dedication, who has been a devoted and true friend, but it doesn't count because that's what fifty bucks will get you).

It's About F*$&ing Time

Let's be honest, we've been waiting way too long for an R-rated philosophy book.

Well now, here you hold it in your hands, so treat it gently, so very, very gently.

Let this naughty little book whisper deep thoughts into your ear. And then, when they get a little hard, really dig in, you know, push it. Don't stop . . . keep going, just grind away at it. Grind, and grind. And if you think it'll end too soon, think about something else for a minute: Ryan Reynolds riding a unicorn across a field of rainbows perhaps (unless that's your thing and you find yourself too distracted). And then, finally, everything goes bright, and there you are, sweating, heaving, and enlightened.

The fact is, Deadpool brings us a (literally) obscene number of philosophical questions. Deadpool fans have known his importance for many years. It has just taken us way too fapping long to get to a book about him. Why? Well probably because we were waiting for a movie to capitalize off of. Outside of that, there's no good reason.

Deadpool makes us question the nature of mortality, morality, and the multiverse. He makes us wonder about killing others, killing ourselves, and killing ideas. He challenges what it means to be a hero, what it means to be a villain, and what it means to be an asshole. And he makes us doubt ourselves . . . like a damned good philosopher.

Let's face it, Deadpool is confusing. He makes us feel bad for laughing, good for doing evil, and worried about the state of our immortal (maybe) souls. It isn't possible to side with Deadpool without feeling a little dirty (and not always in a good way). But we can't just call him a villain, because, dammit, he's often one of the most self-sacrificing, and, honestly, pathetic wanna-be heroes out there. Deadpool is honest, he tells it to us like it is, except when he isn't, and then he asks us why the hell we were listening to him in the first place and flicks us off. Bastard. Damned honest bastard.

Here's the truth . . . Philosophy is honest—at least it used to be. It's about admitting that there are questions so difficult that no one knows the answer. It means being able to laugh when you realize you are wrong, and actually trying to do something about it. Philosophers, are supposed to be a lot more like Deadpool—people who aren't scared to look into the abyss and see reality for what it is. And when they can't make out what scary shit is down there, laugh and jump in anyway. Philosophers shouldn't be afraid of admitting they don't know, and, like Deadpool, they should be willing to tell people what they *do* know (if anything) . . . even if it makes them the villains. In other words, in this book we aren't going to try to be heroes. We aren't going to try to make you like us. For once, we are going to try to do our f*$&ing jobs and share the best questions, and half-answers we can come up with it. And if you don't like it, well, we aren't sorry. (Okay, we are a little . . . please don't return the book).

So here we are, naked before you, ready to lube up and do some philosophy. So, once you've bought a copy, or maybe two . . . light some candles, turn on some WHAM!, strip down and hop into the bath for the most sensual read of your life, 'cause this book is so amazing it might be better than sex. Actually, we will just outright say it's better (after all, this book will still be there for you in the morning). Just remember to wear protection for this one . . . and clean up afterwards (there are some things you just shouldn't do to a book . . .). Are you ready for this shit? 'Cause it's ready for you!

And no, this book is not licensed by Deadpool at all, so he doesn't get a damn penny for it.

Wait . . . What the FUCK???

Sorry, bro.

I

These Timelines Can Get So Confusing

Why I Want to Rub Patrick Stewart's Head

1
Breaking Sixteen Walls

RHIANNON GRANT WITH NO HELP FROM DEADPOOL WHATSOEVER, SERIOUSLY

Deadpool may be the greatest philosopher ever. I also think he'd make an excellent sociologist. The key to his amazing skills in both philosophy and sociology is Deadpool's well-known ability to break the fourth wall (a useful form of critical thinking and not a figment of Deadpool's imagination, whatever Karavitis tries to tell you elsewhere in this book). ***I find Karavitis's lack of faith . . . disturbing. And Deadpool drops the mic . . . StarWars referenced! BAM!***

Hey! You! *The nerd holding this book . . . What are you chuckling at? . . . You're next . . .* Captain Needa. Now shhhhhhhh, the lady's tryin' to write, you rude nerf-herder.

In order to demonstrate that Deadpool is such an amazing philosopher, the first step is for us as readers to accept that Deadpool's broken fourth wall means that he is—and knows he is—fictional. You and I have no such awareness (unless you are, unbeknownst to me, actually Deadpool, *which would be really weird since I'd swear he was right here, or is that extra-large chimichanga with mustard I just ate starting to take a bad turn???)*

We can all have the experience of trying to look at our lives from the outside. Sometimes that's just a bit creepy, like when you feel disassociated or disconnected from what's really happening (this can be mild, like déjà vu, or part of a serious mental health problem); sometimes it's for a laugh, like when your friend makes that pun for the tenth time and you stare off into space as if you were looking into an invisible camera; and sometimes it's the best way to learn about yourself and your world, which is why philosophers and sociologists try to do it. I won't rule out the possibility that we're either mad or joking, but I'm mainly interested in the final sort of "looking at our lives from outside."

How can being able to break the fourth wall make Deadpool the greatest philosopher ever? And can I—or you—do the same thing? In order to understand this and answer these questions, we need two things: a better idea of what happens when Deadpool breaks the fourth wall, and a clearer idea of what philosophers are really trying to do.

When Deadpool breaks the fourth wall, he shows that he's aware that he's a fictional character, and he's able to use resources from outside his fictional world in order to ask new questions about it. Here's an example: when in the 2016 Deadpool movie he's taken off to see Professor X, he asks, "Stewart or McAvoy?" Other characters in the film can't ask this. When they go to see the Professor, he just is Professor X, a.k.a. Charles Xavier—and from their point of view, there is no Patrick Stewart and no James McAvoy. Within the movie universe, Charles Xavier has been, more or less, the same person all along, even if being shot and going bald were a bit traumatic. Outside the movie universe, Charles Xavier has never been a real person at all—however much we want him to, he doesn't exist. Deadpool, though, lives in such a way that he can access both universes: he's going to go and see Professor X, who exists, but he also knows that the Professor has been played by more than one actor, and so is fictional.

When philosophers sit in their dusty, book-lined offices scratching their dandruffy heads over hundreds of pages of weird-looking logic . . . (I'm sorry, my colleagues aren't like that at all. Only one, and she knows who she is.) When philosophers sit around in bars on university campuses debating whether numbers exist and what Descartes thought about soup, they are trying to do much the same thing. Some of them even go so far as to suppose that our world is fictional or only exists in our minds or the mind of God.

A guy called Bishop George Berkeley (1685–1753) is probably best known for trying to turn himself into Deadpool by this method, which is technically known as solipsism. (Hint: it didn't really work out for him, and not only because Deadpool hadn't yet been invented. ***What do you mean invented??? I'm the real deal, lady!*** *No, you're not! You are just another mustard-laden mistake taking a jog through my intestines and a hard left turn in my subconscious).*

Now, most philosophers accept that at least some things about the real world are, well, real, give or take an illusion here and a mirage there and a possible evil telepath somewhere else. But they want to look at the world from outside, or failing that, they want to look at their own lives from outside. One of the most famous philosophers ever, Socrates (about 470–399 B.C.), apparently said that "An unexamined life is not worth living." Well, if we're going to be pedantic, he didn't—for one, he spoke ancient Greek and for another, his buddy Plato wrote it down later—but this is a reasonable translation of his words. He'd just been found guilty of asking awkward questions, and was defending himself: asking questions and thinking about things, he says, is important to living a good life. He then got killed—he'd have been a longer-lived, if not a better, philosopher if he'd also had Deadpool's healing factor. When Deadpool breaks the fourth wall, he's able to ask new questions about his life and what's happening in his world; Socrates would approve.

Deadpool Examines His Life

By breaking the fourth wall, Deadpool is able to examine his life in ways which are not usually available to philosophers. Let's explore this by looking at the moment in the movie when Deadpool breaks the fourth wall within his fourth wall break: "That's, like, sixteen walls." ***I said that. ME.*** Not only is Deadpool examining his life by stepping outside it—moving from his world into ours, and seeing in some ways that his life is fictional—but he's also seeing that stepping *outside* his life is characteristic *of* his life. He can break the fourth wall during his fourth wall break precisely because he is aware that breaking the fourth wall is a habit of his. If you practice looking at your life from outside for long enough, you can eventually look from outside at your decision to look at things from outside. If you aren't confused yet, I'm now going to apply that to philosophers. Philosophers—for this purpose, that includes you reading this book and anyone who is trying to live an examined life—can become aware that wanting to live an examined life is in itself something which needs to be examined.

Some philosophers respond to their sixteen broken walls, the moment when they become aware that they need to examine the habit of examining everything, by studying how to examine things well. This results in lots of textbooks on logic, structures of argument, and how to persuade people to accept that your analysis is better than someone else's. From this perspective, I can win the argument about whether Deadpool really breaks the fourth wall if I can either show for certain that he does, or show that the other guy is wrong to say that he doesn't. This kind of philosophical work has the advantage that it gives you lots of rules for arguing, in the same way that training in multiple martial arts gives Deadpool lots of ways to win fights. The disadvantage is that it doesn't help when people ask why exactly you're arguing or fighting in the first place.

Other philosophers get kind of down on philosophy as a whole, which is ironic when it's paying them. An example of a philosopher who was very down on other people's philosophy was Ludwig Wittgenstein (1889–1951), who compared philosophers to flies in a fly-trap and said that *real* philosophy (in Wittgenstein's opinion the kind Wittgenstein did [he's dead now, so he's not doing much anymore]) aims to show people the way out of the trap (*Philosophical Investigations*, section 309). The specific kind of trap Wittgenstein uses as an example is a fly-bottle—something which has a narrow entrance and a big space inside so that flies, which are a bit stupid and can't see very well, fly in, but can't work out how to get out again. Often, a fly-bottle would also be baited with a bit of fruit or similar, something which smells nice to the kind of flies you're trying to catch. If Deadpool was trapped in a fly-bottle, he might just smash through the side, because Deadpools are much stronger than flies.

Deadpool's knowledge of the fourth wall is kind of like being able to look at the bottle the fly is in *from the outside*. If you're inside a giant bottle with a tiny entrance, it's hard to find that entrance because you have to hunt through the whole space (and flies are terrible at searching in an orderly way, they just fly around at random). If you're outside the bottle, it's pretty easy to say where the entrance is, because you can see the whole thing. Wittgenstein thinks that he can see the whole picture of the 'fly-bottle' which philosophers talk themselves into when they imagine they are searching for the real world but actually just going round and round inside their game of arguments and counter-arguments. By thinking in the same ways, in this case by imagining what someone outside the bottle can see, Deadpool can find his way out of a bottle much better than a fly. If Socrates would approve of Deadpool because Deadpool can examine his life from outside, Wittgenstein would approve of Deadpool because Deadpool can escape traps better than other people. ***"'Cause I'm a rule breaker, heart breaker, love-spanker!" Crap. Those lyrics don't sound right. Rhiannon's got to have the vinyl around here somewhere . . . Damn hipster philosophers. Never a CD around when you need one!***

Morality through the Fourth Wall

It isn't just practical situations (like actual person-sized fly-traps) or abstract philosophical problems (like the nature of the universe) which are helped by living an 'examined life' or looking at oneself from outside. We can also make this try this out in the case of ethical problems. We see Deadpool doing this frequently—he has a strong moral self-awareness even if he doesn't always choose to do good ("I may be super, but I'm no hero"). Thinking about virtue and living the good life were big with Socrates and co., and have been popular with philosophers ever since. Actually, almost everyone has to do this sometimes. There's a sense in which everyone is a philosopher, as you'll know if you've ever walked into a crowded room and asked a key ethical question, like, "Should I make Francis, the guy who ruined my face, into a kebob?" Most popular ways of addressing this sort of question, such as asking whether how much benefit it will create in the long run or whether a virtuous person would do that, rely to some extent on looking at yourself and the situation from outside.

If Deadpool only looks at the question from his own perspective, he might focus on satisfaction as a benefit of making Francis into a kebob, and miss the idea that it's also important to prevent him from ruining anyone else's faces. For Deadpool, it would be characteristic to look at all of this, and also to ask whether Francis is going to be an important plot device in the next movie (and, of course, to make him into a kebob). I know I wouldn't make the guy into a kebob, even if he'd ruined my face, because I'm not that sort of person—if I did, you'd say it was out of character. You, though, are looking at me from outside the fly-bottle. The trick is for me to look at myself from your perspective, outside my own life, in order to be able to assess myself and my chances of winning a sword fight, having left the stove on, or escaping a fly-trap. (Hint: I'm most likely to have left the stove on.)

"Being better at escaping than flies are" isn't, you might well be saying to yourself, all that brilliant. It's a low bar to cross, let's face it. And it's a long, long way from being the greatest philosopher ever, even if Wittgenstein and Socrates would have approved. The trick, though, is in the next part. Once you've looked at yourself in the fly-bottle from outside, you can escape more easily—but you also need to think about what looking at yourself from outside does to you. It makes Deadpool aware that he's a fictional character. It makes me both better and worse at writing job applications, because I'm aware of both my strengths and how they don't stack up very well in comparison to other candidates. In philosophy, it's a strength, because looking at yourself from outside always teaches you something about what's going on. If you want to look at not just yourself but also your community, though, it can tie you up in knots, and this is where sociologists come in: they also learn to break the fourth wall better than most people can.

Deadpool Researches His Team

I heard recently that Deadpool had been given a little bit of funding to write a research project about mercenaries with superpowers and big mouths. (News like this sometimes just slips through cracks in the fourth wall.) Deadpool went to see Professor X for some advice on doing this kind of work—although the Professor is really a geneticist, he's done lots of work on mutants, his own community, which raises many of the same issues. We can think about this problem with the terms 'insider' and 'outsider'—if I do some research on Deadpool fans, I'm an insider, and if I go and do some research on Spider-Man fans I'm an outsider (because I just can't stand Spidey). If Deadpool researches mouthy mercs, he's an insider.

This crack in the wall seems to be staying open, and we can eavesdrop on Deadpool and Professor X chatting about this. *And this is totally real and not the result of my slipping into an insane stupor caused by rancid mustardy burrito chased with a quart of Pepto-Bismol . . .*

PROFESSOR X: Please, have a seat.

DEADPOOL: ***Thanks. Wow, you're all Stewarty today. Not in a bad way.***

PROFESSOR X: What? Never mind, I'll just say thank you. What was it you wanted to see me about?

DEADPOOL: ***Not joining your team, thanks for asking. Serval Industries want a survey of mutant mercs, I guess they're hiring or something, and they've asked me to do some interviews for them, you know, find out people's real opinions and stuff.***

PROFESSOR X: How are you going to do that?

DEADPOOL: ***Ask them?***

PROFESSOR X: Do you think they'll tell the truth?

DEADPOOL: ***Probably not? Why didn't Serval ask a telepath to do this job, anyway? It's not really merc's work.***

PROFESSOR X: You might have insights about the situation that even a telepath wouldn't. You're a mercenary yourself, after all, and your personal experience might shape the questions you ask, enabling you to discover things which wouldn't occur to me.

DEADPOOL: ***Huh? (Seriously, you should have gone with McAvoy instead—great head of hair without all that Star Treky mubo-speak muckin up the dialogue! Oh and while I'm at it, what's with all the Fleetwood Mac layin' around your subconscious, Rhiannon?)***

Deadpool's hesitation and confusion here, articulated as a very understandable "Huh?" echo the hesitations and confusions of many who set out to research communities of people. There is a sense in which, as a person researching people, one is always an insider—in a way that a zoologist who studies lions will never be. On the other hand, sometimes a researcher sets out to study far-off, distant people—at one time, African or South American communities with little contact with the researcher's own culture were popular.

What happens then is that a white man with a university degree, preferably English speaking, goes off to live with and study and write about people of color who have a very different worldview and can't write (in English) about themselves. If Deadpool went off to research conditions in Chinese factories, he'd be in roughly the same position: learning a new language or relying on translators, bringing very different cultural expectations to the situation, and in all sorts of ways looking at the conditions he found from outside the culture in which they arose.

This is a bit like us when we read or watch Deadpool—we look into his (fictional) universe from outside, although of course we're also familiar with many of the things he references (like Deadpool, we've got access to the *X-Men* movies, for example).

On the other hand, though, if Deadpool researches mutated mercs, he's an insider. In the same way, if a philosopher sets out to write a paper about the behavior of philosophers, or a member of the Church of Latter-day Saints studies the beliefs of Mormons, they're insiders. And these examples might make your philosophy-sense tingle, and you might say something like: surely they can't be *objective* about these things?

Objectivity through Maximum Effort

Trying to be objective—to look at things fairly, or as if you aren't involved—is an important aim for many kinds of research. It isn't always possible, of course. In fact, some people would say that it's never possible: your position, as a man or a woman or white or non-white or straight or gay or pansexual or a mutant or a hero or a student or a book-lover or a mercenary or beautiful or hideously disfigured, always affects the way you think about everything.

It turned out, for example, according to Emily Martin, that men looking through microscopes at eggs and sperm had used words which echoed their assumptions about men and women.

There's not much more supposedly objective than looking through a microscope, but if you come in assuming that men penetrate women, you see sperm penetrating eggs. If you look again after you've taken your patriarchal glasses off, you can see the Velcro-like stuff an egg uses to keep hold of a likely-looking sperm. (If Deadpool did the research, it would probably turn out that sperm sing songs by Wham!)

Going to research people who are very different from you lets you have one kind of objectivity. I can easily write a paper about superheroes in a very detached way, being neither super nor a hero, and I can make it sound very factual, perhaps by giving lots of numbers. If I wrote a paper about philosophers, I'd have to work harder to sound detached, and you might assume that I was inclined to be nice about them, since I'm a philosopher. In order to offset that impression, I might end up being extra-rude about philosophers or looking for small things to be critical about. (Is that happening in this chapter?) On the other hand, I probably know what questions to ask philosophers in order to reveal their secrets ("That's *how many* books about Descartes today, Bruce?") while if I went to interview superheroes, I'd have to start with the stupid stuff ("So, err, is heroing good at the moment?"). Professor X has just been explaining this to our favorite Regenerating Degenerate. Pardon me while I pop some Alka Seltzer and beat my head against a wall.

Really? A wall joke inside of a fourth wall break inside of a chapter about breaking the fourth wall? You don't get extra points for maximum effort there Stevie Nicks . . . Witty reference to one's own catch-phrase, though, priceless . . . As Cyborg would say, BOOYAH!

F*%#! Wrong universe. How do I even know who Cyborg is??? Either way, I'll just be happy if the next JL movie doesn't suck. Hear that Zach Snyder? I've got a katana waiting just for you Ol' "Sit and Spin." Okay, back to our episode of "How Stewart Turns" . . . (Get it, 'cause old man smell? Nothing? Really?)

PROFESSOR X: Overall that means that you're very well placed, really. And I hear you can heal from anything, so you'll probably survive even if one of your participants decides to, err, withdraw from the study.

DEADPOOL: ***Yeah, I'm getting it now. It's like having an insider on a heist job, you save all the bother about getting copies of keys and security codes and eyeballs and shit.***

PROFESSOR X: Yes . . . but do remember your research ethics. You're finding things out, not stealing them.

DEADPOOL: ***Serval Industries haven't heard of research ethics, and I'm not sure I have, either.***

PROFESSOR X: Never mind. Just don't blame me if Wolverine does manage to kill you afterwards.

PASSING SOCIOLOGIST: A study on interactions between immortals would be really interesting, especially in a couple of hundred years when they've really had a chance to get to know one another. If I put the application in now, my great-great-grandchild might even have funding for it.

PROFESSOR X: Who's that? How did you get in here?

DEADPOOL: ***I think I may have left a crack in the fourth wall large enough for them to crawl through.***

Deadpool is wrong, of course; sociologists are native to the Marvel Universes just as much as to our own. As he takes his very first baby-steps in his own sociological career, he is using philosophical tools to understand his situation—reflecting on previous experience, such as jewel heists, and making an analogy which helps to explain what's going on. He considers the scope of his own knowledge (even if he's exaggerating for effect; Deadpool actually has, as discussed earlier, a very clear sense of his own ethical positions—such as they are).

Deadpool's ability to break the fourth wall and look at his own life from outside makes him an excellent philosopher. ***Damn right katana-fodder!*** It's also now going to make him an excellent sociologist, because the way that insider researchers get the benefits of both worlds—of working with people you already know and understand because you belong to their community, *and* of working on fresh material where you don't have preconceptions—is to use just this kind of trick to look at their work from both inside and outside. ***I'm a Two-Fer! Philosopher-Sociologist. You can double up on***

me! Wait, I didn't mean that like it sounded . . . Or did I, blue eyes? (Just took a shot in the dark on your eye color there Sinatra, CAUSE I'M JUST A BOOK, but as time goes on you are lookin' more and more like Bea Arthur to me there hot-stuff . . .)

*Sigh,*we can see here that while they work in different buildings, philosophers and sociologists actually have a lot in common and they can both benefit from breaking the fourth wall. You'll also see that the usefulness of trying to break the fourth wall means that people who start thinking about things are usually both insiders and outsiders in some sense; Deadpool can also look at super mercs from outside because he knows that they're fictional, and I can look at my own community from outside by becoming aware of the kinds of critiques outsiders make of it.

PROFESSOR X: I think you should write a book about this.

DEADPOOL: ***With the blood of my enemies? Nah, maybe too dramatic. Sticky doesn't sell well.***

Deadpool may not always use his analytical powers—the skill of examining life which makes him a brilliant philosopher and sociologist—for good. Indeed, I suspect that he rather often uses them for jokes. The structure of a joke often uses that very same change of perspective: "A man walks into a bar. Ow!" Nevertheless, I think it's clear that he may be the greatest philosopher ever (and if he isn't, he will at least outlive the rest). Wittgenstein once said to his friend Norman Malcolm that "a serious and good philosophical work could be written consisting entirely of jokes." When that book is written, many of those jokes will use Deadpool's approach to great philosophy: breaking the fourth wall.

Maybe it's this book . . . the great philosophical work of the next century . . . Ha, who are you kidding, Michaud? Did you read your chapter? I hate haters . . . a lot. [1]

---

[1] Many thanks to Moses Tucker for reading a first draft of this chapter. If there are any errors remaining, we don't have a problem. I have a problem.

2
Deadpool the Dark Angel

CHRISTOPHER KETCHAM WITH HELP FROM THE COSMIC CHIMICHANGA IN THE SKY

> A fourth wall break inside a fourth wall break? That's like, sixteen walls.
>
> —*Deadpool*, 2016

The law of conservation of energy says that information can never be lost, which is why that caustic tweet you unleashed upon the cyber world last year continues to produce bouts of inflamed responses even now.

However, the theory that information could not be lost was severely challenged by the idea of a black hole. Some thought that the black hole was a cosmic shredder that would consume information and destroy it in its heartless black gut. Yet, when physicists did the math they realized that every time the black hole eats something, it gets bigger. This certainly makes sense to anyone with a waistline.

Physicists modified their theory of black holes to say that all information is only found on the surface of things, and when they did the math again, the amount of information on the cosmic chimichanga the black hole just ate fits exactly on the new surface area created by its consumption.

Deadpool on the Surface

> Just promise me you'll do right by me, so I can do right by someone else. And don't make the super suit green. Or animated!
>
> —WADE WILSON, *Deadpool*, 2016

If information is only found on the surface of things, we can easily understand that Deadpool information exists only on the paper surface of a printed comic, or on the surface of a television or movie screen. This is where the fourth wall comes into play. The fourth wall is an idea that comes from the theater. The actors have a floor, sides, and a back to the stage. However, there's an invisible fourth wall in front that separates them from the audience. Breaking that fourth wall is a no-no, unless you are a sweaty rock icon who wants to body surf the crowds in the front rows. The pages of a comic also constitute a wall. Theoretically, no toon can crawl from the comic's pages and hop down onto the floor.

However, Deadpool breaks the fourth wall, and often. As you might surmise, the gravitation pull of information on a page is infinitely smaller than the gravitational pull of a black hole where even light can't escape. Deadpool does not find exiting his comics' pages daunting at all.

However, there are many that still have a problem with this idea. First of all, if information escapes the comic pages or screen, what is left on the page with Deadpool prancing around in the 3D world? Has more information been created or has the page been screen-scraped, so to speak? Let's speculate for a moment that the information produced by Deadpool's escape from the page is holographic. It's 3D alright, but is it a copy of what's on the page?

Most say it most certainly is a copy because the holographic plate is like a recording device that copies the original, although most often in a hazy green glow that would discolor Deadpool's red suit. If it's a copy, we know that information is missing—really important information. Say you put your hand through the projected holograph of Deadpool: he disappears or is severely handicapped by the disappearance of this light information. An awful lot known as Deadpool goes missing in a holograph.

Deadpool's Dimensions

> You're probably thinking "This is a superhero movie, but that guy in the suit just turned that other guy into a fucking kebab." Surprise, this is a different kind of superhero story.
>
> —*Deadpool*, 2016

What if Deadpool's journey outside of the page or screen—his piercing of this fourth wall—is no piercing at all? He's simply been reconstituted in dimensions that we do not see or yet fully understand? String theory suggests that there are ten dimensions. The three we deal with every day: length, width, and height over time, and then there are seven more dimensions curled up so tightly we can't experience them. Let's assume that these dimensions have surface area even if it's miniscule. If these dimensions have surface area and we only experience Deadpool in our three dimensions over time, then doesn't it stand to reason that we too are only getting part of the information about Deadpool? We may be missing a whole lot about him that would be really important to know.

So, if Deadpool escapes the confines of his fourth wall, he can leave behind his information on the toon page or screen and present himself in other than our three experienced dimensions. His information is so tightly curled up in those extra dimensions he can escape his confines without revealing he's gone! We know he has escaped because Deadpool has never been shy about telling us about himself and chastising us for being complete idiots.

We may speculate how Deadpool and, it seems, nobody else has been able to perform such a fourth-wallian feat. Or, we can just chalk up this ability to something that was derived from the process that the Canadian Weapon X, Department K folks used to cure Wade Wilson's cancer and reformulate him as Deadpool with all the powers of regeneration. We can also speculate that anything that slices through Deadpool that would kill an otherwise living subject would only damage his three-dimensional appearance and leave all the other dimensions to fully function even without the former three. Somehow Deadpool has been given the gift of escaping the fourth wall, leaving all his paper-toon information behind in order to exist in the nether dimensions calculated by string theory. Ergo, string theory has been proven.

From Strings to God

From the studio that inexplicably sewed his fucking mouth shut the first time comes five-time Academy Award viewer, Ryan Reynolds in

> an eHarmony date with destiny. Ladies and gentlemen, I give you . . . me! Deadpool.
>
> —*Deadpool*, 2016

Ha! You say. That's the most ridiculous tall tale I've ever heard since I opened my first Deadpool comic and smelled its freshly printed ink.

You need more proof? Here's what I have to offer: through God.

Think about it, God has to work within the rules of physics (God's rules) otherwise things would become awfully peculiar. Then again, even if God wanted to play by different rules, God would be awfully busy trying to sort out all of the strange things that would occur as a result. If he's that busy, who's going to listen to, let alone answer your persistent prayers? Therefore, we can only reasonably assume that God has his own cosmic strings to deal with (and of course strings to pull) just like everyone else.

The folks who messed with Deadpool to enable him to regenerate must have been working within the same rulebook that God works. They just found some new ways of doing things that unlock the separate dimensions so that Deadpool could appear both on the ink and elsewhere without causing a major rent in the fabric of space-time.

You can believe with all the ancient astronaut theorists that, not God, but extra-terrestrials gave the pyramid builders and others great secrets that we have not ever been able to unlock again. As of yet, the evidence produced to link extra-terrestrials to technology our ancients employed seems to me to tug quite hard on the strings of believability. Rather I will turn to the Bible, particularly the traditional Hebrew Bible and the twelfth-century scholar Moses Maimonides (known as "Ramban") who sorted out for us the realm of angels.

Ramban explained that there are ten realms for angels. Beginning to sound familiar? No? Well, consider this: there are ten string dimensions and there are also ten angel realms—coincidence?

There's a lot of gospel that the Bible attributes as coming directly from God. Certainly God knows what's going on in the laws of physics. Even so, angels are metaphysical beings, meaning we can't always see them. We can't ever see the curled up dimensions that string theory posits, but we now know that Deadpool somehow can access these dimensions to break the fourth wall. Hence, if only angels and God could exist in these curled up dimensions, then Deadpool must be either God or an angel. I think it would be a bit presumptuous to make Deadpool the manifestation of God in any dimension, especially ones we experience. I would also suggest that even the most cynical who believe in a vengeful God would not picture God in the form of anyone as dreadful as Deadpool.

On the other hand, we know that angels are not always angels in the Raphael sense of being: chubby pink cherubic nymphs with gossamer wings. Let's all face up to the fact that Satan was an angel before he fell from grace. The ecumenical jury is still out on Deadpool, because one moment he's saving souls and the next instant excoriating, eviscerating, and expunging others from existence upon the Earth. Can I hear an "Amen"?

Angelica

> Wait! You may be wondering why the red suit. Well, that's so bad guys don't see me bleed.
>
> —*Deadpool*, 2016

Here's the angel angle. The God of the original Hebraic books of the Bible is not a sweet deity. Look, God sent plagues out among the Egyptians, God plays favorites and like a Mafia Don requires sacrifices. Why, he almost got Abraham to cut the throat of his son Isaac. Talk about taking one for the team.

God sent hellfire and brimstone upon Sodom and Gomorrah and turned Lot's wife into a pillar of salt. You think that this God is going to have a bunch of fawning cherubs as angels? God's gonna need a posse for all of this mayhem and to keep that junkyard dog Satan in that foul place called Hell. God's gonna need a guy like Deadpool to play the role of Luca Brasi in his gang. Deadpool: angel assassin.

Certainly it's contrary to everything they taught you in Sunday school . . . you can hear the nuns cracking knuckles right now. So be it. Here's the real story. Remember your Bible. Nobody, even the folks like Abraham and Moses who heard from God quite regularly ever really actually *saw* God. The theory is that they would become quite mad or worse if they were to gaze upon God's countenance, that is, of course, if God even has a countenance. Think of it like not directly looking at a King—which of course is the same idea.

God committed arson for Moses by burning a bush, and then Moses went home with carved graffiti tablets for his troubles. Abraham got morality but in a really perverse way after God first told him to kill Isaac and then stepped in to spare the child. So God, just like Deadpool, can somehow manipulate these dimensions higher than the third to visit our three and communicate with us. If we could see God what would it mean? Would it mean that we can experience the dimensions beyond three? If we can't experience anything more than three, would anyone but God be able to prevent these bottled up experiential zones from bursting forth and turning our universe into one really weird place? Or maybe if we had this gift would we just blow the whole thing back to the big bang in order for physics to put the dimensional genie back into the bottle.

Likely not. It appears that accessing these unseen dimension as Deadpool does simply will not controvert the fabric of the universe, well, that we know of any way. There is that thing about him being able to regenerate from any wound which is worrisome scientifically, but as of yet we haven't seen anything untoward come of it (nothing like sucking energy out of perfectly healthy people to fill his needs) at least outside of Deadpool's sphere of influence and his dastardly work.

He could be sucking dark matter out of space or creating new dark energy from another universe which just could upset the cosmological balance. If you recall, the difference in the matter-energy calculation between the universe expanding forever and contracting forever is an infinitesimally small sum—perhaps only + or – five hydrogen atoms. Sigh, we simply cannot go there in this short chapter.

What we can do is bolster the argument about dimensions to look at each of the angel "species" and the realm in which each exist. Each is a different "species." but not where one is human-like and another dog-like. Rather, like any species in nature, each species has a form and function, but in the case of angels, each is suited to a particular dimension's existential duties towards God. Within this discussion we may also be able to find a place for Deadpool, meaning, in what realm does Deadpool as an angel serve God?

All the Ethereal Mumbo-Jumbo

> Whatever they did to me made me totally indestructible and completely unfuckable?
>
> —*Deadpool*, 2016

Maimonides wrote the *Mishneh Torah* in order to explain some things that other rabbis before him had not clearly articulated. One was to explain the three categories of God's universe.

First is our lowly three-dimensional world where things consist of matter and form which *both* arise and then pass away. Second are the things that are of matter and form that do *not* pass away like the stars (Ramban didn't have the Hubble Telescope to see supernovas). Then there is the third category where there is form but *no* matter and this is the meta-realm of the angels. A precocious thinker, Maimonides cogitated something that present-day physicists struggle with. While today's scientists have good mathematical evidence of dark matter and lots of it in the universe, we haven't been able to detect it. Dark matter seems not to have any mass at all—no matter! You see where I'm going, don't you: strings, angels, and dark matter—perhaps there is a connection in all of the unseen dimensions.

It is in these unseen dimensions where Ramban's angels roam. Said Maimonides about angels in *Halacha 5*:

> Since they possess no body, what separates the form [of the angels] from each other? Their existence is not alike. Rather each one is below the level of the other and exists by virtue of its influence, [in a progression of levels,] one above the other. (Mishneh Torah, Yesodei-ha Torah)

If an angel were made up of matter, and matter is something that makes up us and the stars, but the dimensions of strings above the third are curled, infinitesimal and *massless* . . . bringing forth something with mass in those unexperienced dimensions would unleash new matter into the cosmic equation which, as we have explained, is a no-no. Therefore, the angels may have form but not matter (even if it is massless dark 'matter').

This explains a lot. Deadpool, outside of the fourth wall, is not made up of matter which is why he can regenerate himself.

Actually he isn't regenerating himself—it just looks that way. He is only regenerating his form, not matter. For the moment, at least, the ever expanding universe and associated theories are safe from Deadpool's meddling.

From God's Eye to the Mote in Yours

I didn't just get the cure to el cancer, I got the cure to el everything.

—*Deadpool*, 2016

This is all beginning to make sense. We have angels that have form but no matter and each serves God in a different way. Deadpool retained his form and matter in three dimensions but not his matter in the other seven after his transformation from the simple human Wade Wilson.

So far it appears that only angels, Deadpool, and God can access these hidden dimensions. So, can we extrapolate from Deadpool's personality and modus operendi which level of angel is Deadpool? First we must understand what each angel is tasked to do for God.

At the lowest realm (10) are the *ishim* these are the angels who speak to the prophets. They are closest to humans in order to be able to communicate through visions with the prophets. At the highest realm (1), just below God are the *chayyot*, who are capable of understanding all the realms of angels and below, but never that of God.

In between from highest to lowest angel realms are:

2: *ofanim*
3: *er'elim*
4: *chashmalim*
5: *serafim*
6: *mal'achim*
7: *elohim*
8: sons of the *Elohim*
9: *keruvim*

When we turn to the books Ezekiel, Isaiah, and Daniel, we begin to understand the murkiness that surrounds the differentiation between angels in the second through ninth realms.

Through the Bible and the mystical Kabballah, some progress was made in categorizing these angels using the prophet Ezekiel's description of the chariot. Recall that for Ezekiel, this metallic thing came out of the north in a cloud like a fiery thunderstorm complete with flashes of lightning. Out of the midst of this maelstrom he saw four four-faced figures of human form but each with one human face, one of an ox, one of an eagle, and one of a lion. They were straight-legged but their soles of their feet were like those of calf hooves.

Each figure shone like burning coals and each had four wings. The chariot that emerged from the mist had four wheels that moved in concert with the four beings. Inside the chariot was a throne and a gleaming being Ezekiel took as the likeness of God, though likely not God incarnate, rather a *Deus ex machina*—a god out of a machine. The chariot, as Ezekiel spoke about it, seemed to defy the laws of gravity, floating through the air as if supported by and powered by the four-faced winged beings and the four wheels. Wings flapped and wheels turned round and round but the wheels did not turn to steer—the whole thing moved as if one creature, in unison wherever it was wont to go.

We could attribute Ezekiel's vision to some nasty ergot that had infected his bread and created LSD-like hallucinations. We could also say, as the ancient astronaut theorists do, that Ezekiel was just trying to describe a space ship using terms associated with what he knew about his own era's technology. Then again, as we are beginning to realize with our efforts so far, that likely this machination was God harnessing the power of the ten dimensions in order to produce a vision of the realms of angels so that humanity could sort them out.

Certainly the highest realm of God was the being on the throne—not exactly but perhaps a holograph of the same. The next down would be the four-faced winged beasts who seemed to navigate the machination, presumably at the behest of the seated being, and who likely themselves controlled the wheels and so on. Neither Ezekiel nor Maimonides assigned definite tasks to all of the angel species in the hierarchy, so we are left with a mystical hole that will be difficult to fill even with our newfound understanding of string theory.

Seeking Meaning from Chariots and Such

> I should've come and found you sooner, but the guy under this mask, he ain't the same one that you remember.
>
> —*Deadpool*, 2016

Ezekiel's chariot presumably is a construct of God and his realms. Let's assume that it is and each level of angel realm is represented somewhere in the vision. That is in keeping with what Maimonides wanted us to understand. However, humans messed with Deadpool to create his indestructibility which we have already seen as the embodiment of the extra-dimensional. It is quite conceivable, then, that Deadpool has the ability to transit from one realm to another without destroying the hierarchy nor any cosmic balance or tipping point. However, as we see with Deadpool's own personality, transitioning dimensions transforms his personality from one extreme to the other.

Think about it. Before he meets up with the Department K folks, he's framed for his father's death and while on the lam becomes a hit man. Circumstances set his stage even while he's just a regular human. He becomes a mercenary using plastic surgery to alter his countenance. He helps a Japanese crime lord infiltrate the Sumo world of a rival in order to take the rival down. He hangs out with prostitutes . . . Then he gets cancer and becomes involved with the Weapon X project. Up until this point he has vacillated between the dark side and the grey but opportunistic side—but all in the human three-dimensional realm. He's no cherubic angel but we cannot yet call him satanic.

Things are about to change in the grand experiment he is subjected do. He will become a superhuman. That isn't quite Deadpool's style. No, he blows his opportunity in the superhuman training course when he kills his teammate Stayback and is sent to failed superhero rehab. He escapes rehab and tries to better himself, only to fall into his old ways. Someone even tries to convince him it's his destiny to become the Mithras, one who will usher in the golden age of humanity . . .

Well, of course, this vision doesn't take, and rather than try to better himself any further he falls back into his mercenary existence. Doesn't it seem to you that he bounces from one dimension to another? Within each he is confronted by this or that angel, which serves to confuse his identity. He invariably falls back to what he knows best and that's being a mercenary. This is not inconsistent with the thought that a being caught in the intersection in and between the unseen string-theory dimensions must produce some kind of instability and in Deadpool's case, his own fluid sense of identity.

Let's face it, Weapon X, as we see with any other military program, relies on the lowest bidder, unmitigated secrecy, black budgets, the megalomania and hubris of its leaders, and visions of producing a super warrior without regard to consequences beyond the current war construct. Think no further than the minefields wars have left behind that maim and kill innocent farmers years after the soldiers have gone home. Deadpool has been manipulated all his life and now his own existence is in chaotic freefall as he passes from one realm to the other seemingly without any physical difficulty, but with all sorts of cognitive and emotional baggage that he produces along the way.

In one angelic realm he is the human, perhaps one who can speak to the prophets. In another he is a member of a band of super-heroes who want to do good, and in another he is a hitman, albeit one who smites down ignominious enemies which early prophets might have said were in league with Satan and where Deadpool assumes the mantle of a vengeful God. Deadpool could go either way: good or bad.

Perhaps it took Satan an eon or more for his ambition to get the better of him to want to slay his creator and enslave all of God's creatures in the devil's own dungeon we call Hell. Deadpool hasn't been around that long, and as such, it appears that his satanic switch has not yet been locked into the "on" position. Remember, as he traverses the angelic levels, he will likely bump into an angel or two who will whisper subliminally in his ear which may prevent him from turning completely to the dark side.

Casting Aside Disbelief

Here's the thing. Life is an endless series of trainwrecks with only brief commercial-like breaks of happiness. This had been the ultimate commercial break. Which meant it was time to return to our regularly scheduled programming.

—Wade Wilson, *Deadpool*, 2016

I never said I would provide all the answers. A lot of what we have discussed isn't even evident to Deadpool himself.

Incredulity overtakes you. I see it in your eyes, your furled brow, and that ever deepening frown. You see in your mind with this chapter the equivalent of the cover of a grainy tabloid announcing that the starlet du-jour has just delivered an alien baby whose picture graces the cover. As with all celebrities there is a tremendous amount of misinformation about Deadpool circulating in and out of social media and the tabloids. One such outrageous lie is that Deadpool likes chimichangas. He doesn't like chimichangas; he just likes saying "chimichanga." Look it up, people.

Now that you have been disabused from believing one of the most persistent untruths that follows Deadpool around, I urge you to refrain from dismissing the theory of Deadpool as a traveler among unseen dimensions, the realms of the angels. That Deadpool is an angel, but not one confined to a specific level, as Maimonides has taught us, is yet not definitively proven, but we convict murderers on more tenuous threads of evidence than what has been presented here.

While I do urge you to pursue other promising theories about both the epistemological and ontological (philosophical jibber jabber) condition of Deadpool, this new exposition of Deadpool, in the context of string theory, *and* in the realm of the creator deserves rigorous investigation. I would hope, dear reader, that you might be the one to begin such a journey . . .

Wait . . .

> You're still here? It's over. Go home! Oh, you're expecting a teaser for *Deadpool II*. Well, we don't have that kind of money. What are you expecting, Sam Jackson show up with an eyepatch and a saucy little leather number? Go, go. (*Deadpool*, 2016)

3
The *Only* Chapter in This Book You Need to Read!

JOHN V. KARAVITIS (EARTH 616) AND
JOHN V. KARAVITIS (EARTH $e^{i\pi}$)

Welcome to our chapter! We're sure you purchased this stunning entry in the Popular Culture and Philosophy series because of your love of the movie adaptation of Marvel Entertainment's Deadpool. You know, the movie starring "God's Perfect Idiot." You know whom I'm talking about, right?

Brought to rapture and struck dumb by your cinematic experience, you immediately set off on a quest to more deeply understand your beloved snarky *anti*-hero. A quest that ended with the book that you now hold in your trembling hands. Well, we're sure glad that celluloid train wreck led you here to our chapter, which will have *absolutely nothing* to do with that movie. But don't worry. Unlike the movie, here you'll be educated and edified *and* entertained. Promise!

So . . . *Forget the movie*. To get you as deep as possible into the world of Deadpool and what makes him tick, one of my alternate universe selves and I will explore the philosophical issues that can be found in the four-part comic book series *Deadpool Kills Deadpool*.

(He obviously doesn't, since they're still making *Deadpool* comic books. And celluloid train wrecks. So it seems as though Deadpool can't even get a simple thing like killing himself right! And you wonder why American companies outsource their work to Third World hellholes. [Can I say "Third World" in a Popular Culture and Philosophy book? I for one hope that I can!])

Diving into the Deep End of the (Dead)Pool
—The Book of John-$e^{i\pi}$ 1:1

There are an infinite number of universes in Multiversal space, and in each one, there is a slightly different, always unique, version of Deadpool. (Except, of course, for that one universe where there's no Deadpool, right? Or maybe there's an infinite number of those universes, too? It's so easy to lose track of your fingers and your toes when you're counting to infinity.)

While busy battling the giant robot Ultimatum, the Deadpool of the Marvel Universe, the one from your very own Earth-616, is interrupted by the arrival of the Deadpool Corps.[1] He is informed that the Deadpools of all the universes are being hunted and killed. What do you call it when you're killing alternate universe versions of yourself? I mean, it's sort of murder, but also suicide, no? Or is it bad manners? What do you call it when you're killing alternate universe versions of yourself? I mean, it's sort of murder, but also suicide, no? Or is it bad manners?

Surviving an attack by a black-leather-clad Deadpool-murdering Deadpool assassin, he is soon thereafter informed by a Watcher of the reason for this metacidal murder spree in Multiversal space. It all comes down to the belief that "Deadpool is the progenitor of all things." The Watcher explains to Deadpool-616 that a rogue Deadpool in another universe had come to believe that he was "nothing more than a fictional character." This Deadpool wanted to end "his suffering—and the suffering of all fictional beings" by killing them. ALL of them.

Seeing that killing off fictional characters wasn't doing the trick, this Deadpool came to believe that it must be because he, Deadpool, was the source of all things! Of all reality! And thus, to end the suffering of all fictional characters, ALL the Deadpools in Multiversal space must die! Deadpool-616 reflects, "That plan takes a seriously messed up kind of crazy . . . Gotta admit. Sounds like me."

The Watcher notes that this is a situation where all of the Deadpools "struggle against their very selves . . . and never

---

[1] This includes Lady Deadpool (Earth-3010). Which brings to mind the question: what would you call it if Deadpool (Earth-616) and Lady Deadpool "got it on"? Hey, will this question give this chapter an NC-17 rating?!?!

have they faced a more cunning foe." Indeed, it's a "struggle against one's very being!" But if that's the case, that means that Deadpool-616 will have to fight versions of *himself*. This means that he'd have to outsmart himself. Which must be impossible![2]

Deadpool-616, the Deadpool Corps, Pandapool, and the Watcher[3] all collaborate to end the efforts of the Deadpool-murdering Deadpools. At the very end, we see Deadpool-616 prevail.[4] All's swell that ends swell! Except for Pandapool. Poor poor Pandapool. And the hot Lady Deadpool. And the Watcher. And everyone else who decided to show up to this sausage fest. (Memo to future self: stay the HELL away from Deadpool!)

You may not believe me when I tell you that *Deadpool Kills Deadpool* is littered with clues that point to what's really going on in the world of your very own snarky *anti*-hero. All you have to do is see to where all the clues *point*. So let's start at the beginning. The very first scene we encounter has the black-leather-clad Deadpool-murdering Deadpool assassin microwaving an alternate universe version, "Headpool," to death. Right before Headpool explodes (microwave ovens will do that to you), this Deadpool remarks, "Every time I killed one of you . . . others . . . It felt like I was killing a piece of myself." But when this same Deadpool drives a chainsaw into Deadpool-616's chest from behind him, Deadpool-616 survives! And curiously, three pages later, Deadpool's uniform is repaired! An important point, to which we'll return. *If I feel like it*.

Deadpool-616 is told that the alternate universe versions of him "think just like you do." The Watcher Himself appears to break the fourth wall (*which does not exist—more on this later*); and He suggests that the original Deadpool-murdering Deadpool can create all the "soldiers" he could possibly need, which is paradoxical, since that would mean the end of the story before it even began.

---

[2] But Deadpool would finally experience what it's like trying to come to grips with Editor Nicolas Michaud's suggested changes to these wonderful chapters! LOL! Just kidding, Nick! (*No, I'm not! LOL-squared!*)

[3] Yes, the one that watches all the Deadpools. Gotta wonder what the retirement plan is like for a thankless, mind-numbing job like that!

[4] A new and improved Evil Deadpool also survives, watching from a hiding place. But look carefully. I claim that the storyboard panel is incorrect here. Can you spot what I believe is the error? No? Tsk tsk tsk. . . .

Quite a number of the alternate universe versions of Deadpool seem to be based on superheroes and supervillains, for instance we see a Sue Richards (Fantastic Four) version, a Wolverine version, Galactus, and so on. At the end, Deadpool-616 asks the original Deadpool-murdering Deadpool, "Why don't we dream up a better life?" He is told "We both know why. Your subconscious won't let you." Deadpool-616 is "too weak to stop it. To stop . . . yourself . . ."

All of these clues make figuring out what's going on "pretty fricking easy, if you ask me," to steal a phrase from Deadpool-616. You do see where all of these clues are pointing to, don't you? Deadpool is clearly mentally ill. The medical experiments that he was subjected to have driven him insane. He's delusional. He has no real control over his actions. He can't stop doing the same thing over and over again: killing. And even he admits this. "I'm good for one thing. And that's killing chumps." (And being snarky. Always always with the snarky.)

He believes that he's a comic-book character who knows that he's a comic-book character, and that he can talk to his "readers." (Stop thinking that a fourth wall really exists, and that comic-book characters can actually talk to you! Patience! You'll learn soon enough why this is impossible!) He not only thinks he's now fighting and killing alternate universe versions of himself, but he readily admits that the whole crazy idea sounds *just like him*. Finally, he's supposed to be impossible to kill, given his regenerative powers. But now we conveniently have "universal acid . . . flesh-eating nanotech . . . cauterization beams . . . and muta-regenerative overload grenades." You surely must have connected all the dots by now, haven't you? As a fictional character, Deadpool—and there really is *only one* Deadpool—and his true reality—of which there can be *only one*—no need to count to infinity—what's *really* going on here—can be described in just two words:

NARCISSISM and SOLIPSISM

Drowning in a (Dead)Pool of Quicksand

—The Wrong of Way of John-616 2:1

What the . . . ?!?! Did you too just suffer reading through that nonsense? I for one have a dull, throbbing headache, I mean it *really* hurts! You had *nothing* better to do than read this pabulum? You could have at least saved your hard-earned money, saved for your retirement or a trip to wherever, but no, you went out and bought this book! Suckas!

I guess I shouldn't be so mean. I should apologize. (Yeah, right. Wait for that.) I mean, John-$e^{i\pi}$ *is* an alternate universe version of me, so it's not like I don't *understand* his special brand of crazy. And I mean, who *isn't* crazy in today's chaotic, mixed-up, postmodern world?

Well, at least someone is doing their "job" and guiding you (if only John-$e^{i\pi}$ knew the *real* you!) through the philosophical minefield that is *Deadpool Kills Deadpool*. So, let's recap. We've learned that Deadpool is crazy; he thinks there's a "fourth wall" (No, there isn't) and that he can talk to his readers (No, he can't); and he thinks that there are Deadpools killing other Deadpools throughout the Multiverse so as to EndRealityAsWeKnowIt.

By the end of *Deadpool Kills Deadpool*, Deadpool-616 sees himself as the "Last Deadpool standing!", which *has* to mean that *his* universe *really was and is* reality. *All* of reality. *It has to be*. (It's called *common sense*, look into it. Also, if it weren't, then YOU wouldn't be here, reading this chapter. Right? A chapter which is a thousand times more entertaining than that celluloid train wreck you're still enraptured by. Right? Glad you agree.)

So if that's the case (and four-part comic-book series don't lie, they just *can't*, it's part of the Comic Books Code, yes it is, it says so, right there, in invisible ink), *then it's all in crazy ole Deadpool's head. All of it.*

But let's get back to my alternate universe doppelganger/ know-it-all/*idiot* savant, John-$e^{i\pi}$, and have him continue with his philosophical ruminations/idiocy/nonsense about what's really going on in *Deadpool Kills Deadpool*. Which is all in Deadpool's head. Which is really all in our *hands*, since Deadpool is a comic book, and, as you will very soon see, *there is no fourth wall!* I'm just going to kick back and enjoy the rest of the ride for now.

(But . . . Seriously . . . If all of reality *really is* in Deadpool's head . . . Doesn't that make Deadpool *God*? Shouldn't we be covering our *you-know-whats* and start praying to *Him*???) ⮌ ▶ △ ↳ ↔ ◀ ↓ ↸ ⇇ ⇨ △ ⇕ ⤓ ▷ ↑ ⇕ ⇨ △ ◀ ↓ ↔ ⇨ ⇕ ↘ ↓ ⇨ ⇦ ⇕ ⇕ ↗

⇇⇨⇨◁⇨↔⤓↑⇨↙↙⇕▷⇨⇦⇦⇨◀↑◢▽↔⇨△↗◢⇨◀◀↓◀▶⇦⇨↘↘↘[5]

Wading Through a CessPool of Dead Philosophers

—The Book of John-e$^{i\pi}$ 2:1

You may not agree with my conclusion. But then you'd be *wrong*. Deadpool-616 isn't *just* the only Deadpool out there. He's a narcissist; he's mentally ill; and he's in a persistent delusional state. *Yes, it's all in his head. And so are you. All of you. Accept it!* And this means that . . . Drum roll, please . . . THERE—IS—NO—FOURTH—WALL!

There's nothing wrong with looking out for yourself. It's normal to be a bit narcissistic, or as Swiss-French philosopher Jean-Jacques Rousseau (1712–1778) called it, to have "self-love." Self-love is important, because without having at least some positive interest in one's own well-being, a person could not go forth in the world and stand up for oneself. Rousseau called this type of self-love *amour en soi*. It's distinguished from a self-love that has become extreme and pathological, which Rousseau called *amour propre*. Deadpool is caught in an endless cycle of killing, and he's not really interested in understanding other points of view. Deadpool is beyond *amour en soi*, and firmly in the grips of *amour propre*. How deeply? *Deadpool just doesn't care*!

In developing his theory of psychoanalysis, Austrian neurologist Sigmund Freud (1856–1939) saw narcissism as being a part of the normal development of the ego as you progressed from childhood to adulthood. But as with anything psychological, it is possible to either get trapped in a developmental stage, or to regress back to an earlier one. Deadpool has regressed back from adulthood to that developmental stage from where narcissism first sprang. French psychoanalyst Jacques Lacan (1901–1981) also believed that it's during childhood that you first experience a narcissistic phase. Here, you imagine yourself to be powerful by identifying with a more perfect mirror image. We see how deep into narcissism Deadpool is when we

[5] Yes, this means something. Can't you read it? It's in plain English!

notice that some of the alternate universe "Pools" are based on superheroes and supervillains. In fact, Deadpool is so far into his narcissism that he sees himself reflected everywhere! Deadpool even rationalizes this delusion about the other "Pools": "Everybody wants to be the genuine article."

There are also clues to Deadpool's narcissism in how he relates to others. Erich Fromm (1900–1980) believed that a malignant form of narcissism could arise when someone becomes so self-involved that their willfulness becomes extreme. In fact, when this freedom to act becomes too great a burden to bear, a culture that is narcissistic may turn to the security of fascism. And Deadpool is in a sense a fascist. He is incredibly self-involved; he imposes his views on the world by killing; and he does as he wants, when he wants, and without any real concern for the consequences. Did I neglect to mention that Deadpool *just doesn't care*?

Herbert Marcuse (1898–1979), however, took another approach to narcissism. He saw it as an alternative to social control imposed on people through unconscious conformity. Marcuse would claim that Deadpool embraces his inner narcissist because it gives him the ability to defend himself against a world that he perceives is trying to control him. It may be that Deadpool isn't a delusional homicidal narcissistic who just doesn't care. Rather, he's really just rejecting the social order and experiencing *his* reality in a truer, more authentic way!

So, you can look at narcissism from two different perspectives. Narcissism can be beneficial or detrimental. On the one hand, narcissism, at least in moderation, has some psychologically beneficial aspects. It's normal to want to look out for yourself. You may also use narcissism to rebel against what you perceive to be a social order that seeks to place limits on your life. On the other hand, narcissism taken to a pathological extreme results in, among other things, living a life where the plotline, and your future, never change. For Deadpool, this plotline is one of non-stop killing to the tune of a non-stop snarky attitude!

But it's not just narcissism that we find in *Deadpool Kills Deadpool*. We also find solipsism. Solipsism is the philosophical position that there is only one person out there: YOU. And that everything that you think you're experiencing, that you know about the world, is all just in your head. That there is no real world, no reality, outside of what you are thinking at the present moment. And you can even have crazy ideas, like, you're not a real person, but rather a comic book character, an *anti-hero*, if you will, who has amazing regenerative powers, and that you can speak to the people who read the comic books you're "in."

This would also mean that you're the only being with real access to reality, indeed, you create reality—*all* of reality. Deadpool claims that he knows that he's a comic-book character who has readers. We know that he's absolutely correct, but there's no way for him to prove it. And can he really claim to know this if he can never prove it? The original Deadpool-killing Deadpool thought that *he* was the source of all reality; but, since we know that by the end of the story, Deadpool-616 is the *real* Deadpool, then all of reality must be in *his* head! *Yes, we're all just figments of his imagination!*[6] *This* is why Deadpool claims that he can "break the fourth wall."

Seriously, have *you* ever fantasized about talking back to Deadpool when he "breaks the fourth wall?" Did you find yourself "answering back" whenever Deadpool "spoke" to you during that celluloid train wreck you still can't stop gushing over? *Hello Deadpool. How's your day going? Got yourself a bit of the crazies today? Like you do every day?* Wait, you say he can't hear you? Really? Deadpool can't break through the fourth wall because fictional characters CAN'T break through anything! Comic books are simply colored drawings meant to entertain. And whereas everyone has chosen to suspend their disbelief and come to believe that Deadpool can break through the fourth wall, that he's "meta," the fact is that he's just a delusional, insane, fictional character who's an unstoppable killing machine.

It's time to face cold, hard reality. *Deadpool believes that he's breaking through the fourth wall because he's insane.* You see how serious I am about this? About denying the existence of the fourth wall? I've underlined it!!! Yes. The lights are on, but there's no one home. The creators and writers of *Deadpool* have

[6] As in "the fourth wall." Always always with that fourth wall. *Which doesn't exist.* Regardless of how adamant—I mean "confused"—fellow contributor Rhiannon Grant is. (Just ignore her, and her little chapter, too.)

pulled a fast one on you, and you've unwittingly—what do I know, perhaps willingly—become ensnared in their nefarious conspiracy to pull the wool over your eyes. Maybe *you're* narcissistic enough to believe that *a comic-book character would break the fourth wall to talk to you*! "Whatever flies your kite," as Samurai-Deadpool would say.

Yes. It's all just been a terrible lie. No "fourth wall." No "meta." No snarky *anti*-hero who really cares about making a difference, or who even "knows" that you're "really" out there. Earlier in this chapter, my alternate universe self summed up your "condition" quite nicely:

Suckas!

Swimming in the (Dead)Pool of Chum That Is Philosophy

—The Train Wreck That Is John-616 3:1

I'd like to say that's the end of this chapter. But it's not. Far from it. The best is right here in this section. (*My* section. Of course.) Hasn't reading this chapter been a far better experience than watching a celluloid train wreck in a crowded, noisy theater with sticky floors and torn seats? I mean, I haven't distracted you from reading this chapter every five minutes by checking for IMs on my cellphone, have I? Seriously, aren't you glad you stuck it out here? Not that I . . . er, why, yes, I'm glad you did!

Anyway, my alternate universe counterpart has finally shut up—a true miracle, in and of itself, trust me!—so allow me to wrap things up nice and neat. You *will* allow me to wrap things up nice and neat, won't you? *Thank you*. That's so *magnanimous* of you.

Anyway, I have a couple of *twists* that I want to share. (No extra charge.) In *Deadpool Kills Deadpool*, we have demonstrated that Deadpool is a fictional character whose true nature is that he is a narcissist who lives in a delusional, solipsistic world. But if you've studied philosophy for any length of time, you can draw interesting parallels between the themes of narcissism and solipsism in *Deadpool Kills Deadpool* and both the history and the world of Western philosophy. In fact, Steven James Bartlett proposed such parallels in "Narcissism and Philosophy."

Bartlett believes that "the nature of philosophic activity promotes and is encouraged by many qualities of personality which closely resemble qualities that define narcissism." Bartlett notes that in the world of philosophy, there are divergent views about reality, and "no shared universe of discourse in which to assess competing views." Philosophers are willful, in that they create their own view of how the world works, and defend it against every other philosopher who has ever lived or will live. Philosophers do not willingly submit to having others evaluate, and perchance destroy, their construction of reality—*their exclusive, solipsistic world.* This would make Socrates (470–399 B.C.E.) the only true philosopher to have ever lived; and every other person claiming to be a philosopher has simply been either a sophist or a rhetorician. Socrates never claimed to have found the right, *final* answer to any of the questions that he ever asked. Bartlett also notes that "Philosophers seem 'possessed' by a need to be always right," and that criticism reveals more of a desire for "one-upmanship" than for constructive dialog.

So, the history of philosophy contains surprising parallels to what we've seen in *Deadpool Kills Deadpool*. Every philosopher claims to have sole access to the truth, *just doesn't care* whether any other philosopher criticizes his ideas, and ends up having "followers" who take up his clarion call and promote his views. *Metaphorically, every philosopher wants to kill every other philosopher*. Or at least their ideas, which is what makes a philosopher a philosopher, right? Right???

Wow. *Deadpool Kills Deadpool* reads like the history of philosophy. How philosophy has always worked. *Exactly how philosophy works.* And you thought you were just reading a four-part comic-book series about some *anti*-hero clown with a snarky attitude running around in a spandex suit, killing people left and right for the greater glory of his ego! Seriously, aren't you glad you that you read this chapter? Doesn't this stunning world-shattering conclusion fill you with more rapture, bring you to greater heights, than that celluloid train wreck you actually paid money to see? Truly, you've been educated and edified *and* entertained! As promised!

Here's my *second* twist to all of this. Authors of chapters in books in the Popular Culture and Philosophy series (like the book you are now holding in your hands) believe that they should bring *their* philosophy to the poor unwashed masses by demonstrating applications of *their* philosophy to works of fiction, movies, television shows, and also to cultural icons. And that in so doing, the poor unwashed masses will have their lives greatly enriched by having read *their* brilliant ideas. Authors like me and my alternate universe counterparts. *Brilliant* authors.

I know, absolutely *crazy*, isn't it? *Authors?* Huh! *More like complete, utter, shameless, batsh*t-insane narcissists, each living in a delusional, solipsistic world of their own creation.*

Suckas![7]

---

[7] *Deadpool and Philosophy*'s editor, Nicolas Michaud, will be taking a hiatus from helming books in the popular culture and philosophy genre, into the deep, dark, cold abyss. In other words, he'll soon be yet another unemployed PhD serving coffee to people with *real* jobs. Please send your heartfelt charitable contributions, or in the alternative, whatever loose change you find behind your sofa seats, to him, care of publisher Open Court. Thank you. A PhD in Philosophy is *such* a terrible thing to waste!

4

How Much Deadpool Is Too Much Deadpool?

KRISTA BONELLO RUTTER GIAPPONE AND CALEB TURNER AND DEADPOOL AND DOGPOOL AND PANDAPOOL AND ZENPOOL AND DREADPOOL AND GWEN-POOL AND./. WELL YOU GET THE F$&#ING IDEA . . .

How much Deadpool is too much Deadpool? ***This should be good.*** *Never enough, it seems* . . . and this is where *excess* comes in!

Deadpool is excessive in all things, and on the surface this doesn't appear too great for purposes of storytelling. Whenever he's maiming criminal henchmen with joyous abandon, Deadpool's violence comes across as just a little *too* violent for any heroic role model. When cracking wise and cracking skulls, or waxing lyrical or obscene about each kill, ***I DO do that.*** Deadpool's humor is, again, just a little *too* gratuitous for a proper hero.

There's a problem then—Heroes. Are. Meant. To. Be. *Disciplined.* Villains are not. ***Thanks for the update.***

Any hero-vigilante (take your pick: Batman, Spider-Man, Wonder Woman, Daredevil, yada yada yada . . .) properly checks and channels physical aggression, either with a chivalrous tone of humor or dedicated self-restraint, so drawing a line between "necessary" or "unnecessary" levels of violence. ***Hey, I do that too . . . sometimes.***

So, Deadpool's relentlessly escalating superabundance of violence troubles the storytelling process by compromising what it really means to be a disciplined (and morally-driven!) hero. But, if you take anything away from this chapter, it should be this—*Deadpool is entertaining because of, rather than in spite of, his excesses, which define his erratic approach to breaking any or all boundaries of heroic violence, humor, justice and the storytelling structures that shape his movie, game, and comic books.*

Deadpool's antics are exciting precisely because his excesses allow him to rebel against established storytelling conventions of disciplined heroism—which then impact on the readers, viewers, or players of his stories to the point that it ***Here comes the science bit!*** breaks apart the integrity and internal consistency of his comics, videogame, and movie. It is because he is an excess junkie ***I like that*** that Deadpool can keep testing the boundaries and assumptions of genre and medium, through parody, exaggeration, and interruptions, even extending his impact to "our" world.

Extreme Juggling

Near the opening of his 2016 movie, Deadpool leaps into a moving vehicle packed with villainous henchmen on the freeway. As one criminal lackey after another tries to shoot, punch or stab the vigilante in the confines of this car, Deadpool cracks a joke, showing a self-portrait (cum wanted poster) drawn in crayon, declaring "Have you seen this man!?" As the driver loses control, flipping the vehicle over, these hired bodies are hurled onto the road, splattering blood (and I dread to think what else) across the tarmac.

In the midst of this slow-mo spinning upturned crash, Deadpool tentatively pokes his head out through the sunroof of the car, idly pondering "Did I leave the stove on?" as irrelevancies divert his attention from the situation at hand. He then grabs the last remaining bad guy in mid-air, hurling him into a road sign, splattering more blood before the car comes to a stop.

Though impressive, this physical and verbal juggling of violence and humor also reflects something profound about Deadpool's shifting states of mind. Although he may be a mercenary (a.k.a. Wade Wilson), Deadpool is like any other superhero or vigilante crime fighter who juggles excesses of violence (and humor) for his trade. Spider-Man cracks wise in between taking down criminals. Even the firm-jawed Batman will quip a dour one-liner on occasion after defeating his rogues' gallery.

But conventionally, such brutality or humorous banter should *always* be disciplined. Heroes, even anti-heroes, are supposed to use self-control to channel their aggression. Heroes do this to avoid succumbing to the same irrational or self-indulgent sadism frequently enjoyed by villains—to distinguish themselves from those they fight, and to preserve the perceived purity of that opposition.

In the 2016 movie, Deadpool is in pursuit of the heartless scientist Ajax, seeking revenge for the torture and mutilation this sadist inflicted on him. Ajax tortured Wade to stimulate and trigger the anti-hero's dormant mutant healing capabilities. But the torture didn't stop there. Ajax continued to hurt Wade—just for the fun of it. A hero should not give in to the same impulses as the villain. But when Wade eventually captures Ajax, he takes pleasure in the attack, prolonging each strike with variety and humor, giving in to the same emotional excesses as his sadistic adversary. Wade can't change the fact that he was tortured by Ajax and had his face terribly mutilated. What Deadpool *can* change is how he judges and responds to terrible life moments.

The ancient Greek philosopher Zeno of Citium (334–262 B.C.) explained that heroes need *stoicism*—to accept that there are random moments of chaos in life we have no control over, and will never be able to change, but within our control is our rational state of mind to deal with whatever may come our way. Rational acceptance compels Deadpool to protect others from a similar fate. By adopting a stoic mental state he can change things—deciding to stop Ajax from hurting anyone else. Deadpool, like stoic heroes, does not repress past pain, but uses the mental state of stoicism to avoid succumbing to excesses of outrage and disappointment. When Deadpool manages to juggle excesses with stoicism, he is in harmony with forces beyond his control.

This may all be well and good, but Wade still does not juggle emotional excesses in the same way as other stoic heroes. After capturing Ajax, rationally he should hand the villain over to the authorities, or, if Wade "needs" to kill him, then just do it quickly. Wade's stoic control over his emotions got him this far, but (if you remember from earlier) he becomes recklessly brutal, taking a little *too much* time and pleasure over his kicks and punches. He externalizes his excesses in word and deed, releasing them through jokes and violence instead of imposing moderation. Violence often becomes the opportunity for a joke—such as when he's distracted by two passing X-Men, but still manages to absentmindedly throw wheel caps at Ajax's head during the conversation. No longer focused on his task, Wade's lapse in concentration allows the villain to escape.

His juggling act has faltered. A hero's professional courage, in its extreme, becomes too overzealous or reckless, and if it is not effective enough, then it gives way to lack of concentration, or even cowardice. Deadpool's balance between a deficient kind of violence (not forceful enough) and excessive violence (far too forceful) is a juggling act all heroes bear. The desirable midpoint between these two extremes of excess and deficiency is what another ancient Greek philosopher, Aristotle (384–322 B.C.), called the golden mean.

Deadpool's juggling act always tends to lurch towards the excessive end of the scale. He's more driven by impulse than discipline, and becomes unpredictable as a result. In refusing to strictly follow the stoic juggling act, often giving in to reckless sadism and indulgent savagery, Deadpool resists the classical virtues and tropes of heroism. But, although he's a mercenary for hire, he still believes innocents should be protected, and only directs firepower at wrongdoers. This seeming contradiction raises the question of how each of us should balance our own excesses. Should we always apply restraint and stoicism, or can we sometimes indulge ourselves when coping with traumatic events? Deadpool's use of humor gives us a hint of some answers.

Cracking Wise, and Cracking Up

Deadpool. Cracks. Wise . . . All the time. His endless dry wit and outrageously puerile banter is meant to take the edge off his escalating blood-raining ultra-violence, making it more palatable.

To do this he often draws attention to his gyrating crotch, or unleashes a steady stream of butt jokes and innuendos. In the movie, he quips about masturbating after gunning down henchmen ("I'm touching myself tonight") or refers to sex techniques while hurting another henchman with a cigarette lighter ("I've never said this, but don't swallow"). When a criminal lackey shoots Wade in the behind, the hero declares in rage "Right Up Main Street!"

But this wisecracking is delivered with rapid-fire frequency well above that of heroes who simply enjoy a good joke (like the funny man Spider-Man). Wade's screwball vaudevillian humor is not just meant to ease violent tension, but is his way of constantly trying not to crack up mentally. For Wade, a personal blend of anarchic comedy is the best coping mechanism to deal with being mutilated (which almost drove him to lose his sanity altogether). He overcomes personal pain through comedy, sometimes allowing us to forgive his crass behavior.

Deadpool laughs in the face of social prejudice, and mocks what is considered "normal" or "appropriate." Forsaking his inhibitions releases a puerile and offensive brand of humor that Russian philosopher Mikhail Bakhtin (1895–1975) calls carnival excess. Carnivals like Mardi Gras in New Orleans or Rio Carnival in Rio de Janeiro are a time and place of public (often sexualized) revelry not normally permitted in everyday society.

In the carnival, people can wear grotesque masks with gaping laughing mouths, and flamboyant costumes, or not very much at all, proudly displaying barely-covered genitalia, singing and dancing to a riotous procession of loud music—in the spirit of irreverent excess. Deadpool's likability becomes wrapped up in mixing extreme trauma with this kind of humor.

Wade embraces carnival antics, casting off social decency for anarchic fun and cathartic celebration whenever he reminds us of his various orifices (that should really be hidden in "civilized" society). The carnival is a temporary outlet to vent our repressed frustration with the conventions imposed by society, and after it is over, society's stipulations can continue to be imposed as usual. Carnival is a license for free play, perhaps no more than a safe space and time provided by society itself. However, what if the carnival refuses to stick to the set margins?

As you've seen with this book's unhealthy obsession about Deadpool's compulsion to break the fourth wall, currently raging on between Rhiannon Grant, John V. Karavitis, Chris Ketcham, and Shawn McKinney, the guy is either *well* aware or under an impression at least that he exists within the worlds of fictional comic-books, movies, or videogames. He plays within and across mediums, and uses madcap excess that belongs in the carnival to *overspill* these spatial and media boundaries. As Deadpool manipulates the bits and bobs making up his movie set, videogame world, comic panels, or any piece and part attached to these surrounding spaces, this eccentricity reveals to us that he's not only completely aware he exists in a virtual, digital, or illustrated environment, but that he's also aware of how to drift between these different kinds of fictional space, or "storytelling mediums."

Playing Around

Deadpool's first appearance in 1991 had him being FedExed back to sender. Thus does our favorite "Merc with the Mouth" begin his career—with a missed target, unexpected arrival, and turnaround, where error or failure interacts with chance to re-route Deadpool in unceremonious manner, which yet smacks of extravagant flourish.

From the outset, Deadpool is associated with a role which inhabits a zone of "drifting"—a straying element that demonstrates the very possibility of erring from a "proper" path, a possibility which lies even at what may appear to be the heart of any structure. Jacques Derrida (1930–2004) (commenting on Edgar Allan Poe's story "The Purloined Letter") notes that the possibility of non-arrival demonstrates something more radical—that a letter "never truly arrives," beset rather with "internal drifting". What a striking beginning then for Deadpool, literally dispatched and set adrift on a *circuitous re-routing* through a postal system.

Derrida's idea of drifting suggests something about the peculiarity of Deadpool's position. On the one hand, he is entertaining enough, and certainly over-the-top enough, to dominate a scene even when simply sharing an aside with the reader, or to "photo-bomb" (or panel-bomb) an established hero. We would say "steal a scene," but it is rarely that subtle. On the other hand, he has a particular function as comic foil, and his own excesses come across more strongly in contrast with a character of more "traditional" heroic stature. Even his solo outings have featured many moments where he pops up unexpectedly, as if to interrupt or divert the actual heroics.

He is intent on keeping one step ahead of the more efficient X-Men in the *Deadpool* game—a game framed as commissioned, written, and improvised by him *and* which apparently has Deadpool at its center (as he is quick to point out). Yet even here, his role is governed by his capacity for interruption, play, and leading astray—his taste for antics and explosions gets in the X-Men's way, as they attempt to more directly pursue *their* goals. His "story" takes place as intrusion, in the space carved as he derails them—not quite his "own" space. He maintains a cheerful disregard for propriety—when he "borrows" space, he does so without compromise, apology, or proportion.

The Merc with the Mouth is no idle moniker. One of Deadpool's most recognizable–and shall we say, endearing (all the more so, in direct proportion to the annoyance expressed by "in-panel characters")—features is that he *will not shut up.* Ever. Not even death can shut him up—the healing factor ensures he will keep bouncing back. Yet he has also slipped into Lady Death's domain a few times, and managed to sustain conversation (and likely bone-r) there. Deadpool's commentary runs alongside drawing attention to his body in mock-provocative poses, or lavatory humor of the best—that is, crudest—sort.

These, with the liberties Deadpool seems licensed to take, remind us of Bakhtin's idea about carnivals focusing on orifices (including the mouth) and processes involving bodily excess or "downward movement"—gorging on food, gleefully releasing waste products on the world, his action-delaying piss at the urinal in the game, or the ever-extending black-bar-of-censorship when he sits down for a shit (or "stink pickle") (for more on this check out *Rabelais and His World*, p. 370).

The latter example is telling, in its combination of, on the one hand, a "realist" focus on the trivialities and mundanities of everyday existence, and on the other, its (literal) prolonging of them, spinning them into a "meta" joke on the capabilities and flexibilities of the videogame medium. Both Deadpool's bodily flesh and the artificial qualities of the medium are shown to intersect, as Wade refers to this unnaturally elongating black bar of a phallus as counterintuitively "much more realistic." Its implications are likewise extended, for Deadpool is not entirely confined within his videogame world. In the game, Deadpool's name appears everywhere—as co-creator, designer, programmer, ideas man, consultant on almost everything—he spills into the credits, taking credit. He recognizes a player, addressing her/him and commenting on their skill or lack thereof (after several returns to checkpoint, Deadpool commented that perhaps I should hand the controller to a more skilled player—"there's a thought").

Deadpool is also the player, or at least appears to displace the player—sometimes playfully, sometimes forcefully. The game's epilogue zooms out to Deadpool sitting down holding a controller. At another point, a legless Deadpool drops onto a foe and wears the suddenly-sightless staggering villain like a finger puppet—torso over head—rendering action and mobility clumsy and slow. Deadpool, ever the shrewd observer of the obvious, comments: "Dude. We have another dude inside us."

The constraints on movement at this point seem to mimic the stumbles of a player still getting to grips with the game mechanics and Deadpool comments with amusement on the sudden awkwardness of the controls. The excessive self-awareness of this moment blatantly highlights the very mediation which interrupts direct action on the world, a mediation which habitual practice might blind us to.

By declaring there is a "dude inside us", Deadpool seems to suggest that the player—like the floundering opponent—is just as inadequate, and also as dependent on Deadpool as Deadpool seems to be on the player. ***Pretty Meta right?*** Moreover, the relationship isn't one of simply being in-sync, nor one of mere opposition, but rather there is a margin for *cross-purposes*, for difference—Deadpool *is* the player. Deadpool *is not* the player. Deadpool, of course, isn't quite Deadpool, so much as "Deadpool(s)"—a conglomeration-cacophony of voices, a trait established by Daniel Way, who also wrote the game. Deadpool lacks internal integrity, enabling too an externalization of *multiple* Deadpools in the game.

Cullen Bunn's comic run culminates in *Deadpool Kills Deadpool*, as several interdimensional Deadpools come up against each other, with Deadpool revealed to be the "progenitor of all things!", thus the key to both knotting and undoing the comic's structure. These cheeky moves demonstrate a particular property of the character—his threshold position which challenges our assumptions about how boundaries function (and which yet has a peculiar generative force).

Getting a Leg-Up

Whenever Deadpool overspills his comic, movie, or game mediums, he's not quite of "our world"—*nor is he completely of the comic-book-game-movie worlds he moves around in*. He is both "inside" and "outside." But what does this actually do to his storytelling mediums? As you would probably guess by now, Deadpool has little reverence for boundaries ***I just can't help myself! I'll break anything, from lampshades to genre tropes, from smashing apart TV screens to . . . well . . . smashing through any storytelling screen. Can't box me in, baby!*** Deadpool brings in the possibility that any particular medium is not really "pure" in its apparently contained form. The game sometimes uses comic-book format, sometimes as a self-contained feature. You can click on certain characters, such as Cable, to learn more about them—such information is drawn from their comic-book appearances, like dipping into an archive, accessible at the click of a button.

Other times, comic-book conventions play a surprisingly more pivotal role, actually gaining materiality in gameworld terms, and becoming a means to manipulate the world—for example, while *en route* to his destination, Deadpool's proliferating "thought-boxes" materialize into a series of platforms that physically give him a leg-up, so he can cross a wide gap. This inconsistency is however not fully integrated into the game (it is not a consistent possibility at every point in the game, but a rare occurrence for gags). By paradoxically being both part of the game but also in some way disjointed, seeming to emerge from an intersection with another medium, this suggests a threshold riven by inconsistency.

If we were to assert that Deadpool has the ability to utterly separate himself from the world he inhabits, this would suggest a tidy opposition, which doesn't quite hold up to scrutiny. When he tests the device, "Do I still think in those little yellow boxes?" at the end of Gail Simone's "Agent X" story arc (Volume 1, #67), he does it precisely through the medium of yellow thought-boxes. Here, his comment not only applies to the identified comic-book convention, but it is also enabled and conveyed by the device itself.

For Deadpool, humor and violence often remind us of the form of the mediums he appears in, and his gags become *more than is necessary* for the storytelling—done at the expense (and so in excess) of what the plot really needs. Film theorist Kristen Thompson explains that this is how excess works in storytelling mediums: too much attention to stylistic devices occurs at the expense of what the storytelling needs, in effect drawing *too much* attention to the materials of mediums. It's this kind of playful excess that allows Deadpool to reveal the fabric and form of the different mediums that attempt to contain him. The 2016 movie is packed with self-aware gags that depend on him manipulating the frame to surprise viewers, while also encapsulating a quality of the frame.

At one such point in the movie Deadpool forcibly draws our attention to images far too similar in shape to one another. When Wade is kicked sideways into a car for example, arms akimbo, the Merc exclaims "Shit's just gone sideways—in the most colossal way!" The very next image cuts to an earlier Wade (pre-facial mutilation) holding a small toy action-figure of Deadpool, positioned in a similar pose. But this figure is taken from a completely different (and critically-panned) Deadpool film appearance in 2009 (*X-Men Origins: Wolverine*).

Deadpool also comments on how his actor Ryan Reynolds was in another (also critically-panned) superhero movie *Green Lantern* in 2011. This kind of excessive playfulness with allusions does not add anything to the plot—but what it does do is draw our attention to the way Deadpool has been presented across *other* various kinds of media, which requires an excessive delivery of force—and farce—to have this impact on viewers (and readers and gamers). His excessive force also impacts the inhabitants of his various storyworlds, and through parodic exaggeration may also adjust our view on the very nature of vigilante violence and lawful order.

Excessive Farce . . . I Mean Force

The nature of justice and the thorny relation of vigilante justice and violence to law have become central themes in the superhero genre. Superhero-vigilante justice is unauthorized by the legal structure, and unaccountable to it—it seems to *seize* its own justification in dealing with the inadequacies, inefficiencies, and overspill of official law enforcement and judicial systems, finding its *raison d'être* in supplementing existing deficiencies.

Many superheroes may themselves indirectly target the failings of established authority. But, being a mercenary, Deadpool comes into conflict with *both* law and other heroes, and so is *manifestly* in *excess* of what seems necessary—a supplement to the supplement. His lack of discrimination between the law, heroism, vigilantism, or kill-list contracts urges us to question the very nature of justification itself, even where it is less obviously disproportionate.

"Irresponsibility" is a byword of the *Deadpool* movie, parodying (the more chivalrous and morally stoic) Spider-Man's slogan. Yet, Deadpool does have a responsibility—which may run deeper: Deadpool's polyphony of voices, not quite in unison or harmony, provide both chorus and counter-song to the "rules" of the comic-book world. His excesses both typify their own, and exaggerate them—he is their foil, yet shares their attributes as likewise being the product of a structure with exploitable flaws.

Superpowers by definition already exceed the norm, yet are more or less "normalized" in a genre which features them so regularly and prominently, and where ordinary folk (including cops) are generally on the sidelines, curious bystanders, or helpless civilians to be protected, herded out of danger zones, or casualties in the battles of titans. Deadpool is excessive in much the same way, *but* he revels in play for its own sake.

In a 1997 Joe Kelly issue, Deadpool encounters Taskmaster, who can mimic anyone's fighting style—hero or villain's—with systematic accuracy. Deadpool baffles and defeats Taskmaster by breaking into "erratic" dance. Taskmaster has numerous well-defined methods at his command. However, none seems suited to the occasion, as Deadpool departs at an oblique angle from established patterns by indulging in overt play and giving Taskmaster something in excess of expectation. In a way, Taskmaster is emblematic of the underlying structure, stripping back, reproducing patterns, assimilating and readily receiving their impression. He has even run a training school. This is discipline intensified, and it makes him a particularly effective reference-point and foil for Deadpool's excessive and frivolous parody. Deadpool disrupts every well-laid plan, and leaps from frying pan to fire with reckless abandon—indeed, he has a willing hand in sparking most fires.

Can We Ever Have Too Much Deadpool?

All in all, we can never have too much Deadpool—because his irrepressibility and excess are precisely where Deadpool gets his power and particular brand of self-determination. His excesses afford him a certain freedom that we, and even other heroes or vigilantes, are unable to achieve. He rises above the moral stipulations of heroism, then proceeds to play havoc with even the boundaries of the mediums that try to contain his film, game, comic, and TV appearances.

Deadpool finds ways to bend or stretch the rules—perhaps not with finality, since he too is a creature of those rules, and, in the spirit of slapstick comedy, they keep him bouncing back. Yet, he plays with the rigidity of the form, while seeming to offer a possibility of release by indulging in an escalating excess which seems boundless.

This is what makes Deadpool Deadpool—and we can never have too much of his liberating anarchic antics. In a literal overspill, Deadpool comics were recently splashed all over the freeway, in a truck accident from the Plattsburgh Distribution Centre to the Olive Branch Distribution Centre in the US. So, whenever or wherever excessive outbursts occur, be it inside or outside the fictional realm of the Marvel universe, Deadpool won't be far away. And we can't get enough of it . . .

Ah! So THAT'S why I'm so exess-able!!! . . . Can't Contain THIS! . . . Whatever, I'm outta here . . . Maybe go and have a look see at what they're all saying about me in the next chapter . . .

II

I'm No Hero

Seriously, Why Do We Like This Guy? He Has No Redeeming Qualities Other than a Moderately-Sized Dick and I, for One, Would Rather F$#% the Avocado*

5
The Anti-Hero's Journey

ANDY VINK BECAUSE CAPTAIN AMERICA WASN'T AVAILABLE

When you hear the name "Deadpool," *hero* is not the first word that comes to mind. That word or phrase may actually be "merc," "sexiest man alive," "fool," or "@#&#^$."

Most people would consider him an anti-hero, given his villainous origins and moral ambiguity. Yet, in one of the best arcs of the recent Duggan-Posehn run on *Deadpool* in Marvel NOW, we see a new side of the character: we see a Deadpool who grows, struggles, and becomes more heroic. How the hell are we supposed to account for that? Isn't *Deadpool* the comic book we read to get our inappropriate jollies on?

The fact is, Duggan and Posehn's "The Good, the Bad, and the Ugly" has Deadpool follow the hero's journey. If that's the case, you may ask, then why doesn't he get a parade and a sweetheart like most of the other Marvel heroes? If Deadpool really is a hero, why doesn't he get the girl like most pop culture heroes?

The Deadpool We Know and Love

Comic books make room for comedic figures to lighten the mood. Deadpool tends to be this figure in Marvel books. As opposed to traditional heroes like Captain America and Wolverine, Deadpool is a nutty guy who makes light of any situation. He breaks the fourth wall, makes jokes about the Marvel comic book and movie universe, and tells the (sometimes inappropriate) jokes that make us laugh until we bust a rib.

In the "1970s throwback issue" of Marvel NOW *Deadpool*, Pooly breaks out his finest pimp hat and coat to work with Luke Cage and Iron Fist. We tend to read Deadpool as a relief from the more serious storylines of Marvel comics. Even in the dark *Uncanny X-Force* run by Rick Remender, Deadpool was able to keep it light for the most part.

So, should we take Deadpool seriously as a character? I mean, isn't he there just to make us laugh? Is there more to him than the adolescent humor, incessant banter, and overall glee that comes from the endless shenanigans? There is something more to the character than meets the eye; just because Wade plays the fool doesn't mean he is one.

From the beginning, Duggan and Posehn prepare us for this possibility of Deadpool being a deeper character than his foolish persona leads us to believe. After we see Agent Preston's consciousness placed in Deadpool's mind at the end of the "Dead Presidents" arc, we get a unique view into Deadpool's head. Preston's journey through Deadpool's consciousness shows us that there is a dark place in Deadpool's mind that is no laughing matter.

This dark side of Deadpool shows there is a more complex character beneath the surface. His foolish behavior conceals darker emotions, such as rage, injury, isolation, fear, and pain. These emotions reveal a more complex character beneath the mask: one who is capable of change. I'm not trying to say we should ignore the comedic elements of Deadpool and focus only on his deep, brooding storylines. Deadpool's comedy is part of the reason we love him so. I'm only suggesting the world is big enough for both funny stories and serious tales, like "The Good, the Bad, and the Ugly."

Joseph Campbell and the Hero's Journey

The mythology expert Joseph Campbell (1904–1987) follows an approach referred to in religious studies as universalism: a belief that all religions express the same basic truth, but differ in expression and appearance. Campbell thought that Jesus and the Buddha are playing the same role in a larger story. The differences between religions come from the different cultures with different value structures writing the story.

This larger, universal story, called "the hero's journey," can be found in various forms. One of the easiest places to see the hero's journey play out is in what would be Deadpool's favorite example: the original *Star Wars* trilogy. This should be no big surprise, as George Lucas actually crafted the story behind the movies in consultation with Joseph Campbell.

Campbell introduced the hero's journey in his 1949 book, *The Hero of a Thousand Faces*. Here he weaves together various epic stories from cultures all over the world to show a common narrative that underlies them all. While this book is a fascinating read, the explanation it presents of the hero's journey does not fit with Deadpool's narrative in "The Good, the Bad, and the Ugly." This is because the hero's journey has several stages. One of them is talked about in another essay (but of course not as brilliantly in *Maximum Effort*). For example, the hero experiences a call to adventure, and responds with a refusal of that call before changing his or her mind. Deadpool never chooses this adventure. Also, the last stage of the journey, the return with the elixir, claims a hero returns with something that can transform the world in the same way the hero has been transformed. "The Good, the Bad, and the Ugly" does not have this kind of ending. This could be a problem for us, unless we can find another way to bring the hero's journey and Deadpool's journey into discussion.

Fortunately, the answer to our potential problem is in the seminal interview, *The Power of Myth*. Released in 1988, the interview recounts journalist Bill Moyers walking with Campbell through the major ideas of Campbell's body of work. During their conversation, Campbell places a different emphasis on the center of the hero's journey than what we see in *The Hero of a Thousand Faces*. The new focus is in the heroic transformation of a character's consciousness. Under this focus, a character's path to becoming a hero is all about a transformation of consciousness from selfishness to selflessness through trials and revelations.

At this point, Campbell is giving us a philosophical foothold: a definition of the term "hero." The best descriptive definition Campbell supplies is in the following excerpt from *The Power of Myth*: "The moral objective is that of saving a people, or saving a person, or supporting an idea. A hero sacrifices himself for something—that's the morality of it" (p. 156). In other words, we normally find our hero-to-be as a self-centered person who's looking out for #1. Over the course of a journey, the hero encounters trials and revelations that cause the hero to become selfless and willing to sacrifice herself for the sake of some greater good.

This gives us a foundational idea to test whether or not Deadpool actually becomes a hero. First, we will have to establish Deadpool as a selfish or self-centered character at the start of the story. Second, we'll have to identify the trials and revelations Deadpool undergoes that would cause a change. Third and finally, we'll have to find evidence that Deadpool has changed from a self-centered character to a character who is willing to sacrifice himself for a people, an individual, or an idea.

Deadpool's Situation in "The Good, the Bad, and the Ugly"

In "The Good, the Bad, and the Ugly," we find Deadpool (with Agent Preston as a voice in his head) haunted by his past in the Weapons Plus program. Deadpool is captured by a crazed scientist, Dr. Butler. Butler forces Deadpool to undergo more experiments, using the results to create a team of mutates (humans given mutant powers, like Deadpool) for North Korea. Deadpool submits because Butler has Deadpool's former lover and daughter—a child Deadpool didn't believe he had—as hostages and is threating to kill them.

Once freed by one of the mutates, Deadpool rescues two other captives: Captain America and Wolverine. Upon freeing the two Avengers, the three men take down hostage camps, freeing the mutates' families. Tragically, Deadpool finds what he believes to be his family's corpses and seeks revenge on Butler. When Deadpool confronts Butler in an underground bunker, Deadpool discovers a secret project: Butler's sister, who Butler has been trying to keep alive at all costs for years through his experiments without her consent. In a climactic moment, the sick woman allows Deadpool into the panic room, where Deadpool kills Butler and allows Butler's sister to peacefully pass away in accordance with her wishes.

At the end of the day, our Avengers free the mutates from their forced captivity, save most of the mutates' families, and prevent a war between North Korea and the United States. This would count as a win in most superheroes' books. However, for Deadpool this win is countered by the loss of a family he hadn't believe he had and the belief that he has lost his chance to be a father. Deadpool's focus during this time, however, is not just his own pain. He wanted to find justice for the mutates, and any others whom the Weapons Plus program may have harmed. His motivation was justice, not just rage incurred due to loss.

Is Deadpool a Hero?

Does Deadpool's storyline in "The Good, the Bad, and the Ugly" conform to the theory of heroic transformation we outlined above? As a quick refresher, we must prove three things:

1. **that Deadpool begins the narrative as a self-centered character,**
2. **that the trials Deadpool endures and the revelations put before him are things that can and did lead to a transformation of consciousness, and**
3. **that Deadpool has changed into someone who is willing to sacrifice himself to save a person, a people, or an ideal.**

The first criterion is going to be the easiest of the three to prove. Deadpool, by all counts, is portrayed as a self-centered character who is out for his own gain. We only need to look at the issues that predate "The Good, the Bad, and the Ugly" for evidence that this is the case.

The Duggan-Posehn run of Marvel NOW's *Deadpool* opens with the "Dead Presidents" arc, in which Agent Preston enlists Deadpool to kill the zombie Presidents of the United States. Deadpool, however, doesn't agree to do this out of some desire to protect innocents or to aid in protecting the public image of his friends on the Avengers roster. Instead, Deadpool demands payment "in pillowcases with '$' written on them" for his services (p. 17). Deadpool's goal has always been what gets him the most personal gain. Whether it's protecting his bank account, fulfilling his need for revenge, or reuniting with the love of his life, Death, Wade is looking out for number one. Even at the beginning of the story arc in question, he reaches out to Captain American and Wolverine out of fear for his own safety, to people he figured would be concerned about the Weapons Plus program. This affirms that Deadpool does indeed fulfill the first criterion of self-centeredness.

The second criterion deals with the trials and revelations Deadpool experienced during the story, and whether they could and do cause a transformation or not. For the sake of clarity, I will separate the trials from the revelations. The trials Deadpool undergoes are mostly physical torture and human experimentation. While physical pain can do a lot to a normal person, we're talking about Deadpool, who has a nifty healing factor. Given the other horrific bodily injuries Deadpool has endured in his comic career, I think it is safe to say that the pain and torture he endured during this arc has done little to change Deadpool into a less self-centered person.

The other side of this is that there needs to be some kind of permanence in the loss for it to take effect. If Deadpool were to permanently lose a limb, as opposed to regrowing it with that healing factor, then it might have some impact on his worldview. Otherwise, such a horrific injury to him is like breaking a bone for most people: painful, annoying, but something that will heal with little to no side effects.

The revelations, on the other hand, provide a different kind of experience for Deadpool. The first revelation, the confirmation that he has a biological daughter who, along with her mother, are hostages of Butler, is perhaps the most earth-shattering of the two to Deadpool. Part of the reason Deadpool is able to get away with half of the crazy stuff he does is because he has no family that can be used to blackmail him; such a connection could be a liability. Yet, once Deadpool has confirmation from Butler that Eleanor is his daughter, there is a radical change in Deadpool's consciousness as displayed by his interior dialogue with Preston. He is consumed with guilt and fear, frustrated at his inability to protect his child, even though he was uncertain Eleanor was his until Butler's confirmation. Deadpool's concern is not for his own safety and well-being, but for that of his daughter, and, by extension, her mother, Carmelita. This qualifies for fulfilling the second criterion of a revelation that could instigate a change in consciousness.

The second revelation Deadpool experiences is the discovery of the North Korean mutate experiments that Butler is using to fund his research. These men and women, conscripted by the North Korean government, were experimented upon without consent to create a team of X-Men for North Korea. The experiments were, at best, partial successes, leaving the victims disfigured and, in some cases, with malfunctioning powers. These malfunctioning powers can be terrible, such as those of Park, whose overactive healing factor would heal over his mouth and other normal flesh openings.

We see early on in the story that Deadpool has a sensitivity to experimentation. For example, he has nightmares about his time in the Weapons Plus program. This sensitivity transforms into a desire for justice for the mutates and their imprisoned families. It even extends to Butler's sister, who was kept alive by Butler in extreme measures against her will. That transformation may not be as powerful as the one caused by Deadpool learning he is a father, but it still fulfills the second criterion.

Our third and final criterion is whether or not Deadpool has a change in consciousness resulting from these revelations. Judging a person's transformation of consciousness is difficult since we don't have a view into their private thoughts. With Deadpool, it's easy since his private thoughts are displayed on the page for us to read. After these revelations, Deadpool attains a new focus to not only save the lives of those Butler has experimented upon, but also their families. He enlists the help of Captain America and Wolverine to save the innocents and ensure that no harm comes to them. Once he finds what appear to be the corpses of his family, he seeks vengeance on Butler. Yet, Deadpool says his main concern is to stop Butler from making any more killers and from experimenting on people against their will. Deadpool obtains his vengeance, but only as a consequence of freeing Butler's sister from the constant experimentation.

While the actions are altruistic, the question remains of whether or not Deadpool has experienced a change in consciousness. I'll admit to this being a matter of interpretation, but the evidence is strong for Deadpool's change. Given the exchange between Deadpool and Preston at the end of the arc, in which Deadpool emphasizes the importance of family and his desire to get Preston into an autonomous body so she can be with her family, I'd say Deadpool is a changed man and fulfills the third criterion. This new focus on family and a value of relationships with children shows a reorientation of Deadpool's consciousness towards something that goes beyond money or adventure. He's learning to embrace a self-sacrificing understanding of love that only happens when you open yourself up to those willing to love you back. Deadpool regrets not having the opportunity to love Carmelita and Eleanor the way a partner and father should. He seeks to ensure Preston is not deprived of those opportunities with her husband and son. This is a genuine change for Deadpool. He has become a hero.

So . . . Deadpool's a Hero?

Now, we can ask the important question: why doesn't our hero get the girl? After all the torture and violence, he's earned some happy time, right? The sad truth is that the hero, in Campbell's sense of the word, doesn't get the girl. The hero experiences great loss and is willing to sacrifice his life for the sake of a greater good. The hero carries the weight of his journey with him, making it difficult to have the happy ending that cartoon movies promise us.

At the end of this arc, Deadpool fits the role of the hero, and appears to be shouldering the weight quite well. He has moved to thinking about more than himself, and has been motivated to act for the sake of others. Perhaps this story is able to give us pause to rethink what a hero actually is. A hero is someone who's willing to sacrifice health and happiness for the sake of an ideal and the protection of others. Heroism isn't always glorious work, but neither is the work Deadpool does. Maybe Deadpool is the true hero, shouldering the burdens of loss while Captain America and Wolverine can appear to be the sentinels of justice. It may just be the case that the hero never gets the girl after all.

6
The Accidental Hero

Darian Shump . . . Seriously, this one really is just Shump

What makes a hero?

For many of us, it's just a matter of doing the right thing. Helping those who need help. Making sacrifices for others. Taking out the trash. But it's also important to think about how a hero gets the job done. Can a hero lie? Or steal? Is there a grading system? Or is it an all-or-nothing type of deal?

By Western standards, Deadpool's about as far from a hero as you can get. Sometimes he kills for money. Sometimes he kills for fun. Sometimes he even kills the entire Marvel Universe (looking at you, Will). The problem with this way of thinking is that it's boring. The idea that good people, good superheroes don't kill is outdated. Whether we like it or not, issues of morality can't be solved by just comparing body counts.

There are times when heroes might be forced to kill, and there are situations in which people become villains without committing a single murder. To condemn Deadpool for his trigger-happy approach to conflict resolution, then, is really just an unfair (and stereotypical) oversimplification.

So let's switch things up. Instead of judging Deadpool from the West, let's take a look at him from the East. How exactly does the Merc with a Mouth jive with the "peaceful" philosophy of Buddhism? Does his thinking make him a hero? Do his actions make him a villain?

Stay tuned to find out.

How to Get Away with Murder

Before we try to think about what makes Deadpool tick, we have to understand two things about Buddhism. The first, *karma*, probably seems pretty self-explanatory. When most of us in the West hear it, one of a handful of sayings might come to mind: "You reap what you sow," "What goes around, comes around," and, my personal favorite, "Karma's a bitch." In other words, we think that good things happen to good people, and bad things happen to bad people.

But that's not everything. In Buddhism, karma isn't just some kind of spin on The Golden Rule. While the word itself means "action" or "deed," and does have something to do with the belief that all actions have consequences, the Buddhist understanding of "action" is a bit different from our own. We have a habit of viewing actions as purely physical events. Drawing a sword, for example, or pulling the pin on a grenade are both muscular movements before anything else. When they talked about karma, though, early Buddhists were talking about *intentional* actions. The deed was important, but not nearly as much as the reason behind it in the first place. Why was the sword drawn? And was the pin pulled by accident? (Rupert Gethin, "Can Killing a Living Being Ever Be an Act of Compassion?", pp. 167–170).

This makes a pretty big difference. If we don't take the mental factor into consideration, then karma depends only on the nature of the action itself. If Deadpool were to accidentally fall on a miniaturized Ant-Man, for example, we'd think that he'd receive the unwholesome, or "bad," karma that comes from a murder. But in Buddhist thinking, a person can't receive this type of karma from an unintentional action. Since our Mouthy Merc didn't meant to kill something he couldn't see, then he can't really be held responsible.

Of course, deliberately killing someone is another story. According to the early tradition, devoted Buddhists aren't supposed to cause deliberate harm to living beings. And, if they do, there's a sort of hierarchy. Killing a person is worse, in terms of unwholesome karma, than killing an animal, or just simply hurting someone. So, if this is the case, wouldn't it mean that Deadpool is just a murderer? He definitely doesn't have a problem slaughtering his enemies, right?

Well, here's where our second important idea comes into play. In English, it's known as *skillful means*, and is pretty close to the saying that sometimes the end justifies the means. As Buddhism started to grow, early practices were changed to fit new places and new times. The "skillful means" idea was used to explain why these changes were needed.

There were even times when it was used to justify murder. For example, let's put a twist on a well-known Buddhist story and imagine that Deadpool is on a helicarrier full of S.H.I.E.L.D. agents, plus one undercover spy from Hydra. Deadpool overhears the Hydra operative reporting to his commander, explaining that he's set a bomb to destroy the entire ship once he parachutes to safety. Our hero's in a bad spot. If he kills the Hydra operative, then, according to the standards of early Buddhism, he's a murderer and accrues unwholesome karma. If he doesn't, every S.H.I.E.L.D. agent onboard dies (Rupert Gethin, "Can Killing a Living Being Ever Be an Act of Compassion?", pp. 188–89).

If we apply skillful means, though, the murder could be justified. In this scenario, Deadpool knows that murder is the worst crime. As a result, he realizes that the Hydra spy would face the spiritual consequences of hundreds of murders, rather than just one. So, by killing him, Deadpool would not only save everyone from S.H.I.E.L.D. on the helicarrier, but also the would-be murderer himself. Since the Hydra agent never had the chance to act, he wouldn't face the same consequences as a successful mass murderer. The intent was there, but it wasn't given the chance to manifest as a specific action. And because he purposefully killed to save others, Deadpool wouldn't face the same consequences as a mindless assassin.

Letting Actions Speak Louder than Words

Now, the question is whether or not this actually applies to the Deadpool we know from the Marvel NOW! series. Is he really just a mercenary? Does he do or say anything that would make us believe he doesn't just kill for the fun of it?

At first glance, we're shown that the Marvel NOW! Deadpool is Deadpool as we know and love him: a crude, wisecracking, gloriously violent mercenary after money and, at times, recognition. He's hated or disliked by nearly every "real" superhero, pretty much always because of his annoying attitude and willingness to kill.

(Throughout the Marvel NOW! arc, Deadpool admits, or is told, that he's not friends with Thor, The Avengers (as a whole), The Fantastic Four, Superior Spider-Man, Daredevil, Power Man, Iron Fist, Captain America, Wolverine, Odin, and Iron Man. Not to mention the X-Men following their inversion in AXIS.)

In fact, when he's recruited by S.H.I.E.L.D. to dispatch the resurrected presidents, led by George Washington, it's because nobody would expect them to willingly work with the mercenary. Oh, and his payment for that contract? A ridiculous amount of money in cloth sacks with green dollar signs.

Cha-ching.

Still, even as Deadpool slaughters his way through all forty-five issues, we start to see signs that maybe he isn't just a greedy and bloodthirsty mercenary. Agent Preston, Deadpool's contact with S.H.I.E.L.D., seems to be the first to notice that he wants to be seen doing something good. And when she's threatened by George Washington, Deadpool all but begs him not to hurt her. More importantly, it's her subsequent "death" that finally drives Deadpool to defeat Washington. (Spoiler Alert: She didn't die.) So, while their relationship might have started as a professional one, it's obvious that Deadpool actually began to care for Preston. She had treated him fairly, treated him like a friend, and he welcomed it.

On several other occasions, Deadpool points out that he doesn't like to kill innocents. While this might seem surprising for a gun-toting mercenary, it turns out that it's a bit of an understatement. Throughout the series, Deadpool actually goes out of his way to help new friends or even save random people, including a child and a mutant, in the middle of combat. After freeing the North Korean X-Men, he gives Nightcrawler Kim a briefcase full of cash, followed by repeated organ donations and a home in the Monster Metropolis. Around the same time, Evan Sabahnur reverts to Apocalypse and destroys much of New York City, decapitating Deadpool/Zenpool in the process. When the inversion is later reversed and Evan manages to locate Deadpool's head, our hero forgives him and allows Evan to live in hiding in Deadpool's suburban home.

In each of these cases, we see a hint of real compassion. Deadpool is a mercenary, but he's not just an emotionless killer. He doesn't make friends easily, but he's willing to protect the ones that stick with him. And he's far from Captain America, but he's prepared to help the people who can't defend themselves when things get bad. So far, though, we've been talking more about actions than anything else, and, as we figured out earlier, that's not all that makes up karma. If we want to get a better understanding of Deadpool's mind, let's start with another story: The Niagara Bride.

Killing in the Name of Love (and Compassion)

Told as a flashback to one of Deadpool's many marriages, the story of the Niagara Bride is more touching, and more revealing, than the previous acts of heroism. Whether he was helping Evan or pushing a child out of harm's way, we can technically still say that Deadpool wasn't really exerting much extra effort. Maybe shoving the kid was a matter of convenience. Maybe, like any of us, he didn't think anything of giving a friend some extra help.

His encounter with the Niagara Bride was different. She was one of his clients, a cancer victim waiting to die. She wanted to "check out on her own terms," but knew that her parents and kids wouldn't get any life insurance if she did it herself. Or if they knew it was an assisted suicide. Enter Deadpool. According to him, it was all her idea. She did the planning, he just "picked the spot, called in a debt and left a mess so ridiculous" it couldn't be traced back to her. And once everything was said and done, he took her money and donated it to a house for kids with cancer. The end ("The Niagara Bride," issue 27).

Let's start by putting aside the politics of assisted suicide. No matter how you feel about it, the fact is that Deadpool did some serious thinking here. When she came to him, he could've turned her down. But the whole reason he went through Weapon Plus was because of his own cancer. He knew what it felt like to be facing death, and he knew the desire to end it on his own terms. Although he tried to explain it away, he admitted to crying when taking the contract. He called her brave. One of the bravest women he'd ever known.

And this is where we see the difference from those earlier actions. This woman wasn't a friend. She was a stranger. But she was one he could relate with on a personal level. It wasn't an easy kill. Because he didn't take the job for the thought of killing her. He took the job because he enjoyed the thought of freeing her.

Ever the Accidental Hero

Now what do we make of all of this so far? How can Deadpool be a violent mercenary, a caring friend, and, occasionally, a true hero?

Well, that's just it: He's an accidental hero. That's not to say that he does these things by accident; after all, everything we've seen shows that there is a part of him that wants to help people. What it means is that his heroic side, the side that saved the child and Nightcrawler Kim and even the Niagara Bride, isn't part of his essential nature. In other words, it's a sort of add-on. He's a mercenary first and a hero second.

We used Captain America as a guideline for comparison earlier, and it works just as well here. His moral code, his belief in right and wrong, influences everything he does, especially in battle. Even though he's faced off against the Red Skull and Arnim Zola dozens of times, he refuses to kill them. He obviously knows that they're still Nazis, but also knows that killing them is not the "right" thing to do.

Deadpool, on the other hand, doesn't have these same barriers. When he's faced with the choice of killing his enemies or letting them live, he chooses death. It's the easier of the two. But, his willingness to kill doesn't influence every move he makes in the same way that doing the right thing influences Captain America. Which is why it shouldn't be surprising that Deadpool wants to make friends and protect innocents when he can. He's not a cookie-cutter villain, and he's not even an antihero like The Punisher. He's a hero who kills to save others.

It's the Thought that Counts

The fact that Deadpool cares at all should really be more surprising than anything else. He's an outcast, physically and socially. His appearance prevents him from ever fitting in with normal humans, just as his attitude and violent tendencies set him apart from heroes like the Avengers. He has every right to be angry with the world, but he still does things like working with S.H.I.E.L.D. or saving a harmless mutant. Why, then, does he do it?

As Preston said, he wants to be seen doing something good. He wants to love. He wants to be loved. He's an outcast, but he wants to be a part of something bigger. Nearly every time he comes across another hero in the series, whether it's the Superior Spider-Man or Thor or the Heroes for Hire, he tries to label it a team-up. More than once, Deadpool even says that he used to feel worthless or dead inside, and that he never got to experience true happiness. His wedding to Shiklah was the first time that he was really surrounded by friends. Outside of that, he always felt alone.

And, according to him, a large part of those feelings of isolation and loneliness came from his treatment at the hands of Weapon Plus's Bartol Utler, or Butler. When Deadpool finally confronts Butler after years of "bagging and tagging," experimentation, and memory wipes, we get another glimpse into the mercenary's mind. Butler claims that Deadpool has no moral compass, that the experiments are what gave his life meaning. Our hero disagrees:

> I've never had a life because of you. I believe you have no right. I believe no one should spend their life in a tube for someone else's benefit. I believe I would have helped you help your sister, if that were your only goal. But you never stopped making killers. I know so little about myself. I know I've done bad things, but I also know deep down that I'm a good person. Because I stopped helping you. (Gerry Duggan and Brian Posehn, *The Good, The Bad, and the Ugly*, #19).

Pause: Let's recap. So far, we've seen that some of Deadpool's actions, and intentions, contradict what most of us expect from a mercenary. He doesn't have a problem with protecting others. He's capable of compassion. He wants to be seen as a hero. And he'll kill his enemies without hesitation, especially if it means saving the lives of his friends. That is to say, everything we've considered supports the idea that, from a certain Buddhist way of thinking, he's a karmic hero.

But we've been imposing. Regardless of what we might want to think about him, we haven't seen anything to suggest that Deadpool *himself* believes his intentions are good. At least, not until now.

Deadpool's speech is the key to understanding his mentality. He doesn't try to make excuses for what he's done. He admits that he's done bad things, that he's hurt people. However, he still believes that he's good. By refusing to help Butler with his human experiments or random murders, Deadpool believes that he made the right choice. (Butler had Deadpool kill certain targets, including his own parents, before wiping his memories each time.) And although he doesn't say it outright, our hero implies that he continues to try to do the right thing as a mercenary. That's why he saves the child, and the mutant, and Nightcrawler Kim, and Evan, and every other innocent he comes across in the series. He knows that his methods aren't the most wholesome, but they're the only way he can make a positive difference. Skillful means at work.

Zenpool and the Art of Renouncing Violence

Before we finish up, let's take a look at one final piece of Deadpool's mind: Zenpool. During the AXIS storyline, a spell cast by the Red Skull inverts the personalities of numerous heroes and villains, turning the violent peaceful and vice versa. Deadpool, of course, becomes a "pacifist," renaming himself Zenpool and giving up his katana and guns for wooden blades. In the backyard of his home, he builds a rock garden.

In spite of this change, pieces of his old life do remain. The original Deadpool personality, for example, survives in his mind, criticizing the choices of the new Zenpool. He doubts the new approach, pointing out that he's never felt more at peace, or more out-of-place. When Zenpool and the North Korean X-Men are attacked by the inverted X-Men, Deadpool goes so far as to root against his own body.

During this same battle, Zenpool admits that trying to renounce violence was a mistake. He thought that it would make him a better person, but realized that it went against his true, essential nature. Even when he tried to be a pacifist, he beat up two criminals using a frozen turkey. While this non-killing approach might've worked for other heroes, it only made Deadpool feel more at odds with himself. Killing was as much a part of him as his healing factor or suit. Turning away from it meant turning away from his ability to help others, and betraying what made Deadpool Deadpool in the process.

A Violent End?

So, although we're led to believe that Deadpool is anything but a hero, at least in the traditional (Western) sense of the word, a closer look and a different perspective show that there's much more to his story.

Deadpool's the Merc with a Mouth. He's also a friend. And a husband. And a father. He understands compassion, yet he doesn't always know how to relate to others. As we've seen, he can be contradictory, and flawed. He doesn't live by an upright moral code like Captain America (or Daredevil, or Spider-Man). He'll kill his enemies without hesitation, and he'll accept bags of money to do it. At the same time, though, he'll kill them to protect the weak. To save innocent children, or mutants, or anyone else at risk, regardless of the circumstances.

And beyond it all, beyond the physical act of taking or saving a life, Deadpool believes himself to be a good person. He wants to make a positive difference. He wants to do the right thing. He might get there a bit differently than some of the other heroes, and he certainly has alienated a good number of them in the process. But, in the end, that doesn't make his *intentions* any less positive than their own.

With all of this in mind, then, let's ask again: What makes a hero?

And just take a look at Deadpool. You'll find your answer.

7
Why Deadpool Isn't a Hero (Yet?)

MATTHEW BRAKE AND PETER PARKER

If you saw the recent *Deadpool* movie (and let's face it, if you're reading this book, you *did* see it), then you're familiar with Colossus's role within that film.

No, I'm not referring to his inclusion in the movie as a nod to fans, nor of the way in which he serves to show us that a CGI character can make all live actors replaceable. I'm talking about the way Colossus provides a contrast between Deadpool's anti-heroic ways and the actions and attitude of a more traditional and "noble" hero.

This is especially clear in the scene where Deadpool defeats Ajax and is about to shoot him. Colossus gives Wade a speech about the nobility of the hero and tries to talk him out of killing Ajax, and right when you think Deadpool won't pull the trigger. ***Who am you kidding? We all knew I would pull the trigger.*** Deadpool "interrupts" Colossus's speech and hilarious metallic-CGI-vomitus results follow.

But maybe I'm getting ahead of myself. Before there was a successful superhero movie starring Ryan Reynolds; before there was a critically panned, green-themed superhero movie starring Ryan Reynolds; even before there was an even *more* critically panned superhero movie featuring Ryan Reynolds whose name I can't quite remember ***Pulverine Borigins?*** Deadpool was simply a plagiarized, "deep canon" character ***That means a character only super-nerds would know about.*** associated with all of Marvel's X-titles ***You remember those? The ones they're replacing with the Inhumans because Fox owns the movie***

rights to the X-Men and all other mutant-themed properties.

When Deadpool first appeared in *New Mutants* #98 in 1991, he was initially depicted as a supervillain hired to fight Cable and the New Mutants. Over time, the character has been increasingly portrayed in a more heroic light. While often considered an anti-hero, the line between anti-hero and hero sometimes becomes blurred where Deadpool is concerned.

There have been numerous times when he has considered giving up his anti-hero, mercenary ways. Currently, he even appears in *The Uncanny Avengers* as a part of the Avengers Unity Squad—but there's something about Deadpool that causes me to question his hero credentials. Maybe it was the way Ajax's brains got sprayed all over the ground. Maybe not. What is it about Deadpool that keeps him from crossing the threshold to being a fully realized hero?

The Philosophy Part

You knew this was coming. YOU picked up a book entitled *Deadpool and Philosophy*. We aren't just going to geek out about Deadpool. Rather than try to include it nonchalantly with a clever and seamless transition, I'm going to assume you, the reader, are not an idiot and just tell you, "This is it. This is where the philosophy begins." This is where I take something you love ***Me!*** and use it as a pretense to interest you in philosophy by relating it to a thinker *I* care about in philosophy, and that thinker is the Christian philosopher Søren Kierkegaard (1813–1855).

I like Kierkegaard because I am 1. a Christian and 2. sexually frustrated. ***There's a difference?*** Also, I know that nothing sets people more at ease or makes them more receptive to what you have to say than bringing up religion.

Kierkegaard[1] proposed three spheres of existence or three ways of living for human beings: the aesthetic, the ethical, and the religious. The aesthetic person lives for immediate pleasure

[1] Kierkegaard wrote under a number of pseudonyms each of which represented a particular personality or viewpoint. Although the idea of multiple personalities is fitting for Deadpool, it's simpler to just say Kierkegaard. Please don't make me work harder on this thing than I have to.

and is perditious ***That means . . . bad?*** The ethical person strives to live with personal integrity according to society's moral code and conventions.[2] The religious person, among other things, makes a leap of faith or a commitment to a belief that transcends society's everyday moral code and embraces suffering in an attempt to follow the example of Christ. For our purposes (taking my cue from every Superman movie that shows him in a very outstretched-arms-Jesus-symbol kind of way), the religious sphere will be used interchangeably with the idea of the hero, one who commits to a way of life that embraces the suffering that comes with the decision to embrace a higher ideal.

The Hero

We all know characters who seem to fit the cookie-cutter image of what an ideal hero looks like. Deadpool's childhood hero, Captain America, definitely fits this description ***At least, he will again once Marvel explains or retcons the whole "Hail Hydra" thing. Oops! Spoiler Alert!*** How could a person not get chills during Marvel's first *Civil War* comic book event when Spider-Man asks Cap how he can remain resolute when everyone else is against him, and Captain America replies:

> Doesn't matter what the press says. Doesn't matter what the politicians or the mobs say. Doesn't matter if the whole country decides that something wrong is something right. This nation was founded on one principle above all else: the requirement that we stand up for what we believe, no matter the odds or the consequences. When the mob and the press and the whole world tell you to move, your job is to plant yourself like a tree beside the river of truth, and tell the whole world—"No, you move." ***I love him!*** (*Amazing Spider-Man* #537).

This is what Colossus was trying to tell Deadpool in a far less cool way. The hero is someone who commits to a higher ideal, who delays their own gratification and overcomes their own selfishness and discouragement in order to continually do the right thing in the right way. A hero exceeds society's

---

[2] There are multiple accounts of the ethical in Kierkegaard's writings. The one I am using here is that found in *Fear and Trembling*.

"normal" moral expectations and chooses something far more self-sacrificial.

As I already mentioned, I don't think that Deadpool fits the description of the hero, but given Kierkegaard's framework of the spheres of existence, where would "anti-hero" fit in? The aesthetic sphere, or the ethical sphere, or the religious sphere?

I don't think you can say that Deadpool's simply an aesthetic person living for immediate pleasure. After all, he isn't the Purple Man.[3] He certainly is not the ethical person, a normal, average schmuck staying within the boundaries of what's normal for the average person in society. He has certainly dabbled with the heroic, hence the "hero" part of "anti-hero"—but Wade always seems to regress away from the heroic. Why?

The Humor "Thing"

Kierkegaard also discusses two "boundary zones" between the spheres of existence. The first is irony, which falls between the aesthetic and the ethical, and the second is humor, which falls between the ethical and the religious.

We might say that a person in the boundary zone of irony finds himself dissatisfied with a life lived only for immediate pleasure (or villainy) and wants to become a contributing member of society, but they can't come to peace with the contradictions that life presents them with everyday. However, it's the second boundary zone that interests us here. I think that the Merc with a Mouth's lack of standing as a hero can be understood by evaluating how Kierkegaard describes the boundary zone of humor. It is that which sees the contradictions between the way things should be and the way things actually are.

Humor recognizes the limitations of the ethical or the life of the everyday Joe Schmoe and realizes that there is more to life than being a good employee and working a "normal" 9 to 5 everyday; however, while humor may recognize the value of a hero, it can't quite make sense of the hero's life ***Like how Colossus wouldn't let me kill Francis even though it takes care of the problem more efficiently than just***

---

[3] Wait . . . do you get this reference? Kilgrave? From *Jessica Jones*? Okay. Stop reading this, and go watch *that*.

keeping him alive? Humor amuses itself with the irreconcilability between life as it actually works and life as the hero strives to live it.

In his *Concluding Unscientific Postscript to Philosophical Fragments*, Kierkegaard notes that humor borrows from the Christian or the heroic ideal, but it is not the heroic ideal. It may share some of the same terms (superhuman, fearless, daring), but this is also true of the pagan or the villainous (p. 272). In other words, a villain can learn to look and sound heroic, but deep down, he's still not a hero. We can't help but see echoes here of Deadpool's own journey. Having begun as a villain, Deadpool began to adopt an increasingly heroic persona, even attempting to force his way into various super-teams from time to time like the Heroes for Hire and the X-Men ***I AM AN X-MAN!!*** But he's not a hero, and his humor is an indicator of this.

Kierkegaard does not think humor is entirely bad. He understands humor to be present throughout Christianity, and he even writes that humor is an "incognito" or a disguise for the religious (pp. 505–06). Humor, then, is central to us for understanding why Deadpool is not a hero, but it can also be a disguise for the hero. What's the difference?

The "Spider-Man Thing"

To the chagrin of one particular hero in the Marvel Comics universe, Deadpool is often mistaken for him. I am of course referring to everybody's friendly neighborhood Spider-Man ***Heh.*** who is not the biggest fan of Deadpool ("Ninja Spider-Man" as some people like to call him) going so far as to quit the Avengers Unity Squad because of Deadpool's presence on the team.

Why does Spider-Man have such a bone to pick with Deadpool? You would think both of these funny men would get along. Marvel loves to make light of the similarities between the two, like with the cover of *Deadpool* #11, which pays homage to Spider-Man's first appearance in *Amazing Fantasy* #15 (1962). *Wolverine* #73 (2009) plays around with this idea as well. Wolverine's weekly plans are laid out (in part to explain his over-exposure in Marvel's various comics especially at that time):

Monday: A mission with the New Avengers.

Tuesday: A team-up with the Punisher.

Wednesday: A mission with X-Force.

Thursday: A mission with the X-Men.

Friday: A team-up with Spider-Man.

Concerning Friday, Spider-Man appears talking about how excited he is to be with Wolverine, saying, "I love it when we team up," to which Wolverine responds with a terse, "Shut up." The next week, a similar series of events occurs in Logan's life, and on Thursday, we see him with Deadpool, who exclaims, "I love it when we team up," and Wolverine replies again, "Shut up."

Marvel enjoys playing with the idea about how similar the two of them are in their humor and their appearances, but at the end of the day, Peter Parker is a hero while Wade Wilson is not. Why is this true? I believe it has to do with their relationship with suffering. Anyone who has read the Spider-Man comics ***or seen the ever-growing number of reboots . . . talk about a clone saga, amiright?*** knows that for all of Peter Parker's wisecracks during battle, he's really the same fifteen-year-old kid overcoming the guilt he feels about letting his Uncle Ben's killer get away and who is choosing day after day to live up to the famous motto: "With great power comes great responsibility" ***Or the increasingly stupid ways all the reboots try to re-say this without actually saying it. I'm looking at YOU Amazing Spider-man and Captain America: Civil War!*** He constantly carries the responsibility on his shoulders to protect others, no matter how hard or confusing life gets.

This responsibility creates an inner suffering that is essential for the hero to be the hero. Kierkegaard writes about his religious sphere that it "comprehends suffering as essential" to itself (p. 434). Elsewhere, he states, "In his innermost being, the religious person is anything but a humorist; on the contrary, he is absolutely engaged in his relationship with God"—we might say, "his heroic ideal"—which causes this inner suffering (p. 508). It's not that Spider-Man thinks that he is better than others, but he has a driving inner passion that allows him to see the contradiction between everyday life and his ideals, and that passion causes him to decide each day to become the hero that he wants to become. As Kierkegaard writes, "Christianity is the direction forward to becoming a Christian and becoming that by continuing to be that" (p. 602). His humor, then, is an incognito or disguise for the suffering hero within, who is continually choosing to move forward and live according to a heroic ideal even when life gets hard.

By contrast, Deadpool's humor isn't an incognito for a hero's inner suffering. It is a humor that loves the amusing parts of being a hero but not the suffering parts (p. 291). It's not that Deadpool doesn't experience pain and suffering. He certainly takes a fair share of bullets, but his suffering doesn't hold the same weight that it might for a true hero.[4] Even Kierkegaard notes that a humorist recognizes that suffering happens in people's lives, but suffering doesn't mean the same thing to the humorist that it does to the religious person. Kierkegaard writes:

> But it is then that the humorist makes the deceptive turn and revokes the suffering in the form of jest. He comprehends the meaning of suffering in relation to existing, but he does not comprehend the meaning of suffering. He comprehends that it belongs together with existing, but he does not comprehend its meaning otherwise than that suffering belongs together with it . . . He touches the secret of existence in the pain, but then he goes home again. (p. 447)

While the hero recognizes that suffering is an essential part of the life he or she ***Very gender inclusive!*** has chosen, the humorist is able to dismiss the seriousness of suffering with a joke.

Compare Deadpool's run-in with Norman Osborn during Marvel's *Dark Reign* with Spider-Man's on-going conflict with Osborn. Every time Norman Osborn re-enters Peter Parker's world, the Spider-Man comics drip with emotional pathos and

---

[4] I had a friend proofread this for me. She disagreed with this point and said that she thought the Deadpool movie showed that he did experience real suffering when he lost Vanessa, but even here, I think *How It Should Have Ended* does a good job confirming my point about Deadpool and suffering. Check out their videos on YouTube for both *Deadpool* and *The Amazing Spider-Man 2*. Watch how both characters react to the loss of their girlfriends (spoiler alert). They make my point for me. Take that, Jenni! ***Yeah! Take that! . . . Wait, is she hot?***

Peter ends up suffering in some way. Even when the horrible Clone Saga came to an end, Ben Reilly's death at the hands of the resurrected Green Goblin was still kind of sad. However, when Norman Osborn was put in charge of the worldwide security agency H.A.M.M.E.R. ***because of comic-book "reasons"*** and set his sights on Deadpool, a very different dynamic unfolded.

During *Dark Reign*, Norman Osborn set his sights on taking out all of the loose cannons that could threaten his position of power. One of those loose ends was Deadpool. Osborn eventually gets the upper hand, and Deadpool is decapitated in *Thunderbolts* #131 (2009). Osborn commands that the head and body be burned and leaves; however, two pages later, we see Deadpool alive and well with his head sown back on. Osborn becomes aware of this during a TV interview when Deadpool appears behind him with a sign saying ***I love this part!*** "RESPAWN. LOL" (*Deadpool* #10).

Just like that, Deadpool has a little taste of suffering but then laughs it off, and things go right back to normal. Whereas the suffering that Norman Osborn brings upon Spider-Man causes our Kierkegaardian hero to grow as a person and become a better hero moving forward, Deadpool's suffering via Osborn's hands is of little consequence to his growth as a person.

Humor and Moving Backward

Every time Deadpool does seem to take a step forward by doing something heroic, he takes a step backward into his mercenary ways. Instead of moving forward and becoming more of a hero, he remains in the boundary zone of humor. Maybe Deadpool can't help it. His healing factor makes him practically immortal, unlike Spider-Man.

It makes it hard for Deadpool to take anything seriously because his life really isn't at stake. Plus, he knows he's a comic-book character. Unlike Spidey, Deadpool knows that any loss in his life can be undone on the whim of a writer who's run out of ideas. If Uncle Ben were Deadpool's uncle, Deadpool wouldn't have been affected by that loss like Peter Parker was. Deadpool would have simply turned to the reader screaming, "Noooooooo! I'm so heart-broken . . . until Marvel runs out of ideas and retcons this!"

Deadpool's situation seems to be further reflected in Kierkegaard's comments about the humorist. He writes, "Humor is always a revocation (of existence into the eternal by recollection backward, of adulthood to childhood) . . . the humorist always has ample time, because he has eternity's amplitude of time behind him" (p. 602). Deadpool knows that time is on his side. He doesn't need to move forward because he's trapped in a meaningless eternity. He can revoke any heroic forward movement he makes and return to his past ways, which from the heroic perspective is a return to perdition (p. 603) ***. . . also, remember that word from earlier? It means "bad."***

So, is there hope for Deadpool? Can he become a hero? Is it worth putting the "(Yet?)" in the title of this chapter? Maybe. Deadpool and Spider-Man have an interesting interaction in *Spider-Man / Deadpool* #1 that's worth repeating here:

> **DEADPOOL:** It's hard trying to be like more like you. So I thought, maybe . . . if we palled around a bit . . .
>
> **SPIDER-MAN:** That I could teach you to what . . . ? To be . . . good? A "hero"?
>
> **DEADPOOL:** No. Something like that isn't taught. It's earned. I thought if I hung with you. Doing the next right thing, I could *earn* it . . . and maybe your respect, too.

From this conversation, it seems like Deadpool might have a shot at becoming a hero. ***Damn straight!***

But here's the thing, I don't think we can say that Deadpool is a hero yet. After all, the end of *Spider-Man / Deadpool* #1 has Wade taking a contract out on Spider-Man's alter ego, Peter Parker. Deadpool can kick ass with the best of Marvel's heroes, but that doesn't make him a hero. A hero can't have it both ways, beating up the bad guys while making a little extra money from being murder-y on the side. It requires the resolute decision to live selflessly, accepting the unpleasant consequences that come from that decision and experiencing suffering as an opportunity for growth. If you want to be a hero, Deadpool, then you have to stop pulling the trigger on people like Ajax and laughing it off without any consequences. *BAM* ***What was that? I wasn't listening.***

And Now for Something Fourth-Wall-Breaking

Lame . . .

We hope you have enjoyed this attempt at relating philosophy to the pop cultural topic of *(please insert here)*. Your feedback is important to us. Please fill out the following survey by marking the answer that most accurately reflects your thoughts about this chapter with an 'X'. (If this is a library book, please use pencil):

____ A: A well-written work highlighting the importance of pop culture for philosophy.

____ B: An interesting philosophy piece, but who is Deadpool?

____ C: An interesting philosophy piece, but what is Christianity?

____ D: Are you saying heroes have to be religious?

____ E: I feel dumber for having read this.

8

How Shitty Can a Hero Be?

COREY HORN WILL BE LUCKY TO MAKE IT THROUGH TO THE END OF THIS CHAPTER ALIVE!

Deadpool is one shitty hero.

Mr. Pool runs around town destroying everything in his path in order to achieve his final goal. Although cities do get destroyed throughout several comics and superhero movies, none of the heroes are intentionally tearing down buildings and flipping cars to achieve their goal, but Deadpool seems to be turning places inside out wherever he goes, all for his own selfish reasons.

The famous franchise Marvel has created hundreds of superhuman heroes that all follow a similar formula of the heroic epic. Thanks to the *Star Wars* saga, Luke Skywalker has become a household name that every child knows and this is no accident. While writing the original *Star Wars* movies, George Lucas was heavily influenced by Joseph Campbell's book, *The Hero with a Thousand Faces*.

Even though Stan Lee may not have read Joseph Campbell's work, his stories in comic form follow the script very closely. It's not only superhero movies that follow this pattern but many iconic books and movies, such as *Lord of the Rings*, *The Wizard of Oz*, and many more do as well.

Marvel has created a large market for superhero movies over the past decade with films such as *Iron Man*, *Captain America*, and *The Avengers*. Through movies like these, our concepts and understanding of what it is to be a hero continues to be molded and shaped by these characters. Iron Man, for instance, uses his machines as an army of peace keepers, whether it is fighting villains he has created himself, or aliens invading New York; showing us that heroes do not always need superpowers but can rely on technology to protect and serve. Captain America and the Avengers follow in the same tune, upholding justice in the name of good; however, some don't need sophisticated equipment, just their own two giant green hands.

One thing every epic has in common, though, is the concept of some reward. The rewards our heroes typically receive come at the end, and are supplemental to the ultimate goal of the journey. Iron Man gets the girl at the end of his epic, but only after he saves the day; while the Avengers create an organization that will both maximize their potentials while protecting justice. But what of Deadpool? Does this half-baked, sarcastic mercenary fit this script, or does Deadpool get let off too easy? Further, can a self-centered, amoral, mercenary be a hero, or does reward simply not matter?

The Journey

> This is a superhero movie, but that guy in the suit just turned that other guy into a fucking kebab. Surprise. This is a different kind of superhero story.
>
> —DEADPOOL in the movie *Deadpool*

Joseph Campbell (1904–1987) was a famous scholar of mythology. Through his lifelong research of looking into the framework and components of world mythologies, Campbell discovered that there were several patterns that were shared worldwide. The patterns that he discovered and then wrote about in *The Hero with a Thousand Faces* became known as "the monomyth." The monomyth has several stages that may vary in name depending on whose commentary you read, but the stages translate to mean the same idea.

The first part of a hero's journey is the *Ordinary World*. The hero exists in a world that would seemingly look normal to an average citizen, but more than often the character feels out of place. For Luke this was the planet Tatooine, for Frodo it was Hobbiton, and for our friendly neighborhood Deadpool, where else but New York?

Each of these characters felt like he did not belong at home: Luke always had a knack for joining the Rebellion, Frodo a sense of adventure, but Deadpool's reason was far more explicit. He failed to fit in not because he wanted to return a sacred piece of jewelry or stop a guy in a mask from destroying the world, but because his body was burned from head to toe, leaving him looking akin to Freddie Krueger.

The hero of the story doesn't become a hero without an adventure, and the next three stages happen in quick succession. The second stage is the *Call to Adventure*. Circumstances arise in unexpected ways, leading the hero to a new unsuspected world, usually in contrast to or different from the world they are normally used to.

For our man Deadpool, learning that he had cancer was a pretty good push in the adventurous direction. Deadpool's alter ego Wade Wilson learns he has cancer shortly after proposing to his girlfriend Vanessa. During a visit to the bar he's offered the opportunity to be cured and transformed into a superhero, which he refuses.

Which brings us to part three, or *The Refusal*. This stage does not happen in all stories—for example *The Wonderful Wizard of Oz*—but it happens in quite a few of them, including *Deadpool*. The hero is presented with a challenge (often they are the only one who can answer the call) and decides not to accept it. Typically, the world is then thrown into some sort of chaos. This is shown in the movie *Groundhog Day* when Phil Connor refuses to answer his own call to adventure, causing him to enter a cyclical route of reliving the same day over and over. Deadpool rejects the offer by the recruiter in the bar in order to stay with his fiancé and live his final days as a happy couple, but as his cancer progresses, he realizes what this will put each of them through and with that in mind he decides to take the man's offer.

Part Four is known as *The Acceptance of The Call*. Our hero must accept the call since there are no other options. Wade Wilson (Deadpool's alter ego) reaches this point in the journey when he realizes his cancer is about to take his life, and he doesn't want his girlfriend to suffer. So, in the words of our eloquent friend,[1] he hit the "Fuck it!" stage. This is the point where the hero will begin to face their fears, as well as their character pitfalls.

There's always some sort of test or challenge that the hero has to overcome. This is the process the hero undergoes on the

1 Deadpool.

way to their final showdown. For Deadpool, the test is slightly unorthodox, but then again the dead guy himself is not exactly by the book. Deadpool's test of strength was shown by his attempts to find Ajax. In the movie, we see that as he goes through each henchman he gets stronger, quicker, and closer to his final showdown with Ajax. This is also the stage of good versus evil, right versus wrong, or monster versus creator. After rolling through Ajax's henchmen, Deadpool will ultimately face his creator for one last hoorah in order to complete his adventure.

So far Deadpool fits the bill for what it is to be a hero, but every hero has his flaws, and some flaws might be enough to remove the title of good guy in a cape . . . or stretchy pants.

Show Me the Money

That's why we do it, but mostly the money . . .

—DEADPOOL[2]

After conquering Hero Mountain, our hero can return home, prize in hand. Usually, after passing the supreme ordeal someone rewards the hero for his journey, and this could be an entire kingdom, the Holy Grail, or even the girl who has been there all along and playing hard to get. This reward was never promised to the hero to begin with, though. Luke saves the galaxy because he believes in justice, not because in the end he will get paid or become the ruler of the galaxies. Frodo destroys the ring for justice in Middle-earth, and is never promised payment or a girl.

Deadpool is a different story. When we first meet this witty character we get to know him by the name of Wade Wilson, mercenary. He works out of the bar called Sister Margaret's where every day he grabs a drink and a card with someone's name on it. The card is a job. He does not care who it is or what they have done, just get the job done and get paid. In quick succeeding scenes, Wade completes a job for a young lady in which she tells him "I have no money . . ." and proceeds to hug Mr. Wilson and responds with the quote that opened this particular section. Later, he takes the card back to the bar and asks for every cent owed to him and he "doesn't want any babysitting money."[3]

[2] Deadpool.

[3] *Deadpool.*

When Wade becomes Deadpool, he's not working for the X-Men, but for himself. He could care less about the damage he creates and the lives he steals on his mission to find Ajax. Deadpool's journey is fueled simply by reward and not the good that will come from apprehending his enemy. Even when Deadpool's girlfriend gets kidnapped by Ajax and his sidekick, he is still in search of his enemy, a "sack full of assholes," for personal reasons.

Throughout heroic stories, especially ones that follow Joseph Campbell's model, heroes are supposed to be the ones who uphold justice. The goal of their journey should be to right wrongs. However, Deadpool's journey seems to be a selfish one, and one that does not attempt to take on a "just" role like we see in his counterparts such as Iron Man or the Avengers. It aims for a personal goal that does not extend past himself.

Superhero or Bust?

> The day I decide to become a crime-fighting shit-swizzler who rooms with forty-four other little whiners at the Neverland mansion of some creepy old bald Heavens-Gate-looking mother-fucker . . . on that day I'll send your shiny, happy ass a friend request. Until then I'm gonna do what I came here to do.
>
> —Deadpool[4]

First we need to examine the difference between two types of rewards, intrinsic versus instrumental and what sort of motivation would influence each end, or goal. After finding which reward system applies to Deadpool, we should ask: Can Deadpool be a hero under the guidelines we set in place?

Alasdair MacIntyre, a Scottish philosopher born in 1929, is a leading philosopher in the field of virtue ethics, and in his book *After Virtue*, he gives a good example of what justice would look like between the two types of rewards. MacIntyre is famous for his chess example, which basically goes like this . . .

> Blind Al wishes to play chess with Deadpool who does not appreciate playing the game. So, in order to get him to play, Blind Al offers a reward, which is instrumental to Deadpool playing. Without the bribe

---

[4] *Deadpool.*

> of a reward Deadpool would not play with her, so he's not playing the game for the sake of the game but merely for the reward he will get in the end.

This, McIntyre says is not virtuous since they are not playing for the sake of playing but for some other purpose unrelated to the virtues of playing chess in an excellent way.

What the opposite would look like then is Deadpool playing with Blind Al for the sake of playing chess, or intrinsic reward, because of the good that playing chess brings about. Whether that is better problem-solving skills, learning chess strategies, or developing more patience (since we all know chess is the game old people play at the park when they have nothing to do but waste time), he plays the game with no reward in mind, just merely for the game itself.

MacIntyre does point out that a person can move from one reward system to the other, or in other words, someone could begin doing an action because they are given something in return and slowly continue performing that action simply for that action's sake. In fact, instrumental actions are how most people learn right from wrong, or how we teach our pets not to pee on everything we own inside.

With the understanding of what type of reward could be virtuous, Deadpool could possibly be a hero. As described by MacIntyre, someone could start out as an instrumental actor, but move towards an intrinsic one. So, although Deadpool is acting selfishly currently, as long as he makes the move towards selfless acts then Deadpool could be a potential hero in New York. As Deadpool shifts around the Big Apple he may at first be acting for his own reasons, but if he begins to do favors for others, or act in accordance to with the X-Men, then he could become more of that textbook Campbell hero.

If MacIntyre were to use Deadpool as one of his case studies I believe that he would agree that Mr. Wilson is on his way to being a hero, we all can look to. However, what motivates someone to act like a hero, and is there any overlap between motivation and reward?

In order to explain motivation, we turn to the German philosopher Immanuel Kant (1724–1804). According to Kant, there are two types of motivation, that by duty and that by motives. Motivation by motives would be actions such as self-interest, or happiness. So, if someone performs an action purely out of self-interest, and they would not have performed that action without that self-interest, then that action was not moral or done for good purposes. Motivation by duty then is the opposite of the former. When someone performs an action out of duty, they are doing that action for the sake of the duty itself.

So, if Deadpool caught a thief in order to collect the reward money, but would not have caught him if the reward had not been offered, then this would have been motivation by a self-interested motive. Although the action was good, it was not moral. However, if Deadpool caught the thief in the name of justice, or because it was the right thing to do, with no intention of receiving something from the action, then this would be motivation by duty, and thus moral.

When comparing Kant's motivational reasoning behind some action and MacIntyre's chess example of rewards, there tends to be some overlap. With Kant's motivation to do some action for that actions sake and MacIntyre's intrinsic reward, in both instances Deadpool acted for selfless reasons; while Kant's motivation by motives and MacIntyre's instrumental reward, Deadpool acted in a selfish manner.

With instrumental reward the person seeks personal gain, while with intrinsic reward he performs the good action for its own sake, because it is good. How does Deadpool measure up? Deadpool enters his journey with one thing in mind: to capture Ajax and make him fix his horrific face, so he is motivated by self-interested reasons. Deadpool does not enter the journey to stop Ajax for the sake of humanity or because of the people he watched burn alive in the laboratory, but to try and reverse his transformation so he can go back to being with his bangin' girlfriend.

Given that he only entered the journey for self-interested reasons, Deadpool would not be viewed as a hero through the eyes of either MacIntyre or Kant, since Deadpool does it purely for the instrumental outcome. What his actions show is that if the body change had never happened during the testing he underwent, Wade Wilson would never have become Deadpool, since he would have seen no reason to hunt after Ajax.

Aren't We All a Little Super?

> Four or five moments. That's all it takes . . . to be a hero. Everyone thinks it's a full-time job. Wake up a hero. Brush your teeth a hero. Go to work a hero. Not true. Over a lifetime, there are only four or five moments that really matter.
>
> —Colossus[5]

Assuming that MacIntyre is correct, there's still hope for our deathless mercenary. Although Deadpool acts out of selfish desires now, there is nothing that stands in the way of his beginning to act in a selfless manner.

In exchange for Colossus's and Negasonic Teenage Warhead's help at the shipyard, Deadpool told them he would consider joining the X-Men. That step alone shows that Deadpool is already thinking about putting his powers to good use for justice, not just his own life.

No one's perfect and we all have our flaws, but the outline MacIntyre offers allows for anyone who has the ability to be virtuous (which could be anyone) to become a superhero. Despite Kant's belief that someone is either selfish or selfless, MacIntyre allows for mistakes which allows for Deadpool to be a hero. Deadpool's heroic journey lands him one action closer to becoming an Iron Man or Captain America figure, but as shown by his final action of shooting Francis in the head at the end of the movie, Deadpool clearly has a long road ahead of him.

All it takes are those four or five moments in your life, when you protect someone from being wronged, or save a life in danger. Deadpool is the most accurate depiction of a hero, and one that we can most likely connect with on a personal level because he is someone who can both act in selfish ways for his own personal gain, but also be a hero when we need one most.

Deadpool is a different type of superhero, albeit possibly a shitty one, but a superhero none the less.

---

[5] *Deadpool.*

III

Wade, Is That You?

Is It Just Me Who's Getting Tired of That F$%ing Avocado Joke?*

9
Is Headless Deadpool Still Deadpool?

BEN FULMAN AND DEADPOOL OR A CHIMICHANGA . . . WHO THE HELL CAN TELL THE DIFFERENCE?

Deadpool can't die, he will never die, and probably will only die when humanity is extinct. You know what? Even if the writers decided they couldn't care less about him and were tired of his shenanigans, they still wouldn't be able to kill him.

Yes, they could stop writing his comics, and stop illustrating his magnificent but appalling figure. And yes, Hollywood could potentially—if the franchise lost money, or Ryan Reynolds gets caught up in a scandal—cancel the movies.

Well, you ask yourself: "How can that be possible?! We know Deadpool has regenerative powers. He can recuperate from anything: getting his head blown off; even being smashed into atoms." You get the gist. So do please solve our mystery: How the hell can Deadpool retain his identity and continue to be Deadpool? Quite easily: his memories are stored in the audience via the fourth wall, which means that to kill Deadpool, you need to kill all the people who have read and watched Deadpool. There needs to be a meteor shower, similar to the one that killed the dinosaurs, that will kill all of us and only then will Deadpool die. And that'll be the day. Only then will Deadpool stop being Deadpool!

If Deadpool Equals Deadpool, then Who Is Deadpool?!

The question isn't whether or not Deadpool can die, but the more philosophical and psychological question of personal identity. Deadpool's personal identity. How can we tell whether

Deadpool is indeed Deadpool over time? When can we say that a person starts and ends?

Is personal identity a consequence of our body being the same, over time? Is it a psychological awareness of our past instantiations? Or is a block of Deadpool's parts sewn together enough for us to say that he is the same Deadpool? Let me make it clearer: if the Punisher were to blow Deadpool's head to smithereens—like he did in *Deadpool: Suicide Kings* #2, blasting a hole in his head where his right eye and brain used to be—and then Deadpool's regenerative powers grew him a new one (including his brain parts), could we say that this is the same Deadpool, because he still has the same body as before?

Tough question indeed. Let's see what we can do about it. Let's blow, chop, dismember the poor bastard and find out if he's still Deadpool. Or are we talking about an endless hydra of Deadpools?

Let's say that Deadpool is Deadpool due to the parts that make him Deadpool. Let's take a part of him, which often happens in the comics. Imagine that the Punisher chops his hands, say, like pastrami on a rye bread. Then the logical conclusion is that Deadpool ceases to be Deadpool. What would happen if Deadpool deteriorated into a blub of flesh and then into to a mound of atoms (which happened in *Deadpool: Agent of Weapon X* #60)? Could we still say that the goo on the floor is Deadpool if he no longer took the shape of a sturdy and strong super human?

I Blew Deadpool's Head Off and All I Got Was This Lousy T-shirt

So, how can we determine whether Deadpool persists over time? How can we tell that Deadpool of comic book #1 is in fact Deadpool of comic book #2? A tough question indeed, especially when it comes to Deadpool, the superhuman who can regenerate himself, who cannot die. "Cursed with life," as Thanos once said.

Philosopher John Locke obviously had a thing for Deadpool, especially with regard to the idea of personal identity. In *An Essay Concerning Human Understanding*, Locke writes that Deadpool's personal identity relies on whether Deadpool_1 can remember $Deadpool_2$. Let's say $Deadpool_1$ is the Deadpool from his origin story, where he gets tormented and his regenerative gene kicks in, so that he can heal himself. And let's say that $Deadpool_2$ is the bastard that captured and tormented Blind Al (Deadpool #1). Can we honestly say that both Deadpools are one and the same? Clearly time has passed, and they have changed. Right?! Well Locke had something else in mind for Deadpool. In order for Deadpool to be identical to himself Locke says there must be some sort of continuous awareness of the person's being the same person, or in other words: psychological continuity including memory. Deadpool, Locke claims, not only has a soul and a body, but also consciousness that is separate from both and which is responsible for his personal identity.

Take a glimpse at this surreal conversation from ~~*Cable*~~ *Wolverine & Deadpool*, #44:

BOB: (Hydra—Agent from Earth—616) You cut off his head.

WOLVERINE: Yeah. Adamantium claws. What can you do?

What just happened?! Did Wolverine cut Deadpool's head off? Apparently yes. Well I guess that's the end of Deadpool and the comics, and this chapter, and the whole book.

Well, no in fact. Deadpool, a.k.a. the Merc with the Mouth, has an amazing ability: he can heal himself incredibly quickly. Due to the Weapon X experiments, which utilized Wolverine's special genetic anomaly, he is able to rejuvenate his cells at superhuman speed, making him almost immortal. The main benefit of this mutant gene is that Deadpool can misbehave and get decapitated, but when his head is re-attached he regains himself.

But what about Deadpool's personal identity? If his head is severed is he still Deadpool? Or does he stop being Deadpool until his head is re-attached, as Wolverine promised to do as soon as the commotion stops? Locke was adamant that Deadpool is Deadpool if and only if $Deadpool_2$ (the one that is further down the road, temporality wise) has a vivid recollection of being $Deadpool_1$ (a former Deadpool in time).

Locke thinks that Deadpool has a soul and a body (a thinking substance), and to that he adds a consciousness that is responsible for reminiscence of past Deadpool's actions—

ensuring Deadpool's identity over time. So Locke is convinced that we can transfer Deadpool's personality from one body to another and still retain Deadpool's personal identity. As long as Deadpool retains psychological continuity he will continue to be the same Deadpool. The moment his head is cut off there is no person that can remember past instances of Deadpool—other than us—so at that moment Deadpool will stop existing. But he can go back to being identical to himself when his head is back on his shoulders.

Scottish philosopher Thomas Reid (1710–1796) did not much care for Deadpool's severed head. Reid considered Deadpool a nuisance. He even named a paradox after him, called "the Deadpool paradox." Imagine that! Well it goes as follows: $Deadpool_1$ is Wade Wilson at the time when he was a young mercenary killing people for money; $Deadpool_2$ is the Deadpool that has learned that he has cancer, breaks up with his girlfriend, Vanessa Carlysle, and goes on to participate in the Weapon X experiment; and $Deadpool_3$ is the Deadpool that fled from the hospice where he was held after he was thrown out of the experiments and already has regenerative powers.

Now, Reid tells us that something weird happens when we apply logical thinking to personal identity, like Locke does. What we get is indeed weird: $Deadpool_2$ remembers $Deadpool_1$, while $Deadpool_3$ only remembers $Deadpool_2$, and cannot for the life of him remember $Deadpool_1$. It seems that the Merc with the Dead Mouth is both identical and not identical to his past incarnations. Cancer Deadpool is identical to young Wade Wilson, and the regenerative degenerate is identical to cancer Deadpool, so by association the degenerate is identical to the Deadpool of youth. But at the same time the degenerate has no direct memory of youth Deadpool, so he is not identical to him. Dealing with paradoxes is indeed confusing stuff, particularly a Deadpool paradox.

Imagine what happens to the idea that Deadpool must be aware of his past instances to be able to say that he's the same Deadpool if some evil mastermind splits Deadpool into four different people? No need to use your imagination. It did happen. In the series *Deadpool: Funeral for a Freak*, Parts 1–4, the villain T-Ray is able to perform something unbelievable, and resurrect dead Deadpool while urinating on his grave; but by doing so he splits Deadpool's personality into four. The original Deadpool suffers from amnesia, and still doesn't get who the hell those other guys are. T-Ray uses the Gemini Star to extract Deadpool's personalities, ". . . TO LEAVE YOU NOTHING BUT A BORING SHELL." So the big question is whether Deadpool continues to be Deadpool if his so-called personalities are expelled?

Philosopher Roderick M. Chisholm (1916–1999), who obviously read the comics, has a lot to say on the matter. He thinks that Deadpool's identity consists of his essential parts. Deadpool's muscular body is an essential part of Deadpool. Perhaps Deadpool's existence is not essential in itself, but his parts are fundamental parts that make Deadpool Deadpool. Take one of them away and we no longer have Deadpool, but another person.

I think we can extend Chisholm's fetish with Deadpool's organs to his mental characteristics. There cannot be a Deadpool without his wonderful traits, such his love of killing, his insatiable appetite for chimichangas, his desire for women and sex. Yes, yes, I can immediately hear your objections. What about that time the Hulk eviscerated Deadpool? Didn't he take away a part that was essential to Deadpool and that stopped Deadpool from being the same?

Wait! Did you just say that the Hulk killed Deadpool?! No way! Well, way! In *Deadpool* Volume 2, #38, Deadpool decides he has had enough of life. Immediately he faces a problem: that damn regenerative healing power prevents him from dying. So he decides to find one of Marvell's strongest heroes to literally smash the life out of him. Yep! The Hulk was the perfect candidate, so Deadpool took care of business and pushed the Hulk to the limit of his anger and strength.

Talking to his beloved Death mistress—the same one Thanos also loves—while he momentarily died he told her about his plans: "I'm gonna do it, baby, I swear. I'm gonna get Hulk to kill the hell outta me—smash me to a bloody pulp till I'm nothin' but a red smear on the concrete. Nothin' left to regenerate." And in *Deadpool* Volume 2, #39, the Hulk succeeds and crushes, smashes Deadpool to smithereens. Nothin' is left of him. Of course, later we find out that he regenerated, so you need not worry. But going back to Deadpool's wish to die, we must ask: is the Deadpool before the Hulk smashed his head the same as the Deadpool after he was smashed and then regenerated?

Since Chisholm loves our Deadpool so, he claims that in ordinary language it would be nonsensical to say that it is the same Deadpool, since obviously his parts were changed. Even if his mind can regenerate, and he can grow back his limbs, they aren't the same ones as before. But philosophically speaking, what we get are different Deadpools. Every time Deadpool's body parts are cut off and then rejuvenate, we actually get a "new" Deadpool, but still it's a Deadpool, and not a chimichanga. Confused? Me too!

I guess we have to find something other than psychological arguments about personal identity to think about personal identity, or we might lose Deadpool altogether—he might just stop existing, and then who will kill people? Who will make us laugh while doing it? Let's let the material aspect of personal identity shine on our crazy chimichanga.

I'd Say I Want a Piece of You . . . But I've Already Got a Full Set

Okay, okay. I get it. It's a bit confusing. If Deadpool gets his head blown off is he still Deadpool or is he another version, similar, but yet different? I guess there's no clear answer. But that shouldn't put us off complicating things even more.

In *Deadpool* Volume 2, #44, "Okay, She is the Crazy One?", Deadpool finds some disturbing things floating around in his lover Dr. Ella Whitby's refrigerator. Although, being the great dick he is ("dick is a slang word for detective, right?"), he should have known from the stink the moment he broke into her house that something was fishy. Or should I say dead fish. Or dead cat heads. Or Deadpool dead parts. Never mind.

It seems that Dr. Whitby is obsessed with Deadpool and in the time he spent in the mental institution under her supervision she managed to keep, stored in her refrigerator, various body parts that belonged to Deadpool. Opening the fridge, with no idea what he might find, looking for the source of the dreadful smell oozing into the apartment, Deadpool mumbles to himself: "It's the *fridge*. Probably fulla *dead cats*. OR, Y'KNOW, A BUNCHA SEVERED HEADS . . . HA! NOPE. JUST ONE SEVERED HEAD. MINE. THAT'S . . . THAT'S . . . US. In *pieces*. THERE'S GOTTA BE A WHOLE BODY'S WORTH OF PARTS IN THERE!"

Deadpool is right; there are lots of his dismembered body parts. Detached from one another. Stored in the fridge. Later he puts them all, including his severed head, into a plastic bag, wraps it up and throws it outside Dr. Whitby's apartment into the dumpster. Unfortunately, and unbeknownst to him, in that moment Deadpool created Evil Deadpool, another Merc with a Mouth, constituted of all the body parts that once made up Deadpool. How did that happen?

We get the answer in *Deadpool* Volume 2, #45, "What ~~Who~~ Is Evil Deadpool?" The regeneratin' Degenerate is able to regenerate himself. Well it seems that this ability is not restricted to the Deadpool we know as Wade Wilson, whom from now on I'll call Deadpool$_1$. It seems that this ability can revitalize another Deadpool if enough essential body parts are in proximity to one another.

Philosophy loves puzzles as much as Deadpool loves chimichangas. So consider the following puzzle of personal identity. If Deadpool$_1$, our own beloved Wade Wilson, gets carved up every now and then, including his head, torso, heart, blood, skin, hands and legs—you get the drift. And eventually gets thrown into the garbage. Imagine this Deadpool$_1$ has a regenerative ability, and soon it kicks in and his members form together so that we get a "new" Deadpool, one I shall call Deadpool$_2$, a.k.a. Evil Deadpool. What prevents us from arguing that Deadpool$_2$ and Deadpool$_1$ are one and the same Deadpool?

This paradox, "The Ship of Theseus," is famous in the history of philosophy and dates back to Ancient Greece, beginning with Heraclitus (around 535–c. 475 B.C.E.). But it was Plutarch (around A.D. 46–120) who first put it to paper. Simply put, the Theseus paradox goes as follows: "if all of the planks of which a ship is composed are replaced, one by one, is the resulting ship the same ship?" Or, as we might ask: "if all the body parts of which a Deadpool is composed are replaced, one by one, is the resulting Deadpool the same Deadpool?" This is a tough question. I guess for answers we must go to the ultimate source, the comics, and ask: Does Deadpool$_1$ = Deadpool$_2$?

Philosopher Theodore Sider might shout out: "Of course Deadpool$_1$ equals Deadpool$_2$!" In fact there is no need to number them, they are the same object. That is the reasonable conclusion of this paradox. If they share the same body parts, even genitalia, then they are the same. If they occupy the same space, the same mass, velocity, and love of chimichangas, then obviously they are one and the same. In *Deadpool* Volume 2, #45, Evil Deadpool makes a lot of effort to get from England to New Jersey, USA, to the place that serves the best chimichangas in the world, Pablito Balibrea's. So if $Deadpool_2$'s love of chimichangas drives him to go that far for them, isn't this enough to indicate that they're identical to one another?

Well, a couple of things are not in order here. First, the name: Evil Deadpool. How come $Deadpool_2$ is considered more evil than $Deadpool_1$? Mmmm . . . that's not a hard question. $Deadpool_2$ just hijacked a plane and killed a rich passenger because he couldn't get him pretzels. While taunting him he uttered: "BUT YOU? YOU'RE PREETY MUCH USELESS." And this comes right after the guy offered him billions.

Soon after, we find out that $Deadpool_2$ crashed the plane into a bridge, without even working up a sweat. A pure sociopath. No moral compass at all. And that's a tad different from the moral sociopath we have come to know as $Deadpool_1$. Meanwhile, $Deadpool_1$ arriving at New Jersey by freight, finds out that a group of women have been abducted, probably to be forced into sex work, and he saves them by slaughtering the entire crew of the freight. $Deadpool_1$ is still a sociopath. When asked by one of the girls, "You . . . take us back to home?" he answers "NO, BUT I'LL TAKE YA TO NEW YORK . . . I KNOW A GUY IN THE RUSSIAN CONSULATE . . . HE'S A GOOD GUY—I KILLED HIS GREASY BROTHER-IN-LAW FOR HIM." A maniac indeed.

But what if Sider had a split personality and after reading *Deadpool* Volume 2, #45 and #46 went on a rant, saying: "No way are they the same Deadpool. How can two Deadpools share the same space and have the same body parts? That is inconceivable. They should be unequal to each other. The verdict is in: $Deadpool_1 \neq Deadpool_2$, and that's final."

Philosopher David Wiggins is pretty adamant when it comes to the Deadpool case, and seems to have a solution to Sider's split personality. Wiggins suggests that if we cut Deadpool's brain into two halves and transplant them into two different persons, what we get is essentially the same Deadpool in two separate bodies. Let's see what Deadpool has to say on that matter. Deadpool and Evil Deadpool meet and fight each other. "HE LOOKS LIKE . . . US" says $Deadpool_1$, or so-called non-Evil Deadpool.

It seems they have the same body parts, but not exactly in the same order, which is apparent since they don't necessarily look alike. $Deadpool_2$ has "A BACKWARD ARM?!", and all in all just looks funny, like a chucky doll (from the movie *Child's Play*) of Deadpool. But they do share the same memories. Muscle memories at least, as $Deadpool_1$ gets beaten like a rag doll because "THIS GUY KNOWS ALL OUR MOVES BEFORE WE EVEN MAKE 'EM!"

Okay, the verdict is in: $Deadpool_1$ and $Deadpool_2$ are the same. No need to philosophize anymore. They share everything.

Well, no. I don't buy into the idea that $Deadpool_2$ has no conscience. $Deadpool_1$ has done some horrific stuff along the way. And evidently both of them are nuts and ruthless murderers. But sadly Wiggins didn't know that his thought-experiment is incomplete. What happens if Deadpool's head is chopped off and a couple of years go by, and only then his body parts heal themselves, and revitalize $Deadpool_2$? And to top that, $Deadpool_2$ won't have memories of the years that have gone by since $Deadpool_1$'s head was severed. Wiggins might find himself in quite a pickle. He shouts:

> $Deadpool_1$, you ass, don't patronize your other $Deadpool_2$, you can be split into parts and combined into one, and still be the same person. Why is that you ask? Well it all boils down to the fact that, while both Deadpools share the same space, they aren't the same thing. I mean, I can say they have the same inner thoughts, feelings, judgments, yet one is Evil Deadpool and the other is Deadpool. The same thing but different reference. Not only is $Deadpool_1$ the one that existed before $Deadpool_2$, it was the former that created the latter.

Philosopher Harold Noonan thinks in a similar way to Wiggins that $Deadpool_1$ and $Deadpool_2$ aren't that different after all. They are both part of the family of Deadpool. They share Deadpoolness. They drink from the fountain of the pool of Deadpool. So in what way are they different? After all, even if we reject the evilness of Evil Deadpool as being something extraordinary, $Deadpool_2$ can teleport himself out of a crashing jet, or evade getting hit by a truck driven by $Deadpool_1$ by teleportation.

Noonan agrees that $Deadpool_2$ differs when it comes to the idea that $Deadpool_1$ and $Deadpool_2$ share the same inner structure. In a way, for $Deadpool_1$ to be identical to $Deadpool_2$ the former must be identically the same, down to the atom, as the latter. And obviously that is not the case. $Deadpool_2$'s head was detached from $Deadpool_1$'s body, so it didn't have the thoughts, memories, and feelings of $Deadpool_1$ during the time it was detached from a body. That's why $Deadpool_1$ can outsmart $Deadpool_2$ and the latter is unaware of the fact that $Deadpool_1$ rigged the car where he had stashed his best weapons, which caused $Deadpool_2$ to get hit by the explosion.

What then happens to both Deadpools from the moment they exist simultaneously? If we take Wiggins's advice when it comes to the all-Deadpool-dudeness, then even if the particles of both aren't the same, the Deadpoolness is. And if so, the fact that $Deadpool_2$ crashed a jet into a bridge and at the same time $Deadpool_1$ saved a bunch of women while killing the crew of the ship indicates that both have different histories. These histories affect the way that Deadpool is shaped, so in a sense Wiggins leads us to think that they are the same but yet their histories cause them to be different. I believe that Deadpool's head would have exploded if he had had to deal with the question of personal identity.

Last Chance to Save Deadpool's Personal Identity

I guess y'all want to save Deadpool and continue seeing him get crazy about chimichangas, right? Well, bear with me.

A possible answer to the problem of Deadpool's personal identity lies in the breaking of the fourth wall. "Breaking the fourth wall" means that the imaginary wall that separates us, the audience, the readers, from the characters in the story is dismantled and the characters approach us—they become aware of us by addressing us.

I got this idea while reading a thread on Reddit.com called "When Deadpool/Wolverine's head gets completely destroyed, how do they retain memories?" dated August 2014. The discussion was primarily about Wolverine's loss of memory and how plausible it is that he has regenerative healing power yet cannot heal the hippocampus that stores memories. One user,

Wanna-be_Jedi, argued that "Deadpool stores his memories in us when we read anything about him. He then accesses it through us when he needs to remember anything."

Well, I'm sure you ask yourself how that can solve our Deadpool predicament. For that we need the help of philosopher Herbert Paul Grice (1913–1988). Grice did have a soft spot for our beloved Deadpool. Instead of thinking about personal identity, in terms of $Deadpool_1$ being able to remember $Deadpool_2$, like Locke, Grice suggests that we consider leaving Deadpool be, and not forcing him to be identical to himself. But what personal identity actually consists in is that at a certain time $Deadpool_2$ has some of the memories of $Deadpool_1$, and those memories overlap, and this continues also for $Deadpool_3$ who has certain memories of $Deadpool_2$. So what we get is not a logical equation of $Deadpool_2 = Deadpool_1$ and $Deadpool_3 = Deadpool_2$, meaning that $Deadpool_3 = Deadpool_1$, but a set of memories that continues and is amalgamated, which makes Deadpool Deadpool.

Brilliant, indeed! Grice just saved Deadpool from being lost in the paradox of personal identity. There's no need for the later version of Deadpool to remember his past incarnations because the transition between different instances of Deadpool's series of memories does the job for us.

But another philosopher, John R. Perry, had other things in mind for Deadpool, or perhaps for Grice. Perry did not agree with Grice that the series of memories is enough for Deadpool to retain his personal identity. The argument is circular. How can we tell that someone hasn't implanted thoughts into Deadpool? In *Cable & Deadpool* #15, *Enema of the State: Part 1*, the mysterious villain Black Box manages to brainwash Deadpool, turn him into a brainless puppet with the sole purpose of killing Cable. Two characters who serve Black Box discuss Deadpool's biology.

Black suit person: Wade's got an accelerated metabolism—part of a healing factor—makes him virtually indestructible.

Trench coat person: But it's made his brain a little squirrelly. Crazy, but also a borderline amnesiac.

Black suit person: Or at the very least, a selective memory that conveniently excuses his actions and alleviates all his guilt.

In this instance, Deadpool's regenerative powers do not withstand the surgical procedure performed by Black Box. For this reason, Perry believes that for Deadpool to rely on a set of memories to make him Deadpool requires him to be the same person who remembers the same set of memories. In that case, if Black Box put thoughts into Deadpool's head, we would be mistaken in thinking that Deadpool is the same Deadpool. He would have memories that aren't his, but he would believe that they are his. Quite a pickle.

Here comes the suggestion from the beginning of this chapter. What if we consider Deadpool to be more than just a regular superhuman, chimichanga-loving, merciless killer, anti-hero, comedian, regenerative maniac? What happens if we take him to be an entity that includes the comics, and movies, the cartoonists, and of course the readers? Perhaps it was not by chance that Deadpool broke the fourth wall, the same block that is erected to allow the reader to immerse herself in the comics without being conscious of the fact that they are not "reality," but something else.

If continuity is determined by Deadpool's being the one who remembers, and requires a set of memories that overlap over time, let us imagine that Deadpool stores his memories in the readers. In fact, we have more than what Deadpool simply wants us to know. We get the ambience of the events Deadpool experiences. We witness his inner thoughts, and the thoughts he shares with us. We get to differentiate Deadpool's addressee in his inner conversations, so we can then unify Deadpool for him, and tell him: "Yo! You blabbering degenerate, you are at times a sociopath, and sometimes a caring person, most of the time you are a ruthless killer—but always a funny guy who loves chimichangas."

Deadpool might object to this solution. Wade Wilson wouldn't like it that we, philosophers, bloggers, movie viewers and comics reader, are responsible for his personal identity over time. I fear he might even want to hurt us since he is a kind of sociopath. If Deadpool's personal identity is depended on external factors, Deadpool's identity becomes somewhat a "non-personal identity." His contribution to the persistence of his identity over time turns out to be less important than most Deadpool philosophers hitherto have argued. Consider this: What would happen to Deadpool if he forgets his love for chimichangas and only we, the viewers, have a recollection of it? In a way we're forced to say that Deadpool's forgetfulness of his love of chimichangas render him not Deadpool as he has no memory of something which is a fundamental part of him. This might come across as nonsensical since our own experience indicates that we know that we are who we are, and even if we don't have any recollection of our previous selves we're still the same person. Perhaps the fourth-wall-breaking is Deadpool's way to tell us that personal identity over time is a mutual thing, it depends on other people recognizing us as us. Wade Wilson's continues to be the same person as long as we—external to Deadpool—recognize him as the Deadpool.

Another way to understand Deadpool's personal identity is to consider there is a multiplicity of Deadpools. When Deadpool cuts his hand cut off in the motion picture, he creates another instance of himself. True, he can grow a new arm, but a new harm makes him a new Deadpool, he is not the same old Deadpool. Well, some of you might argue that every comic release and movie picture renders a different instantiation of Deadpool. A different Deadpool is created each and every time a comic is created. Wouldn't it be equal as saying that Deadpool never existed over time? But what we get is many variations of Deadpool created every time a new Deadpool is portrayed.

If we combine these two ideas that there are multiple Deadpools and that their personal identity over time is depended on external factors, then every time, *you the reader closes the comic book or pause the movie you end up killing your favorite merc with the mouth*. Well, shame on you!!!

We become the cornerstone that, together with Deadpool himself and the cartoonist, sustains his personal identity. The equation should be: Deadpool loves chimichangas equals Deadpool loves chimichangas. And that's how you solve the problem of Deadpool's personal identity over time.

10
Always a Pallbearer, Never the Corpse

HEIDI SAMUELSON AND SOME OLD DEPRESSING DEAD GUY

The world is an indifferent, irrational, and meaningless place. It has to be, right? Bea Arthur is dead, and we're clinging to Betty White like the ship is going down.

Suppose you've been diagnosed with terminal cancer and then agree to be experimented on by a government project that tells you it will heal you, but is actually testing a drug on you to see whether mutant powers will emerge in you. Suppose the experiment leaves you with an amazing healing ability, but with a face that no one's mother could love—this sounds absurd, right? It's supposed to. This is Deadpool's origin story, and it's also a perfect example of absurdity.

If you're twentieth-century French philosopher Albert Camus (1913–1960), you would say that the whole world is absurd, but you should live with it and enjoy it anyway. Camus explains that the world is meaningless and valueless, and human beings are stuck looking for meaning that they are never going to find. It's not that we're incapable of finding meaning or understanding the world, there just *isn't* a rational, objective explanation of the world—period. This is the philosophical theory of absurdism.

It might sound bleak at first, but Camus says there's a chance for you to become a hero in this absurd world. I say—***with some help from me, your pal Deadpool***—that you can go Camus one better and become an absurd superhero, or at least a certain mercenary in a red suit can—***Aw, you're making me blush.***

The Absurd
—Sounds like something from an informercial.

Camus explains "the absurd" like this:

> If I see a man armed only with a sword attack a group of machine guns, I shall consider his act to be absurd. But it is so solely by virtue of the disproportion between his intention and the reality he will encounter, of the contradiction I notice between his true strength and the aim he has in view. (*The Myth of Sisyphus*, p. 29)

If this man is dressed head-to-toe in red spandex, then he might be Deadpool. If he's cracking jokes and hitting on everyone around him, then he's *definitely* Deadpool.

You can see the absurd when you compare the intention of your actions and the reality of the consequences. It would be absurd for a man to go into a firefight against multiple cars full of heavily-armed men with only twelve bullets and intend to win. Of course, this is exactly what Deadpool does in his movie—***I told them they'd have to share!*** It would also be absurd for one man to be completely dismembered (*Deadpool vs. Carnage*), impaled by a bull African elephant tusk (*Deadpool* Volume 3, #2), ripped apart and feasted on by zombies (*Night of the Living Deadpool*), shot through the head with an arrow (by Bullseye in *Dark Reign*), shot through the eye with a bullet (by Punisher in *Deadpool* "Suicide Kings"), literally blown into pieces by a future-tech rifle (by Cable in *Deadpool vs. The X-Force*), completely liquefied and swallowed (also by Cable, in *Cable & Deadpool* #5), and survive each and every time. But Deadpool does.

The difference between expectations (certain death) and reality (no death) shows that there's a difference between the meaning and truth we *want* to find, and the *lack* of meaning and truth we *actually* find in the world. Even though Deadpool is a fictional character and people don't normally survive gunshot wounds to the head, let alone being liquefied, Deadpool's knowledge of the world outside of his comic books helps to show us the absurdity in our own lives. You might read comic books as a way to lose yourself in a different reality, and meanwhile the comic book character you are reading tells you that "none of this is actually happening. There is a man. At a typewriter.

This is all his twisted imagination" (*Deadpool* Volume 1, #34)—***Kind of absurd, right? I think I'm getting it.***

Problems start to happen when you think about how we can live in situations where reality doesn't line up with what we intend to do, where meaning is nowhere to be found, and where there is so much absurdity that you question why you should keep living at all. Camus tackles these problems and shows that certain traits are found in the people who embrace absurdity, including a sense of purpose, compassion, and humor. The traits of the absurd man come together for Camus in the absurd hero, and I contend that Deadpool epitomizes this absurd hero by being an absurd *super*hero.

The Question of Suicide

—*Who commits suicide with a bow and arrow?*

Bows are for, like, long-distance killing, not up-close killing. Now that that's settled, Deadpool, there is *another* question of suicide, and, for Camus, it was critical to answer it in order to face the absurd. He famously wrote in *The Myth of Sisyphus*, "there is only one real philosophical problem, and that is suicide" (p. 3). In other words, because life is meaningless and we don't understand it, you have to ask yourself: why not just end my life?

Suicide comes up as a possibility when you recognize "the absence of any profound reason for living, the insane character of that daily agitation, and the uselessness of suffering" (p. 6). This is the feeling of absurdity. It's a feeling that Deadpool knows well, and it is one that Camus says we should embrace.

Deadpool has faced suicide not as a philosophical problem, but as an actual one. In *Deadpool* Volume 2, #37, Deadpool decides he wants to die. He tries to kill himself in the only way that seems plausible—death by Incredible Hulk—though his attempt ultimately fails. What adds a bit of absurdity to Deadpool's attempt at suicide is that he wants to die so he can be with Death, or the personified mistress of death. Death wants Deadpool's soul and Deadpool decides to join her, but because he can't die, death isn't an option. Because Deadpool wants to die for absurd reasons, he's even more absurd than someone unsure whether they should keep living.

For Camus, facing suicide means confronting your fear of death, which comes from a combination of other things we fear: time, the future, and the unknown. Deadpool is canonically afraid of cows—***What? I find their stare chilling***, but Deadpool writer Daniel Way has suggested that Deadpool thinks his biggest fear is to end up alone, no one paying attention to him, fading out of existence (Ben Morse, "Fear Files: Deadpool"). Because death is the ultimate unknown, something we can't really have an experience of, then looking death in the face, or for Deadpool his fear of being alone, is part of embracing the absurd.

When you have an accelerated healing factor and you're more or less immortal like our masked mercenary, you don't have much of an option when it comes to suicide—as Deadpool himself says, "I'm always a pallbearer, never the corpse!" (*Cable & Deadpool* #19). But by ultimately rejecting death by Hulk and the mistress of Death, this allows Deadpool to keep living his life in a Camus-approved way, in spite of his fears and his very few options for death.

Even though Camus insists that life has no meaning, this doesn't mean that life isn't worth living. Human lives are full of confrontations with the absurd, like dead presidents coming back to life (*Deadpool* Volume 3, #1), having a S.H.I.E.L.D. agent's consciousness inside your brain (*Deadpool* Volume 3, #6), getting your DNA mixed up with a time-traveling hero named Cable (*Cable & Deadpool* #5), knowing that you're actually a comic-book character—***Take your pick!***

Absurdity connects man to the world, because we keep confronting the world even though it's indifferent to us. When we make a choice to keep on living, we're choosing to try and find meaning and a rational explanation for the world, even though we know the world will respond with silence. Some of us choose to fill that silence by talking—a lot.

Once you've resolved this question of suicide, Camus thought there were two possible ways to face life: either embrace a dogma or accept the absurdity of the world. Camus rejects dogma—like religion—outright, because to take that path you have to knowingly accept something untrue and pretend that it is true. Doing that contradicts the whole point of absurdism: there *isn't* one big truth to be found in a meaningless universe. It might make you feel better as you live your day-to-day life, but it's ultimately living in denial, and eventually you will have to confront that your "truth" is just an illusion. You also might have to deal with the people around you not realizing they exist on comic-book pages. ***—Forget it—it's too hard to explain.***

For Camus, the only legitimate option was simply to embrace the absurd, and this is the path that Deadpool takes. In his job as a mercenary, Deadpool's usual response to death is to cause it. He "unalives" bad guys, sometimes for free, and this gives him a sense of purpose, even in an absurd world. In Camus's famous novel *The Stranger*, Meursault kills a man on the beach, but it wasn't intentional or purposeful—he was just distracted. What Camus meant by this is still debated, but Camus seems to disapprove of indifferent killing (something Deadpool doesn't do—he goes after bad guys) and supports certain forms of violence. Deadpool chose not to commit actual suicide, and Camus might say Deadpool chose not to commit philosophical suicide by not choosing a spiritual path.

By choosing absurdity, Camus's absurd man demands "to live *solely* with what he knows, to accommodate himself to what is, and to bring in nothing that is not certain. He is told that nothing is. But this at least is a certainty" (p. 53). In the comic book canon, Deadpool doesn't remember much of his past, and he doesn't really question it. He accepts his situation, which follows Camus, who argues that life is lived better if it has no meaning and you should just accept your life as it unfolds. This almost sounds like you're chained to particular consequences, but accepting absurdity is not the same thing as accepting a pre-determined fate that has been decided for you. For Camus, you aren't resigning yourself to one path—you can freely act in an absurd world. Deadpool actually argues Camus's point for him to Evan Sabahnur—a clone of Apocalypse whom Deadpool rescued—by telling him that he still has a choice to be his own person and is not destined to be evil just because of his DNA (*Uncanny X-Force* Volume 1, #35).

By rejecting suicide as an option and accepting that life is going to unfold in an absurd way, it puts you in charge of giving your life a sense of purpose for yourself. For Camus, you should live and continue to look for meaning that is impossible to find rather than believe that some bigger, greater meaning exists. And there are various ways to live an absurd life—including being a comic book mercenary.

Revolt, Freedom, Compassion
—Are we about to kiss?

Spidey says never, but I'll wear him down eventually. Other than hitting on Spider-Man, the best way to live in an absurd world is to keep the absurd alive and to revolt against meaning and truth. You should live, says Camus, by constantly confronting the meaninglessness of the world (p. 54). An absurd life includes being aware that some things are out of your control and some things you won't understand, but without you feeling resigned to it or unsettled by it. According to Camus, there are three characteristics of properly living an absurd life: revolt, freedom, and passion.

By facing your life head on, your everyday life becomes a revolt, because every day you are rejecting suicide and dogmatic truth. Living an absurd life also includes recognizing that freedom doesn't mean the freedom to create meaning or the freedom to hope. Deadpool would agree; he never could afford to have hope—ever. Rather, you are free to accept the meaningless universe and draw your strength from its indifference. In *Cable & Deadpool* #19, Deadpool tells Cable about his unfortunate childhood and then, in a Camus-like way, says, "So what was I gonna do, cry all mopey for having been dealt a crappy hand? Frig that. Just play the cards, right?"

The way to face this indifferent world is to have a variety of experiences—***I've got that covered***—and to live in the present without wanting a particular future, and Camus says you should do this with "the passionate flames of human revolt" (p. 64).

Camus explains these characteristics as they appear in particular types of "absurd men." With so many different ways to show revolt, freedom, and passion, embracing an absurd life will not (and should not) look the same for everyone. Camus looks at absurd figures like a lover, an actor, a conqueror, and a creator, who each represent a style of an absurd life. Though Deadpool definitely has his own style, he does have traits found in Camus's examples. If you are a conqueror, you see that action is useless and human beings continue to be vulnerable—even if you put on a fancy red suit and swoop in and save them—but you can't help but feel pity and compassion for them anyway. Camus says it's only the most daring people who feel compassion this strongly, and these feelings don't make them any less strong.

You might not think it to look at him, but Deadpool, in spite of being a mercenary, has a strong sense of compassion. Before Francis turned him into a testicle with teeth, Wade Wilson was a mercenary who showed his soft spot by helping others. Even after his transformation into Deadpool, and in spite of his own mental instability, he's a protector of the weak and of his friends—well, he calls them friends—***Hey! I'm practically an Avenger!***

Deadpool's most enduring relationship—albeit a bizarre one of dubious origins—is the family-like closeness he has with Blind Al, the elderly, blind woman living in his house. Blind Al is sort of a prisoner (though, in Deadpool's defense, he *was* hired to kill her at one point) and sort of a confidant for him. Deadpool also has a long-term friendship with an arms dealer named Weasel, who even publically acknowledges that Wade is a friend. Deadpool also has a soft spot for children, including his own daughter, whom he takes trick-or-treating (*Hawkeye vs. Deadpool*), and Evan, whom Deadpool has fatherly feelings for—well, he gives Evan some dirty magazines (*Uncanny X-Force* Volume 1, #35)—***Eh, close enough?***

Set aside the fact that Deadpool once killed the Marvel universe—***We all have slip-ups.***—he has also helped them, and sometimes he ends up being quite considerate. One of his favorite brothers-in-arms is Spider-Man. Deadpool once wore Spider-Man's costume and offered to lift the mask if he had to kill anyone, because he didn't want to hurt Spider-Man's reputation (*Deadpool Annual* #2). Deadpool's compassion even extends to considerately lifting up his mask enough so Hawkeye, who is deaf, can read his lips, and he uses sign language to communicate with him (*Hawkeye vs. Deadpool*).

Ultimately there is not one way to be an absurd man or to recognize that you live an absurd life. Revolt, freedom, and passion have many forms. Deadpool revolts when he doesn't follow the path of other mutants, mostly works alone, and doesn't choose to follow a moral code. He also uses freedom by expressing weakness and vulnerability when he doesn't have to by showing compassion for others. This compassion is something you wouldn't expect from a mercenary, and so it gives us another example of Camus's absurd ways of living. Sometimes Deadpool's conscience is fleeting, but consistency and certainty aren't features of the absurd world, and you cannot deny that time and again, Deadpool reveals himself to be a merc with a heart.

The Absurd (Super)Hero
—I don't know who that is, but okay.

The absurd life can look different depending on the person, but Camus suggests that there is an ideal, heroic version of the absurd man. For Camus, the absurd hero is best seen in Sisyphus, from Greek mythology, but Deadpool is an even better example.

Let's start with Sisyphus. In Greek myth, Sisyphus was accused by the gods of levity—sound like a certain merc you know and love? Sisyphus doesn't follow the rules or respect the authority of the gods—he tries to wheel and deal with them. He goes to the underworld and puts Death in chains, then convinces the gods to bring him back up to Earth so he can see firsthand that his wife betrayed him (by not giving him a proper funeral), and then he just refuses to go back. So the gods punish him for his disrespect. They order him to push a rock up a hill only to have it roll back down so he has to push it back up. Why does this make him a hero to Camus?

For one, the gods in Greek myth are great examples of the absurd and meaningless world; mere mortal humans could *try* to find meaning and order in the gods' actions, but it would be pointless. Not to mention, the gods wouldn't like you to try to find reason in their actions—case in point: Sisyphus exploited them to escape the underworld, and they punished him for it. Sisyphus is an absurd combination of passion and revolt, and his eternal punishment is fittingly absurd. Camus explains: "His scorn of the gods, his hatred of death, and his passion for life won him that unspeakable penalty in which the whole being is exerted toward accomplishing nothing" (p. 120). Sisyphus is clearly an absurd character, but there's another trait he exhibits that makes him a hero according to Camus—his punishment brings him a silent joy, because "his fate belongs to him. His rock is his thing" (p. 121). In other words, Sisyphus decides that if he is stuck pushing a boulder up a hill for all eternity, then he's going to own his fate and enjoy it.

This description certainly isn't what you traditionally consider "heroic," but if you add all these traits up, there's another candidate who fits the bill, isn't there? One Wade Winston Wilson. Even though Deadpool works for money, which some—***Cough, Wolverine, cough***—argue prevents him from being a true hero, his occasional selfishness does not prevent him from being an absurd hero. Camus even sets him up for it: "All great deeds and all great thoughts have a ridiculous beginning" (p. 12). Regardless of which origin story you choose, Deadpool fits this bill, and it's an origin story worthy of an absurd hero. We have seen that Deadpool is willing to face death, has his own freely-acquired sense of purpose as a mercenary, has a sense of compassion that drives him, has an uncanny knack to tell the Olsen twins apart, and, like Sisyphus, he has accepted the absurdity of his existence to the point where he can joke about it and take joy in his situation.

It is when Sisyphus realizes that he does not have to feel resigned to his fate, and can claim that all is well, that he becomes the absurd hero. Likewise, Deadpool realizes that he is a mercenary fated to kill bad guys and accepts that he was given a healing factor that makes him nearly indestructible—like Sisyphus's rock, this is Deadpool's thing. But it's crucial for absurdism that this isn't just giving yourself up to fate. Deadpool has moments where he doubts the meaning of life, particularly when he considers what it really means to be a comic book character. In a weak moment, burdened by the fact that he knows he exists as a comic-book character for our entertainment, Deadpool does say, "I now realize I've never experienced happiness," but he recognizes his entrapment and carries on anyway (*Deadpool Kills the Marvel Universe*). Yet he still does celebratory dances after killing bad guys, gets amusement out of life, and finds ways to crack jokes even in dire situations. He's not known as the "Merc with a Mouth" for no reason. Yes, sometimes he's the only one laughing—***Sorry, I use humor to deflect my insecurities. Plus, I'm hilarious, so don't hate.***—but the absurd hero doesn't have to share his joy.

Camus says that we "must imagine Sisyphus happy" (p. 123). Being the absurd hero requires finding enjoyment in the absurd, and that's why Sisyphus is the ideal candidate for Camus. But Deadpool is an even better candidate, isn't he?

Sisyphus never talks about the absurdity of his situation, but Deadpool does. He says, "When you're confronted with a horrible situation, there are only two reactions that make sense: laughter or tears. And laughter, after all, is nature's anesthesia" (*X-Men Origins: Deadpool* #1). If you don't think these words make him an absurd superhero, well, if it helps, you can pretend he's Wolverine.

11
Immortality Is Misery

JOHN ALTMANN WITH SOME HELP FROM THE REGENERATE DEGENERATE

Death is a terrifying thing even for philosophers like me who think about it more than most. We do this to strip away the awe that death possesses. In the end though, understanding death is an impossible task—mainly because death is such a personal experience and we all have loved ones we don't want to live without or dreams we can't handle seeing unlived.

Because of these fears that the human animal has about death, you would think that immortality would prove to be very attractive. After all, no matter what disease may try and infect you or what disaster you may find yourself in, with immortality you know you're going to keep on living and no force of man or nature can stop you. Immortality sounds amazing doesn't it? Well not so fast, because this chapter is going to examine that belief through the life of one of Marvel's greatest antiheroes. The man, who has suffered swords through the stomach and bullets in the head, all the while knowing he'd never end up dead, the man whose soulmate is Death herself in a love that can never be, and the man whose immortality in the form of a regenerative healing factor gave him the name Regenerate Degenerate: Deadpool.

Hi everybody! Man I cannot tell you how exciting it is to be here in this book! Granted my entrance could have had a better introduction but that's what you get for dealing with a philosopher and not a professional ring announcer right? I must say though, this book has taught me so much about philosophy

and philosophers! The biggest lesson is that there are actually philosophers who don't work at fast food joints for a living!

Anyway. . . as I was saying, Deadpool, thanks to being an unwilling participant in the Weapon X program, was granted a regenerative healing factor that makes him near-invincible. Deadpool gets sliced by Wolverine's adamantium claws? There's a regenerative healing factor for that. Deadpool gets shot in the head by a zombie Abraham Lincoln? There's a regenerative healing factor for that. When we see Deadpool taking on mercenary jobs or facing extraordinary obstacles all the while possessing his regenerative healing factor, we're seeing the possibilities of immortality come to life in the most imaginative circumstances that only a comic book could capture. We think to ourselves how amazing it would be to be immortal and all the things we could do with that power. Who could possibly argue against the appeal that being immortal clearly possesses? The answer to that question is, I could.

What a twist! You're truly the M. Night Shyamalan of Philosophy!

Thanks . . . but I won't be doing it alone. Behind me will be the strength of the ideas of three philosophers all from different points in human history. The first two, Jeremy Bentham and Friedrich Nietzsche, will actually be arguing in favor of Deadpool's regenerative healing factor.

So they are fans of me then? I like them already! Almost as much as I like Spider-Man, but definitely more than I like Logan!

No, Deadpool, they don't know you because they can't read comic books, because they're dead! So would you just be quiet over there?! The last philosopher, Bernard Williams, offers a devastating argument against immortality and one that I believe shows the fatal mistake Nietzsche and Bentham make in their arguments.

Fatal as in, I get to cut their heads off with my katana when this chapter ends?

No, you psycho! Put the weapons away and pay attention, Deadpool. Even your brain, which is as chaotic as any roller-coaster, might learn something.

If there's No Killing You, What's the Most Good You Can Do?

We begin with the English philosopher Jeremy Bentham (1748–1832) and he developed an idea known as utilitarianism. In Jeremy Bentham's view, what's moral is what causes happiness for the greatest number of people and what's immoral is what causes suffering for the greatest number of people. The happiness or sadness of the majority is the idea of morality that utilitarianism is founded on.

That is the stupidest idea I have ever heard and I once thought of dressing up as Marilyn Monroe to trap a zombie John F. Kennedy to kill him.

Utilitarianism isn't stupid, Deadpool.

Yes it is. If I have to worry about how many people are affected by the jobs I take on as a mercenary, how would I ever get paid? Money is my favorite thing so you'd never catch me being a utilitarian!

It's funny you say that Deadpool because in your very first comic you actually were a utilitarian! In the first Deadpool solo comic that was released in the 1990s, there was a character named Walter Langkowski also known as Sasquatch who was a member of the Canadian superhero team Alpha Flight. Sasquatch was working on a project whose end goal was to make a facility be fully powered by gamma energy that is harnessed by a gamma core. Around the same time, Deadpool was assigned a job to kill Sasquatch.

I remember that job, Sasquatch's ugliness made it more difficult to complete than the usual job.

Oh please, Deadpool, you can say it was Sasquatch's ugliness and while I agree he'll never win any beauty pageants, we both know the real reason you failed that job that night is because while you were fighting Sasquatch, you damaged his gamma core and created a huge threat for the Southern Hemisphere. With the gamma core now on the brink of a meltdown, that left the Southern Hemisphere at risk of exposure to dangerous levels of fatal gamma radiation. Wide-scale death would have resulted, and the "lucky" ones would have had to deal with cancer and disfigurement.

Oh come on John, it's not all bad. That meltdown

would've caused quite an increase in Deadpool cosplayers at future comic cons!

Your idiocy aside, you and I both know that in the end, you didn't let a meltdown happen: when Sasquatch told you how many people would be killed and how many more would have cancer, skin damage, and the rest, you dived into the gamma radiation headfirst and swam to contain the core's meltdown.

I told Sasquatch if he told anybody about what I did I would shave him down like a French poodle!

You would've been better off threatening the writers, Deadpool. ***You're actually right for once, which is about time considering you're the philosopher here.***

You make your jokes, but you and I both know you saved countless lives that day at great personal risk to yourself but that risk was diminished thanks to your regenerative healing factor. Bentham and others, who believe themselves to be utilitarian in their actions, would see your immortality as a gift because if you can live through swimming in gamma radiation and save millions of lives, there is no limit to the good you can do. Remember, to a utilitarian what's morally right is what makes the greatest number of people happy while what is immoral is what causes suffering to the most people.

So Bentham would have you use your immortality and join up with a group like the Avengers who are globally recognized and have superior resources to help people, to be a hero across the entire globe knowing you can't die. He wouldn't have you use your immortality for mercenary work, because that is solely benefiting you because you're getting paid while a utilitarian would have you do all of your jobs for free because you're the only one who benefits getting paid and you have no real risk because of your immortality, while the greater good isn't financially wealthy and it would bring them greater happiness to know a hero was protecting them at no cost. Your being immortal would mean that you alone would bear the greatest suffering while you would always be bringing the greatest happiness to the greatest number of people by protecting them. Your immortality would leave any utilitarian drooling knowing the good they could protect people from if they possessed it.

Yeah whatever—I'm still not convinced. Living life selflessly for others and always thinking of others before myself? I'll pass both on being a utilitarian

and a sword right through your neck if you feed me garbage like that again.

So Bentham and Utilitarianism isn't your cup of tea, perhaps then you would rather be a Superman, a Nietzschean superman that is.

Eh, Batman still seems more appealing, but who the heck is Nietzsche?

From Regenerate Degenerate to . . . ÜberPool!

Friedrich Nietzsche (1844–1900) was a German philosopher who was quite critical of what he called "herd morality."

Herd morality meaning the kinds of morals cattle subscribe to?

No, Deadpool, herd morality is when a person doesn't carve out their own values and instead simply identifies with the values of a particular group. People who embrace herd morality do so at the cost of making their own unique identity and goals in life and the result is that the meaning of a particular herd becomes the meaning of that person's life.

So it's like if I joined the herd known as the X-Men and adopted all of their principles as my own without much thought or objection?

While I wouldn't necessarily call the X-Men a herd, you actually have the right idea, Deadpool.

That sounds absolutely awful then. I would have to become a . . . a hero! No way am I following the herd.

Nietzsche would agree. He believed strongly in the idea of individuality and that people should create their own values and decide for themselves what fulfills their own lives. People not afraid to live the life they want and not submitting to the principles and ideals of any group or proclaimed authority. People like you for instance Deadpool, who Nietzsche would regard as a living breathing Übermensch!

Übermensch, that's the driving service right? No . . . to Nietzsche, the Übermensch was someone who not only created their own values instead of adopting the values of entities like God or a group like the Democratic party, but also protected the future against these same entities and groups from causing herd morality to exist within communities so that people could maintain their individuality and use it as they see fit. The Übermensch does this by possessing great energy and great power. The kind of power that say, being immortal would allow you to have. Deadpool, you're an Übermensch because you prevented a global-wide herd morality from taking root. When the Messiah was coming to Earth, you were supposed to make sure the Messiah got there safely as a member of the Mithras Directive. But when you realized the Messiah takes away people's free will in order to be able to give the Earth world peace, you made your own decision and chose a future where humans could freely decide their own future whether that was creating art or creating war.

Man, the Mithras Directive was always so annoying talking about my cosmic destiny and making me believe that I could actually be a hero. Yeah, some hero! I was going to let a hideous alien covered in eyeballs take away the free will of the entire planet. It's bad enough I'm controlled by the writers, I wasn't about to give up what little freedom I do have to that cosmic creep!

Spoken like a true Nietzschean! Nietzsche would value your immortality precisely because of the freedom it gives you. The most important freedom being to Nietzsche, the freedom to both destroy and create values, whether on a personal level or on a wider scale. You've used your immortality to create the personal meaning for your life of acquiring wealth, killing selected targets for those who pay you, and annoying all of your comic book brethren with your constant breaking of the fourth wall. You've also used that immortality to make sure others can also decide what their lives are to be by preventing an entity like the Messiah from taking away their free will, even for a worthy cause like world peace. Nietzsche would have you use your immortality to become a symbol of what it means to truly overcome your humanity and experience absolute freedom. To create and destroy values in a never ending cycle while making sure others had the power to do the same. That power would ensure that no one religion, political party, or other value system could take root thus keeping the people free and away from becoming a part of a greater herd.

Look, I'm all about individuality because I do what I want when I want so long as I don't catch the writers after their latest comic idea got laughed at in the writer's room, but how Nietzsche would use my immortality sounds like the whole being-a-hero thing in different packaging. Again, I'm not interested and it would bore me to tears keeping everyone's free will safe all the time.

Bore you, huh? Yeah, boredom really is one of the worst things human beings or even super beings like you, Deadpool, can experience. I just couldn't imagine how I would feel if that boredom never ended. Lucky for us though, there was one philosopher who thought about just that possibility and he concluded that immortality is a punishment and not a power.

Well it is about time! I was starting to dread that this chapter was going to be nothing but a kumbaya session!

An Eternity of Ennui

Bernard Williams (1929–2003) was a philosopher who looked at the problem of immortality from a different angle than just a fear of dying or un-fulfillment. Williams was more concerned with immortality from a psychological perspective and specifically the relationship between how the human personality operates and the idea of immortality. Williams believes that as we grow into our identities and become who we are now, we become set in many things.

Whether it's something as simple as our food preferences, or more complex subjects such as religious belief, Williams believes that there comes a point in all of our personalities where we are just locked into them and can't change them. You're a unique case of this fact, Deadpool, as you personally don't even determine how your personality grows or becomes set in. That's all thanks to the writers.

Thanks for rubbing it in, you jerk.

I'm not trying to be mean Deadpool, but I am pointing out that you fit Williams's idea of a personality perfectly. You're a mercenary who loves violence, making money, and eating chimichangas. That hasn't changed in the countless Deadpool comic-book series that have been produced and just when it seems like it might, such as with the Zenpool arc, you either turn back into the old Deadpool or the series just ends without warning. The writers don't want you to be good, compassionate, charitable, or anything. and with the little freedom you do have with breaking the fourth wall, you've always expressed joy at the money you made or how you were going to make guts splatter.

Well, you've got me there. I love the sound a spleen makes when it is sliced out!

Williams is against immortality for this very reason. If human personalities can't change and human beings after a certain point in their lives become set in their ways as you have, then immortality becomes boring and depressing. Because after a certain point, argues Williams, we'll have done everything while immortal that would've made our particular personalities happy and the more we repeat these activities, the more the initial happiness diminishes and we become miserable.

The only way we could avoid this boredom is if we radically changed our personalities. Vegans would have to become meat eaters, Republicans would have to become Democrats, and you would have to go from a self-loathing mercenary who loves money, to a man that respects himself and the people around him enough to put the guns down, stop spilling blood, and to be at peace with yourself. Only then can your immortality be anything other than a source of misery.

That still sounds like a bunch of New Age hippie garbage that gets pushed out at bookstores like they're some kind of life solutions. Williams doesn't know me, you certainly don't know me, and frankly I'm tired of you blathering on about my immortality! It's time I controlled the conversation! So step aside you glorified burger flipper! It's time Deadpool laid down the law!

To Be Immortal or Not Immortal, That Is the Question

Starting with Jeremy Bentham, who believes in an idea known as utilitarianism which basically says forget about being impaled with your own katana, Deadpool, think of the greater good! Well Bentham, what has the greater good ever done for me? I can save the entire Southern Hemisphere from suffering

cancer and disfigurement, but do any one of them go out the next day and buy a Deadpool shirt?! No they just sit around geeking out in front of their My Little Pony collection to the latest X-Men movie trailer! Logan, isn't that great alright? My movie was so much better and it single-handedly saved a man's career! But that's not good enough for Bentham, who would have me use my immortality to save orphanages and crime-filled communities all day like some do gooder in the Avengers! This guy is so morally self-righteous it makes me sick!

Next we come to Nietzsche, who believed that being an individual is the next best thing to apple pie. Nietzsche was very critical of what he called herd morality and felt that human beings were better than just being followers to whatever group makes them feel like special snowflakes. Nietzsche has this vision of humanity known as the Übermensch, which is a type of being that overcomes the dominant moral principles of their time and sets about creating new values while also using their great power and energy to do the same.

When I stopped the Messiah during my time in the Mithras Directive from coming to Earth to steal people's free will in exchange for world peace, I became an Übermensch, because I refused to have the entire world take up the Messiah's vision of humanity as their own. Nietzsche would have me use my immortality to stop creatures like the Mithras all the time and to use my power to spread the word to the people about the strength that comes from living life as you truly are. I have better things to do than to be a walking self-esteem PSA, like shooting people for money for instance. So I'll pass on being an Übermensch, and relying on Über pickups while I'm at it because I'm not fond of going broke either.

Bernard Williams is nothing more than a Dr. Phil ripoff with his "profound insight" about immortality and human nature. Williams believed that personalities aren't very likely to change after a certain point when we've grown into our identities. So if I've been

a murdering, money grubbing, self-loathing, sarcastic, chimichanga-eating jerk for many Deadpool comics, chances are in Williams's eyes I will always be a murdering, money grubbing, self-loathing, sarcastic, chimichanga eating jerk.

Because of this, Williams believes that being immortal would eventually lead to boredom. The only way we could avoid this fate is if we radically changed our personalities. So I would have to go back to being Zenpool for instance to make my immortality more bearable and I can tell you, I would rather have the writers put me in a comic book series with Wolverine than go through that again. So Williams can kindly eat lead as far as I'm concerned.

Though, while I'm speaking of Zenpool, there was one philosopher by the name of Angel Gonzalez who I read during the Zenpool arc who had a quote I want to end with. "The greatest kind of self-sufficiency is born from prolonged suffering."

I've suffered for years and will suffer for years more, but that's what makes me the greatest Marvel character ever. Because I've endured it all on my own and have never needed a team to do it and I've got a movie and a book to show for it! Bite me, X-Men! Especially you, Logan!

Now if you'll excuse me, I'm going to slice John here with my katana. Enjoy the book!

12
Only Deadpool Is Sane

CHAD WILLIAM TIMM ALL BY HIMSELF

Deadpool is perhaps the most complex and misunderstood character in Marvel Comics. To use Winston Churchill's phrase describing Soviet Russia, he is "a riddle, wrapped in a mystery, inside an enigma" (Radio Broadcast, 1st October 1939).

The antiheroic "Merc with the Mouth" is a ruthless killer, a witty comedian, a hero and a villain often vacillating between these extremes within a single scene. It's not uncommon for Deadpool to crack jokes as he mercilessly kills both friend and foe.

Not only is Deadpool a walking contradiction, his mental health is repeatedly called into question. Nearly everyone in the Marvel World thinks he's crazy, including Deadpool himself! After all, only an insane person would attempt to kill everyone in the universe, including himself, to prove that the universe is the figment of an author's imagination. Then again, doesn't this awareness of his own fictionality represent a level of brilliant awareness that sets him apart from any other character? Does that make him an insane genius?

When you take a step back and look at the big picture the notion of sanity can't have any meaning at all in a multidimensional universe with genetically modified super-human characters prone to killing, destroying, and causing general mayhem. I don't believe Deadpool is insane at all, but I do believe that people in power have labeled him insane in order to control and discredit him.

What in the Name of Namor's Bikini Briefs Is Going On?

Insanity is a complicated and controversial concept, but French philosopher Michel Foucault (1926–1984) provides an important perspective on the subject. Instead of trying to uncover the truth about a person's sanity, like whether or not Deadpool is clinically insane, Foucault based his efforts on analyzing the historical circumstances under which the idea of insanity originates and is used. Foucault called this method of historical investigation "genealogy."

Our modern understanding of madness or insanity isn't grounded in history. Instead, what is or isn't clinically insane is determined by criteria set forth by experts from the American Psychiatric Association and published in a diagnostic manual, the *Diagnostic and Statistical Manual*. As a result, whether or not someone is diagnosed as clinically insane depends on how that person's symptoms align with the experts' established criteria. This gives the experts who design and interpret the manual a tremendous amount of power, since their decisions shape society's understanding of mental illness. Expert power is rarely questioned, because they are best positioned to determine the criteria.

The unquestioned power of diagnosis concerned Michel Foucault, who meticulously traced the ways in which the definition of sanity or insanity evolved throughout history and changed based on social and political conditions, like who had the power to define it. While the more common notion of mental illness is linked closely to the work of Georg Hegel (1770–1831), where humanity is continuously progressing towards a more "true" understanding of insanity due to advancements in science and technology, according to Foucault, "Truth' is linked in a circular relation with systems of power which produce and sustain it, and to effects of power which induces it and which extend it" (*Power / Knowledge*).

Power decides what's true and possessing the truth gives a person power, a relationship creating what Foucault called a "regime of truth." These regimes of truth appear in the Marvel Universe when certain individuals use their expertise to exert the power to decide whether or not Deadpool is insane.

According to Foucault's *History of Madness*, in the modern age insanity became an issue to be studied and the field of psychiatry developed in order explain it. Individuals deemed qualified experts used their positions of authority to arbitrarily define the characteristics of insane individuals, which in turn gave them more power because leaders looked to them to help solve the problem of insanity.

Using Foucault's historical analysis helps to shed light on insanity in the Marvel Universe because Wade Wilson is regularly characterized as insane or crazy by so-called mental health experts. Like the time Professor Xavier and the rest of the X-Men took Wade to Ravenscroft Asylum, "a place for healing shattered, tortured souls." The resident psychiatrist, Dr. Benjamin Brighton, utilized "a new treatment designed to ease troubled minds" and exclaimed "I have had great success in rehabilitating individuals just like Mr. Wilson" (*Deadpool Kills the Marvel Universe*, p. 10). Thus the individual identified as the expert issues their diagnosis, and then the person deemed insane, in this case Wade Wilson, is institutionalized.

Foucault's analysis of the history of madness helps to uncover the role that power plays in deciding what is true about insanity, but let's stop for a minute and address one obvious question: isn't Deadpool really crazy? On one occasion he attempted to kill the entire Marvel Universe and on another he kills all of the Deadpools in each alternate universe in order to end the misery of knowing he's a comic-book character. These do not seem like the actions of a sane individual.

But what if, in fact, he isn't crazy? What if he's one of the only sane characters in the whole universe but has been labeled "insane" by those with the credentials to make that determination and the power to act on it? By diagnosing Deadpool as insane, powerful individuals thereby link all of his actions to a lack of mental health. If he attacks someone, it's because he's insane. If he seeks revenge, he must be crazy. By labeling Deadpool crazy or insane the doctors, therapist, and even government officials then create the identity of the insane person. Because of the expert's power and authority everyone then associates insanity with the person identified as crazy.

Powerful labeling clearly occurred when authorities arrested Deadpool after he tried to trick the Hulk into killing him with nuclear weapons. Prosecutors in Deadpool's trial attempted to convince a judge to sentence the Merc with a Mouth to The Raft, an infamous maximum security prison for those with super powers. Deadpool's attorney Jennifer Walters, also known as She-Hulk, instead claimed that he should be placed in Crossmore Prison, a psychiatric hospital. Walters made her case by relying on Deadpool's psychological assessment "Prepared by government experts who examined my client during pre-trial discovery." According to the psychological assessment, Deadpool "has no super-powers; only a biological aberration directly caused by experimentation upon my client by agents of the US Government" ("Institutionalized: Part One," p. 4). In labeling Deadpool's psychological state, "government experts" used their power to construct the criteria for identifying insanity and in turn crafted an identity for Deadpool—the identity of a man driven insane by a biological aberration.

In his analysis of the history of madness Foucault referred to this process of labeling and sorting used on Deadpool as the knowledge/power nexus. Because a person with certain credentials names the characteristics of a category, they are perceived as knowledgeable or an expert on the subject. As a result, their expertise gives them additional power to continue naming and categorizing.

Nutty Shenanigans

Is calling someone insane or crazy really a big deal? When he realizes Deadpool's desire to die instead of living with the knowledge that he's a fictional cartoon character, The Hulk says "You're insane . . . deeply, dangerously disturbed" ("Operation Annihilation Part Three," p. 17). But who cares if the Hulk calls you insane? I mean, the Hulk is . . . a gigantic raging lunatic of radioactive proportions! When we call someone or something crazy, it's usually just a harmless recognition that what we 'e witnessing is outside of what we might see on a daily basis. Perhaps something is abnormal. It becomes a big deal, however, when the naming is done in a systematic way as a means of controlling or discrediting an individual or group, especially when it's in order to justify your own questionable actions. Labeling to control is exactly what happens to Deadpool on numerous occasions.

For example, Deadpool's actions in his recent battle with the Hulk are systematically defined as insane by Dr. Ellen Whitby at

Crossmore Prison in *Institutionalized*. Dr. Whitby, the institution's resident psychologist, describes Deadpool as "A profoundly troubled man who has suffered psychological trauma so severe it's a wonder he can even move, let alone speak" ("Institutionalized: Part One," p. 12). Your friends, or enemies, calling you crazy is one thing. You can just ignore them or, like Deadpool, crack a witty and inappropriate joke. Institutionalization in an asylum like Crossmore, however, represents a systematic policy of identifying criteria for insanity, sorting sane from insane, and then acting on those determined to be mad.

Foucault first uncovered the systematic practice of naming in the seventeenth-century field of medicine, where physicians sought to prevent the spread of sickness. In order to do so, experts first needed to name the symptoms of the particular sickness and then identify those who were sick. Naming reflected a position of power because once identified and labeled, the sick could then be sorted or separated from the rest of the population. According to Foucault, "Knowledge is not made for understanding: It is made for cutting" (*The Foucault Reader*, p. 88). While the medical field was concerned about understanding the sick they were also concerned about wielding power over their subjects, identifying, classifying, and then treating them in ways they saw fit.

In the case of Deadpool the mental health expert, Dr. Whitby, determined that his actions were unhealthy and dangerous when he flipped out after other inmates laughed at his grotesquely burned face. She reported that Deadpool "was having a psychotic episode brought on by a paranoid delusion—he thought he was being made a spectacle of . . . in order for me to treat him, he must first trust me" ("Institutionalized: Part One," p. 18). Dr. Whitby's expertise as a mental health expert gave her the authority to link Deadpool's violent act to a diagnosis of insanity.

Foucault explains the phenomenon of linking crime and mental illness as a fiction. Nineteenth-century psychiatry invented crime caused by insanity and in the process invented insanity. In other words, prior to the nineteenth century, the clinical concept of insanity did not exist. In fact, during medieval times those who saw the world differently or abnormally often served as advisors, seers, or shamans.

During the nineteenth century the early psychiatric movement also sought to solidify its position of power by proving its own necessity. Psychiatry did this by linking criminal behavior with mental illness. Foucault explains that psychiatrists' interest in crime became less about gaining knowledge to understand it, but rather to gain power and secure the relevance of their field. By linking crime and insanity, especially murder, psychiatrists made it clear that mental illness should be feared. Since you never know whether someone who is mentally ill might get violent, it's best if they are institutionalized to keep everyone else safe. As Warden Aimes of the Crossmore Mental Asylum concludes, Deadpool is "One of the most violent and mentally unstable probates on the planet," (p. 4), formally linking his violent behavior to potential criminal activity.

Technologies of the Self

Foucault's genealogy reveals that the process of linking madness with crime through the field of psychiatry reflected a change in the art of governing that swept Europe in the seventeenth and eighteenth centuries. Up to that point, the primary methods used by governments to keep populations under control involved outward public displays of punishment, like torture and execution, or what Foucault calls sovereign power. Over time these public and brutal forms of punishment actually had the reverse effect: people rose up and overthrew their governments. Conversely, linking insanity with crime served as a new and powerful form of social control because it justified the incarceration of those labeled insane, allowing governors and governments to exert more subtle forms of control. But disciplinary power is far more insidious because it actually encouraged people to discipline and control themselves. Deadpool is impossible to control and his power of regeneration makes killing him out of the question. If those in power could convince him to believe he's insane, however, he could control himself!

This new form of power, called disciplinary power, encouraged the criminal or person labeled insane to see themselves as mentally ill. For example, at the Crossmore prison for the mentally ill, Dr. Whitby used a unique kind of therapy to encourage her patients to confront their crimes and see themselves as criminally insane. She forced her patients to put together puzzles that were actually graphic photographs of the crimes they were accused of committing.

One of her patients, Dr. Cereus, convicted of mass murderous gas attacks, tells her "I do not like these puzzles Dr. Whitby!" Her response, "Well I'm glad to hear that Mr. Cereus, you're not supposed to ("Institutionalized: Part One," p. 14) reflects her goal of making the patient uncomfortable by seeing the insanity of their crimes. I am not arguing that killing is socially acceptable or should be allowed, or that Dr. Cereus or Deadpool should be released from prison. What I'm questioning is the automatic linking of their criminal behavior to mental illness. Just because someone commits a crime does not automatically mean they are crazy.

By convincing people that their actions or thoughts are insane, the expert takes the external diagnosis of criminal insanity and moves it inward in the form of a self-image of a crazy person, a process Foucault referred to as "technologies of the self." By diagnosing and labeling a person as mad, crazy, or insane, the expert begins the process of disciplining the patient's mind. Patients are encouraged to critically analyze themselves and change their conduct or way of being in the hopes of being seen by others as rehabilitated. Expert diagnoses of insanity affected Deadpool to the point that he sees himself as insane.

Insanity Is Good . . . It Keeps Me Sane

I talk to myself often. In fact, I had a long conversation with myself about whether I should admit that I talk to myself. Despite my admission, I have no concerns about my own mental health. Deadpool talks to himself and as a result he questions his sanity. In *Deep End Part I* the voice in his head says "Dear Diary, I think I might actually be crazy." Deadpool responds to the voice with "What! I'm not crazy. I have a vivid imagination is all!" ("The Deep End: Part One," p. 6).

Questioning his sanity is a regular occurrence for Deadpool. In *Deep End Part II*, Wolverine says "You know what your problem is, Deadpool? You never learned to take anything seriously." Deadpool responds with "I thought my problem was that I was crazy" (Issue 36, p. 6). In *Collecting Deadpool #36*, Deadpool is literally on a suicide mission, attempting to get his friends to finally kill him for good. He tells his periodic sidekick, Bob, "I think I might actually be insane" ("Operation

Annihilation Part Three," p. 17). In *Deadpool Kills Deadpool,* Wade Wilson says "I speak fluent raging psychopath," and describing his plan to destroy all the versions of himself in each universe, remarks "That plan takes a seriously messed up kind of crazy . . . Love me daddy kind of nuts . . . Gotta admit. Sounds like me."

These are just a few examples of the influence of disciplinary power on Deadpool, where he internalizes the imposed identity of a madman. Here disciplinary power acts as something like a self-fulfilling prophecy. The labeling, sorting, and treating creates an identity of insanity, and might actually cause a person to behave that way! As Foucault describes, "He is mad because that is what people tell him and because he has been treated as such. 'They wanted me to be ridiculous, so that is what I became'." Deadpool acts crazy because everyone expects him to!

Uhh . . . This Chick's Crazy!

Deadpool's Marvel Universe is rife with power-hungry so-called experts who repeatedly use their positions of power and authority to cause mayhem. While institutionalized at Ravenscroft Asylum, resident psychiatrist Dr. Brighton remarks "My techniques are unorthodox, but I've had great success in rehabilitating individuals just like Mr. Wilson" (*Deadpool Kills the Marvel Universe*, p. 10). "Unorthodox" is a gross understatement, as Deadpool discovers that Dr. Brighton is actually just a robotic shell inhabited by Psycho Man, who uses mind control to create a "force of willing soldiers."

Deadpool's experience with power-hungry megalomaniacs with advanced degrees in the sciences actually goes way back to when we knew him as Wade Wilson. Wade acquired his regeneration ability as a result of horrific experiments conducted by the Weapon X geneticist, Dr. Killebrew. While conducting his experiments, Dr. Killebrew told Wade that "I'm the man that collects the rejects and finds uses for them . . . You see, I have work to do, important work, and for that I need test subjects." When Wade's heart is ripped out by Dr. Killebrew's henchman, Ajax, his desire for vengeance kick starts his regeneration powers and, according to legend, creates the madman Deadpool.

While at Crossmore prison, Dr. Whitby's puzzle therapy makes the voices in Deadpool's head temporarily disappear. Dr. Whitby asks him "Do you 'hear' voices in your head? Or did you literally 'see' words and then read them, as if you're reading a comic?" Deadpool's response, "How'd you make the boxes go away . . . you did something—you're a doctor, you know how to do things like that . . . like put things in their brains and take things out" ("Institutionalized: Part Two," p. 5) reflects his belief that doctors can abuse their position of influence. Dr. Whitby turns out to be no exception. In fact, Dr. Whitby has secretly been collecting Deadpool's severed body parts and storing them in her apartment refrigerator because she's madly in love with the Merc with the Mouth! When Deadpool discovers this he states, ironically, "Uhh . . . This chick's crazy, right? Not sexy crazy but, like—scary ugly crazy."

I'm a Mercenary, Not a Murderer!

Is someone who acts unreasonably or illogically crazy? After all, Deadpool repeatedly kills, maims, and even tries to commit suicide. These actions certainly defy logic and reason, leading us to wonder whether Deadpool is indeed whack-a-doodle crazy. Then again, even the heroes in the Marvel Universe kill, maim, and contemplate their own deaths.

Why is Deadpool repeatedly institutionalized and diagnosed as mentally ill when so many others are similarly or more deserving? For Pete's sake, aren't Wolverine, Bruce Banner, Peter Parker, Venom, Loki, and Nick Fury all on the insanity spectrum?

Foucault isn't claiming that insanity or mental illness do not exist. On the contrary, mental illness is real and deserves our serious attention. Funding for mental health services, especially for children and adolescents, is constantly being cut, which is no doubt a travesty. Foucault's point, however, is that any process of labeling, sorting, and then acting on individuals is an act of power. Acts of power can be abusive. In perhaps his most famous quote, Foucault claimed that "The point is not that everything is bad, but that everything is dangerous, which is not the same as bad. If everything is dangerous, then we always have something to do" (*The Essential Foucault*, p. 104). Instead of blindly accepting the expert's diagnosis of Deadpool as insane, we should question the role that power plays in the decision.

Foucault's work helps us see that insanity is defined arbitrarily in the Marvel Universe. I mean, the authors of Deadpool literally construct notions of sane and insane. What we "know" about Wade Wilson comes from vague and often contradictory descriptions of a violent childhood and confused identities. In "The Price Is Right," the writers describe him as "crazier than a sack of ferrets," "by-product of a government-sponsored weapons program gone horribly wrong," and "a trash-talking mercenary of world renown who suffers from violent hallucinations and delusions of grandeur" (p. 1). The writers use their "knowledge" of Deadpool, constructed by themselves, and the power that comes with the pen to create the rules for sanity and insanity in his world.

Foucault's work demonstrates similarly how experts created the criteria for insanity and mental illness throughout history. From the mad fool to the dangerous individual, the madman and definitions of insanity changed over time depending on who was doing the defining. As a result we should question the power that allows experts to determine madness in our own world. Just as we question the way madness is defined in Deadpool's Marvel Universe, we must also question the foundation for our present understanding of mental illness.

The purpose is not to deny the existence of mental illness or deny the mental health support to those who so desperately need it. Instead, our awareness of the danger inherent in categorizing someone as mentally ill due to subjective social norms could help avoid gross abuses of power, like current attempts to link gender identification to mental instability. Through his philosophical genealogy of madness, Foucault "wanted to show the traumatizing quality that our societies still possess" because "our society still excludes the madmen" (*The Essential Foucault*, p. 376).

Our society still identifies those outside narrowly defined rules of normalcy as deviant or abnormal and deprives them of rights. The current resistance to transgender students using the school restroom of their choice is an example. Foucault shows us that the role of the philosopher of madness "is to show people that they are much freer than they feel, that people accept as truth, as evidence, some themes which have been built up at a certain moment in history, and this so called evidence can be criticized and destroyed" ("Truth, Power, Self"). Thus we should question the claims of truth about mental illness in order to expose potential abuses of freedom, as there is a fine line between sanity and insanity.

Despite internalizing an identity of insanity, Deadpool's violation of the fourth wall and his unique ability to address the reader directly may represent an awareness of the smokescreen of sanity created by the Marvel authors. His awareness is most apparent in *Deadpool Kills the Marvel Universe*, when our hero is institutionalized and labeled insane for believing that he and all the other Marvel characters are nothing but figments of comic-book imagination. When Deadpool exclaims "I'm the only person in the world who sees things clearly" and "I can see through the bull##$% and see the world how it really is" he is critiquing the very idea of the comic book.

"Don't you get it? We're puppets" he says, and asserts "They always thought I was crazy . . . but they never realized I saw the world the way it is" (*Deadpool Kills the Marvel Universe*, p. 10). What if you see the world the way it "really" is, but are viewed others as a crazy lunatic?

While Foucault's philosophy has the potential to paralyze us with fear that all truth claims and assumptions about labels and categories are dangerous, his work also contains hope that conscious awareness can lead to justice. Although being labeled a madman and then institutionalized no doubt influenced Deadpool's identity, his recognition of the power wielded by comic book authors shows us that we are not automatic losers. He even goes so far to challenge the authors themselves to wake up and recognize their own constructed identities when he tells the reader "Even the progenitors of our universe may be nothing more than the playthings for other entities" (p. 19).

If experts in positions of power used their credentials to label Deadpool insane, then what about us? There are regimes of truth operating on each of us as we speak. Teachers label our children as "at risk" or "deficient" while sorting them into groups. In order to receive special education services a child must have a diagnosis from a medical expert. Who labels *you* in order to categorize you and influence how you view yourself?

We must question regimes of truth and work to change or reform them to ensure justice, because Foucault reminds us:

> It is therefore not a matter of describing what knowledge is and what power is and how one would repress the other or how the other would abuse the one, but rather, a nexus of knowledge-power has to be described so that we can grasp what constitutes the acceptability of a system, be it the mental health system, the penal system, delinquency, sexuality, etc. (*The Essential Foucault*, p. 275)

Remaining vigilant in questioning the relations of power and knowledge and recognizing their role in society can prevent abuses of power. Challenging accepted notions of sanity can also cause us to evaluate our own identities and how we view those individuals' society labels as mentally ill. In this way Foucault's work directly calls us to live an examined life, forever questioning who we are, how we make sense of the world, and what power relations influence us.

The philosophical giant, Socrates, (469–399 B.C.) devoted his life to examining himself and everyone else, which ultimately led to his trial, conviction, and death. As you examine your own life, and your sanity, be careful whom you tell: you never know if an expert's listening.

BOO!

13
Weapon X Machina

COLE BOWMAN AND
WADE WILSON, PHD, DDS, MI6, TGIF

Deadpool is the ultimate comic-book badass. A weapons expert, a mercenary, and a ***red-blooded Canadian*** man with extraordinary healing powers, Deadpool has challenged the boundaries of the Marvel Universe since the moment he graduated from the Weapon-X program. From his inception in the 1991 *New Mutants #98* comic book, Deadpool has been a complex and unsubtle character. He disrupts the world around him ***Like I'm doing right now?,*** toying with the readers of his comic books and manipulating even the very structures of the panels around him. He has a supernatural agency in all of his manifestations that sets him apart from all the rest—even the other supernatural ones. He speaks to the readers as equals ***How*** **dare** ***you call us equals?!,*** to the authors as a mouthpiece and to himself as a critic of comic form.

Because of his unique position in the world, Deadpool has become extraordinarily talented at being a tongue-in-cheek commentator on the state of comic-book culture, creativity, and characters. In fact, the Merc with a Mouth might be the very best the industry has to offer when it comes to critiquing itself despite the fact that they made him up in the first place. To get to the heart of the matter, we must first look at what makes Deadpool, *Deadpool*. **Chimichangas.** His freedom. ***Oh, that.*** Deadpool is entirely free in a way that not even we are because of his place in the Marvel Universe, his agency, and his ability to peer past the fourth wall. Though he has been oftentimes dismissed as insane or even a trickster, he's important in a way unrecognized by his Marvel brethren. Deadpool is something more than the rest of them—he's the *deus ex machina* of the Marvel Universe.

~~Phenomenology and the Deus Ex Machina~~
Deadpool in the Machine

To kick this party off, we need to sort a few things out: what exactly does *deus ex machina* mean and why is it important that Deadpool is one? *Deus ex machina* is a phrase borrowed from Latin that translates roughly as "god out of the machine." While literature uses the *deus* as a denotation of fate, power and of the freedom of self, philosophy looks at this kind of agent just a little bit differently. We'll get into the grit of it a little later on, but for now, our definition of it comes from philosophical idea of cause and effect, where a person ***Me!*** can remove themselves entirely from this causal chain. Deadpool being a *deus ex machina* would effectively mean that he has ultimate control over not only his life, but everyone else's around him. And maybe even *yours*.

So, how the hell did we get here? ***She sounds worried. Are you worried?*** To understand, we first need to talk about Deadpool for a second. Put through the Weapon X program to become the ultimate weapon, Deadpool combines a number of classic superhero traits in a very new way. Not only does Deadpool have powers like super strength and regeneration, he also has a personality that could make hardened war criminals blush. Though he has made appearances in several iterations of Marvel Universe media, he has never really been known to play nicely once he's in them. Originally conceived as a villain by Fabian Nicieza and Rob Liefeld, he has since evolved into something of a chaotic superhero at best and a self-serving antihero at worst. He is also completely out of his mind. ***Are you just going to let her talk to you like that, Wolverine?!***

The fact that Deadpool appears to be utterly unhinged (even to the audience) is one of the defining parts of his character. There's no Deadpool without a little schizophrenia and disorderly conduct. But can any of us really blame him? From Deadpool's perspective, he's a simple comic character imagined by some ***really weird*** guys in the Nineties, and subjected to the constant whims of new artists and creators. Every time a new artist comes along, his entire appearance changes. Every time a new writer picks up a pen, his circumstances and even his very mode of thinking is altered. And to top it all off, he's one of the only people he knows who can conceive of this as even being an issue. Add that to his already tormented existence, and you have the perfect catalyst for alienating a person beyond the normal expectation of life and comfort. It would kinda make perfect sense then that he would be driven to act out against the world around him. But, wait, you might caution my reckless tirade: How does he know any of this in the first place?

For this, we turn to the noble branch of phenomenology, a core concept in philosophy. Phenomenology is the story of our consciousness's relationship to our experiences. So, how our mind deals with the stuff (phenomenon) it encounters along the way. For example, Deadpool can confirm that Ajax—***Ahem* Francis*** exists because he slams a six-foot length of rebar deep into his body. Deadpool's receiving "data" of a sort from his neurons, relaying the immense pain of a traumatic chest injury to his brain as a means to confirm that Francis is, like it or not, probably real. This sort of "perception confirms existence" concept is the foundation of phenomenology, which points out the necessary connection between a body and a mind for human experience.

Phenomenologically, a strong argument can be made for there being a deep schism ***Heh!*** dividing Deadpool's body from his mind. Because of his unique experiences of his body, Deadpool's mind has been alienated from his physical form. He's in constant pain from his cancer, but can never die. ***Thanks for the reminder.*** He can cut off his own hand and grow a tiny, hilarious one back later. This dynamic of self means that Deadpool's perception of his own body would be quite different than our own. Deadpool sees his body as something of an object rather than as a part of *himself*.

There are oodles of examples of Deadpool using his body as a prop gag or a tool rather than the precious, delicate flesh vessel it is for the rest of us. In the 2016 *Deadpool* movie, he does both at the same time by cutting his arm off to escape the manacle Colossus put him into and then using the dismembered hand to flip the aforementioned silver behemoth the bird. ***Hey! He didn't ask what my safeword was before putting me into that thing!*** Have you ever been so mad at a guy that you cut your own limb off to make a point? ***Yes!*** I sincerely hope not. Deadpool's objectification of body necessarily changes his phenomenological perception of the world around him. This is why he's able to perceive things in a completely different way than us regular people who lack a supernatural healing factor.

Deadpool's phenomenological standpoint is both challenged and accentuated by his good ol' buddy Wolverine. In literary criticism, the two mutants would be considered "foils" to each other. ***Wolvie's covered in adamantium not aluminum, dummy.*** Foils are two characters that complement each other, but also contrast each other at the same time. Usually, a foil has a very similar biography or characteristic to their counterpart, serving ultimately to illustrate the failings of one of the characters. Given that Deadpool was literally built to be an improvement on the "instantly healing super soldier" project that turned Wolverine into the beloved adamantium-clad ***You only know that because I told you . . .*** X-Man he is today, it's pretty easy to see the similarities between them.

So, why is it then that Wolverine doesn't crack like Deadpool does? ***It's the sideburns.*** He can't die either, but he doesn't go around screaming about pickles. ***NO PICKLES!*** The answer to this brings us back to their origins. Deadpool is fully aware of his ability to heal, while Wolverine hasn't always been. Deadpool has known from the getgo that he can bounce back from nearly anything, while Wolverine has suffered through at least two serious bouts of amnesia. Because of this, their motivations are completely different. Wolverine is heavily motivated by rediscovering his past and preserving a legacy for the future of mutant-kind. Deadpool, however, has no such compulsions. He's completely conscious of the fact that he cannot be killed and has used it to test the limits of his own existence by *embracing* his phenomenological disconnect. This is also why he has so much agency within the Marvel Universe, and ultimately the thing that causes him to be able to exert so much control over it. This is also the first baby step he took into becoming the *deus ex machina.* But, before we delve further into this idea, we must first fit another Deadpool-shaped puzzle piece into place: Deadpool's agency.

~~The Role of Agency in Deus Ex~~
Secret Agency Man

Deadpool's weird body ***That's hurtful!*** makes it so that he has a remarkable amount of control over his actions within the basic confines of his comic, but he's better known for being able to overcome these confines entirely. From being able to free-fall off of an overpass at the exact right moment to be carted away by an empty truck bed, to talking to the readers directly, Deadpool's unlike almost all of the other characters in the Marvel Universe. Persistently, he breaks the fourth wall in all forms of media ***Like in the movie? When I broke the fourth wall inside a fourth wall break?*** hinting that he has a greater amount of control over his circumstances than he first appears. ***Hold on a second! If I break the fourth wall by talking about a fourth wall break within a fourth wall break while she's talking about me breaking the fourth wall, how many walls is that?! 256?***

Early twentieth-century French philosopher Jean-Paul Sartre suggested an idea that fits Deadpool like an avocado-faced super soldier does a pleather suit. If Deadpool is the *deus ex machina*, then he's also the perfect argument against the nature of a philosophical problem called *determinism*. Determinism is the philosophical equivalent of destiny, where all of the events of your life are already laid out in front of you. Everything is already *determined* ***Get it?*** usually by some kind of creator or magical force. Sartre believed determinism was hogwash. Instead, he suggested that all people have what he referred to as "radical freedom." What this meant was that rather than being at the mercy of some kind of fate, we could actually just kinda do anything we wanted. Like, *anything*.

Sartre insisted that there was no predetermination to life at all. Instead, there's a simple system of cause and effect, without the unnecessary mess of a deity or other force guiding the actions. As long as a person was willing to accept the necessary consequences of whatever it was that they said or did, they could (and should) do whatever the hell they felt like. This theory came in the face of many other thinkers who insisted that there must be some sort of meaningful reason behind our every action. Sartre thought that all of our actions were our own responsibility, no matter what. When we act in any way, it's because we have made decisions to do so, be they conscious or unconscious. So, to get back to our favorite red-suited killing machine—Deadpool's not necessarily constrained by what the writers want him to do.

But wait, how can that be possible if the character is literally being drawn by the creator? That's where things get really philosophically interesting—because characters can far outlast their creators. Really good characters will, simply by having certain personalities, control the way that a story should go. Deadpool was originally written by Fabian Nicieza and drawn by Rob Liefeld. Later, he was written by Gail Simone, Mark Waid, Joe Kelly, Daniel Way, Victor Gischler, Christopher J. Priest and *many, many more*. Each of these writers almost necessarily changed some little aspects to Deadpool as a character, be it simply the tone in which he speaks, whether or not he's Canadian, or the way that he sees the world. Literary theorists suggest that there's a certain virility to characters who can outlast even the most concerted efforts of the original creator—giving them something close to autonomy.

The way a character evolves just a little bit from his original model (Nicieza's) through each subsequent writer is what specifically makes so many comic-book characters dynamic. The character's very essence is distilled so that the character drives the writers, not the other way around. This is, of also partly due to the audience. Hardcore fans of a character will hold writers and artists to certain standards, just by the voracity of their love for the character. This relationship between the character and the audience is something that has not escaped Deadpoo ***. . . she said ominously . . .*** What stands is that Deadpool harnesses the reigns of his own creation better than just about any other character ever written.

Remember *X-Men Origins: Wolverine*? Yeah I know, you were trying desperately to suppress that memory. ***Me, too!*** Despite its failings, it's the perfect example of a character being driven by something other than their creator. The writers of this movie had conceived of an interpretation of Deadpool that was so reviled by fans that the Marvel studio *no longer considers the movie canon*. Deadpool's depiction in that movie has been discarded as a credible piece of his story and has been mocked repeatedly for its failure to hold true to the spirit of the character—as seen in several allusions to it in the 2016 *Deadpool* adaptation. This evinces the fact that a character can transcend their creators, despite the apparent control they have over them.

Deadpool's most defining characteristic didn't emerge until well after his original run with Liefeld and Nicieza had ended. ***But at what cost? I lost all my little pockets!*** Known mostly for his ability to break the fourth wall (the "unseen perimeter" dividing the audience from the story) ***You know, the thing I'm doing now*** Deadpool didn't gain this ability until his story was taken over by Joe Kelly in the early 2000s. This is perhaps the greatest indicator of Deadpool's own radical freedom according to Sartre, because he is free to ignore the potential bonds of his place in the world. He's free to look beyond the wall and shout obscene comments to the people looking back. ***#$@*&!!!!!!***

But Deadpool's ability to look beyond the fourth wall is not entirely unique. Many other characters can do the same thing—the Marvel universe alone has about a dozen such people. Howard the Duck, Uatu the Watcher, Loki, and She-Hulk are some other Marvel characters who can engage with the very fact that they are in a movie or a comic book. But that ability alone doesn't make them anything like Deadpool. ***For starters, they need better aliases. Who's going to be impressed by a Duck named HOWARD?***

~~Mauvais Fois and Agency~~
I Think We Made Out Once

So, what makes Deadpool so different than, say, She-Hulk, who also breaks the fourth wall several times during her run? ***My uniform is waaaay less revealing.*** The biggest difference is simply what Deadpool *does* with that power. She-Hulk's run with *Sensational She-Hulk* would use the device mostly for laughs. Albeit they were hilarious—that was pretty much it for her. While yes, Deadpool's agency is usually for comic effect, his use of the fourth wall has often gone well past that. With it, he attacks the core of his plight ***the imperial system?*** the creators of the series and then the audience that keeps him trapped in the confines of his weird little existence. With it, he destroys the entire Marvel Universe. With it, he grapples with the very fibers of his own existence. ***Polyester, you bastard!!!!!!***

Sartre would argue that the essential difference between Deadpool's radical freedom and She-Hulk's lack of it is what he called *mauvais fois*. ***I'm sure my liver is worse than hers is . . .*** *Mauvais fois* is the secondary principle of Sartre's concept freedom—the antithetical reason that most people are constrained by their circumstances. Translating to "bad faith," the concept behind *mauvais fois* is that we are all essentially bound by our unwillingness to accept the consequences of our freedom and take the reins of our own existence.

She-Hulk's awareness of the fact that she's a comic-book character is an example of this. She ***Hulk*** knows that she's in the pages of a comic book, *but* she ***Hulk*** only uses this knowledge in small ways, where it could be used for her advantage *within the context of the story*. In *Sensational She-Hulk #59,* She-Hulk is confronted by a group of self-proclaimed super-villains and she ***Hulk*** reminds her assailant Porcupine that he was killed off in a previous issue. At this point, Porcupine—reminded that he's supposed to be dead—keels over and dies on the spot. This is *freaking funny*. As a bonus, it's also convenient for She-Hulk, because she ***Hulk*** doesn't end up having to fight him. At no point does she ***Hulk*** stop, however, and realize that this awareness she ***Hulk*** has of the universe outside of the immediate frames she's in provoke her to seek out anything else, as it does for Deadpool. She's stopped up by her own bad faith and unable to reach further outside of her paradigm. Deadpool, however, takes hold of this knowledge and runs away with it.

This is perhaps the biggest reason for Deadpool's characteristic personality. As the only *really* self-aware character, Deadpool looks crazy to his comrades. When he speaks to the audience instead of his fellows, Deadpool appears to be out of his damn mind to the others around him. But to him, talking to the audience is just a natural extension of his authentic experience. ***It'd be weirder if I didn't say something! They're just sitting there looking at me with their beady little eyes for pages!***

And while the majority of Deadpool's interaction with the outside world is benign, there has been a very notable instance of him going far beyond the boundaries of his own comic. In

Deadpool Kills the Marvel Universe, he goes after both the writers and then his own fans in an effort to finally be able to die. Because Deadpool has been able to see past the fourth wall into the real world, he has come to understand that the writers and the readers of his comics are responsible for driving his tormented existence. Neither work, but this attempt highlights the vestiges of his drive to control his own reality. If he can die, then he was no longer the folly of the exterior gaze of the writers or the readers themselves.

So far, we know that Deadpool is phenomenologically different than the rest of his brethren, even the other ones that can regenerate. We also know that he's aware of the narrative framework of his own existence and takes advantage of it in a way that the rest of the self-aware characters never do. But how does any of this make him into something more than a deranged, super strong immortal with the charm of a hysterical ferret? There's just one more piece to fit into place: the machine itself.

~~Comparative Deus Models~~
Rage Against the Machine

From here, it's important to look next at noted German Enlightenment philosopher, polymath, astrophysicist ***and probable playboy*** Gottfried Leibniz (1646–1716). In his work *Primary Truths*, Leibniz discusses the necessary implications of God's control in a deterministic system. Not unlike Sartre, Leibniz believed that there must be some other theory that explained authentic experience, as all situations in which a God controlled everything effectively reduced all people and things to mere extensions of God. More plainly, this means that the only really *real* thing is God if such an all-powerful creator exists. If a person has any real control within a system overseen by a God, the whole system breaks apart. Leibniz argues that the only way to solve the existence of God while allowing for some sort of agency is for there to be a *deus ex machina* that emerges. This is where things start coming up aces for our rebellious Merc, because according to Leibniz, Deadpool's agency makes him the perfect candidate for the job.

Leibniz's argument is especially important when it comes to Deadpool because he and all of the other comic-book characters that make up his universe are so very controlled by their own "Gods"—their creators. This is where Deadpool's distinction amongst the rest of the characters really takes hold. Deadpool has motivations that are outside of the creator's best interests, as we discussed before. He then uses this agency to challenge the norms to which even other characters are held. But because these characters are held to the designs of the comic-book gods, Deadpool becomes *necessary* in Leibniz's theory. Because Deadpool is the *deus ex machina* that can destroy the machinery that has created him.

Leibniz's definition places the *deus* as a being who can break free from the chain of cause and effect to exert control over the chain. One clear example of this happens in *Deadpool Team Up* Volume 1, #885, when Deadpool takes out his katana and uses it to cut through the previous pages of the comic book in order to warn his past self to keep Hellcow out of the sun. ***It only took me, like, sixty tries. And we had tasty Hellcowburgers from all my failures to celebrate!*** There's one other historical precedent for the *deus* that makes discussing the merits of such a character something of a challenge. Referring to the practice of ancient Greek playwrights orchestrating a manifested "god" to enter the stage on a mechanical contraption stationed above, it has cemented an image of divine intervention into the works that it takes place within. More often than not, these gods would bring with them the magical conclusion to the play. One such example comes from Euripides's play *Medea*, where Apollo descends on a golden chariot in order to whisk his niece Medea away from the torment of her situation. ***Who else was going to do it? Spider-Man wouldn't be created for another 2,393 years*** This figurative god (Apollo) literally descended onto the literal stage with literal machinery.

Over the past two and a half millennia, this tactic took on a metaphorical connotation: divine intervention to solve a convoluted plot. *Deus ex machina* came to refer to the action an author might take when nothing short of a miracle could solve the issues laid before the characters. ***Are you there, Apollo? It's me, Deadpool.*** It's because of this that the primary concern about a *deus* in artistic criticism is that it uses an outside, unseen force to magically fix the main problems of the story. This can be super-frustrating to an audience, because it works as a kind of plot patch where parts leading up to that moment usually have no connection to the resolution. Just when Medea is saved by Apollo, the audience finds out that the two just *happen to be related*. That's not a satisfying ending for a modern audience because it's just too *convenient* for us to take seriously. This is the reason why many thinkers have condemned the practice of using a *deus*.

But Deadpool is not Apollo, no matter how many times he lights himself on fire and soars through the sky. ***Don't you dare try to stomp on my dreams!*** But he can be a *deus*, at least in an evolved sense. Because Leibniz's suggestion for a supernatural resolution to causation is the basis for his idea of the *deus,* any "supernatural" force that can disrupt a causal chain, can be this *deus*. This perspective from Leibniz necessarily changed the future virility of the very concept of a *deus*, especially as an agent outside of aesthetics.

While the later philosopher Friedrich Nietzsche (1844–1900) ***Wasn't that the guy with the mustache?*** would bring the concept back home to the poetical use in his revolutionary work *The Birth of Tragedy*, he could not help but be influenced by Leibniz's change of perspective. Nietzsche writes that:

> tragedy is, in the strict sense of the term, dead: for out of what are people now supposed to be able to create that metaphysical consolation? Consequently, people looked for an earthly solution to tragic dissonance. After the hero was sufficiently tortured by fate, he received a well-earned reward in an impressive marriage, in divine tributes. The hero became a gladiator, to whom people occasionally gave his freedom, after he had been well beaten and was covered with wounds. The deus ex machina moved in to take the place of metaphysical consolation. ***Why does mustache guy get a block quote?***

Nietzsche is further describing the mechanism of the literary *deus*. The hero of a story is given to solving his problems by reaching outside of an earthly solution. In this way, the *deus* takes the place of the resolution, causing a false sense of consolation of plot.

What's different about Deadpool from the previous examples of *deus*-hood, is that he's coming from *inside the comic*. This thwarts the concern of an out-of-context intervention that has no real meaning to the story at all. The classical criticisms don't really apply to this new kind of *deus*, because his motivation and onus ***Heh*** is different than the traditional view. If a comic book writer were to write themselves into a scene in order to magically fix the problems going on with the characters, *that* would be something else entirely. ***Jeepers! Someone tell Stan Lee*** The powerful outside force swooping in to save the day is much less conducive to a good story than the crazy comic-book character who understands how to manipulate the panels and has the power to actually do so, effectively finding his own metaphysical consolation.

~~Aesthetics and The Deus~~
Why Deadpool Is Pretty

There's one final important point that all of Deadpool's shenanigans bring to mind when you're considering his place in the Marvel Universe ***How much more flattering leather is than spandex?*** If Deadpool has gained this supernatural agency as a result of his apparent immortality, what does it mean for us foolish mortals? If we were given thousands of do overs, would we inevitably be able to achieve this godlike status as well? If so, would we go also go crazy?

Literature has a great deal to say about the importance and prevalence of a *deus*, specifically how it acts as a go-between for the artist and the creation. It closes the gap a little bit between the expression and the expresser, making the piece much more visceral and (especially) more personal when a character can occupy both their story and the outside world. This connection is extremely important to the legacy of a *deus* like Deadpool because it not only justifies his place within the universe he was created in, but also makes his commentary on comic books much more important to the reader. When Deadpool gives the audience a sultry "come hither" look from the silver screen, it draws both of you closer together, making his narrative a shared experience. ***Come hither, Philosophy Nerd.***

What happens with the modern *deus* is that they challenge the course of things from within their own story. Deadpool is the insurgent character who, as far as we're aware, *cannot die*. Therefore, he's free to try as many times as necessary to break out of the confines of his own narrative. This is an actualization of self that manifests in a way that no one else could possibly achieve. ***Except maybe the stupid duck.***

While an argument can be made that god-hood is simply for comic relief and convenience, it is unlikely. Yes, the *deus* agent is helpful given the actual structure of the comic form. Because comic books have such limited space to tell such complex storylines, this can help to bring resolution to a very complex plot in a tidy (and often contrived) manner. Many more modern literary theorist, however, say that the role of the *deus* is actually quite more subversive than previously thought. Rather than neatly tying together the strands of a complex plot, the modern *deus* challenges these plots. The modern *deus* exists to complicate plots, not to fix them. ***Are you talking about Wolverine again?!*** This subversion is equally satisfying and frustrating, taking the measure of convenience out of the creator's' hands.

Deadpool acting as this ghost in the comic machine is what makes him so interesting in the context of actual real life. The creators even made sure to make him able to kill *them*. This, of course, is explained in his long-fraught desire to be able to die. The very fact that this is feasible for him in the first place shows his unique relationship with our world. Not only can he break the fourth wall by commentating on things outside of his specific comic book, he can utterly demolish it, walk over the rubble and go after the people who built it in the first place. In this way Deadpool is truly free, unlike the rest of the Marvel characters, because he embraces his radical freedom and uses it to exert control over his world and our own. Or, as our friend Sartre would say: "Freedom is what you do with what's been done to you." ***I'm going to go get a taco, wanna come?***

IV

Looks Aren't Everything

Why Ryan Reynolds Can't Act

14
I'm an X-Man!

DANIEL MALLOY (AND NO HE'S NOT)

Deadpool owns an X-Men costume. Several, actually. They range in appropriateness from a simple variation on his usual red-and-black with a few X-Men logos to a variant of Jean Grey's old Marvel Girl outfit (at least, I hope it's a variant. Knowing 'Pool, it may well be the original).

The thing is, though, Deadpool isn't an X-Man. Never has been. Never been invited. In fact, he's been explicitly rejected on multiple occasions by multiple X-Men. And yet he persists. He pulls the same sort of antics of trying to join up whenever he's around the Avengers and even in his rare encounters with the Fantastic Four. The Merc with the Mouth keeps trying to join up with the premier superteams of the Marvel Universe, in spite of repeated explicit (and sometimes lethal) rejections.

Some whiny fanboys tell me that Deadpool has joined the X-Men a couple of times, but what do they know? Can't tell a chimichanga from a burrito. What matters is Deadpool wants to be an X-Man, cool? Good. Moving on.

On the face of it, this is puzzling. 'Pool's a bit of a loner and definitely not a team player. Being an X-Man or an Avenger would undermine his cred and earning ability as a merc, if not destroy that career completely. So why does Wade keep insisting "I'm an X-Man!" at every opportunity? What's his angle?

Maybe Wade's attempts to join are nothing more than his motormouth doing its thing. Wade's brain's a chaotic place, and of course he has no filter, so it makes sense that he'd talk about joining a superteam when he's in their company. He's got to talk about something, right? But the fact that it comes up almost every single time should make us think twice. Wade talks about joining the X-Men and Avengers more than he talks about chimichangas and Bea Arthur combined. So there's a real desire underlying these encounters. You can almost smell the desperation—and the chimichangas, of course—when Deadpool encounters members of Marvel's premiere superteams. He's always either trying to get an invitation to join them, or acting like he's already a member.

But why does the Merc with the Mouth want to be a part of one of the do-gooder-in-tights crews? He's a good merc, one of the best, but being a merc and being a hero aren't really compatible. Spidey or Cap would never save someone's life and then send them a bill. That's part of the reason that Peter Parker is usually broke. If anything, being a hero would hurt Wade's earning potential—if it got out, people would expect him to work for free. He says it himself during good Samaritan missions: if it ever got out that he wasn't being paid, he'd be ruined.

The thing is, even though Wade's mind is definitely on his money, his heart is in heroism. Deadpool wants to be a hero. And he's got what it takes to do it, except for one thing: recognition. That's why he wants to join a superhero outfit: it's the ultimate sign of acceptance, the final seal of approval that he has truly and finally made it as a hero. Recognition might seem like a minor thing, but it really isn't. In fact, Deadpool can't be a hero without recognition. It's a kind of uncomfortable thought, but part of what makes us who we are is the acknowledgement of others. We need it, and so does Wade.

Out in the Cold

But maybe I'm wrong. Maybe what Wade wants isn't to be a hero. He just wants to be thought of as a hero. He wants the benefits without the sacrifices. Like the first incarnation of the Thunderbolts, Deadpool wants to appear to be a hero without actually being one. Maybe being a hero is a choice anyone can make. Whether you're a hero is up to you. Wade can be a hero anytime he likes, he just has to choose to act like one. The fact that he acts the way he does—like a hyperactive, brain-addled jackass—is on him.

This argument depends on a particular understanding of the term "hero." Deadpool can be a hero in two senses. In one sense, a hero is someone who acts in certain ways: heroes are selfless and brave and conscientious. They do the right thing because it's the right thing and don't count the cost. Heroes, in this sense, don't expect praise or recognition. If that's what a hero is, then Wade can just choose to be one. But in the Marvel Universe, "hero" also has another meaning. The heroes of Marvel are a kind of community. And you can't join a community without the community's acceptance. In some cases, that's a trivial thing; if a club rejects your application, no big deal. But in other cases, belonging to community and being recognized as a member makes us who we are. It's not a small thing to be shut out from one's country or one's family. That's the kind of case Deadpool faces in his attempts to be a hero.

These things aren't simple. Humans (using the term very loosely) are social beings. As Aristotle (384–322 B.C.E.) put it, "He who is unable to live in society, or who has no need because he is sufficient for himself, must be either a beast or a god" (*Politics*, p. 29). Accusations aside, Wade isn't a beast. And he sure as anything isn't a god. If the voices in his head and his rotating cast of supporting characters prove anything it's that Wade, like the rest of us, is a social being.

Being a social being has a lot of benefits, but also a few drawbacks. The main one is that we can't simply define ourselves. Wade can't just decide one day that he's going to be a hero, any more than you can decide that you're a surgeon. Others have a say in what we are and can be. We get input, sure, but the final judgment is always a compromise between ourselves and others. Who gets a say depends on what community we want to be a part of. In Wade's case, he wants to join the hero community, so he needs to convince heroes that he's one of them.

There are different sorts of recognition Wade could get. The general public might call him a hero; some villain or other might think of him that way. But recognition from them wouldn't mean much. It would simply be an acknowledgement that 'Pool sometimes acts like a hero. Lots of people do that who aren't heroes. Dr. Doom's been known to be kind to puppies; it doesn't make him a hero.

What's wrong with the recognition that civilians and villains can offer Wade is that it isn't mutual. Recognition in the sense that's important here isn't a one-way street. It goes both ways. Wade needs people that he recognizes as heroes to recognize him as a hero as well. This element of recognition was first recognized and analyzed by philosopher Georg Hegel (1770–1831) in his *Phenomenology of Spirit* (pp. 111–149). According to Hegel, mutual recognition is a key factor in the development of our identities. The only way we can become ourselves is through interactions with others like us. Struggles with others shape us and mold us and end up making us who we are.

So, aside from convincing himself and the voices in his head that he's a hero and acting like a hero, the one group Deadpool really has to persuade to acknowledge him as a hero is other heroes. Wade needs people he recognizes as heroes to recognize him as a hero. The superhero community has been happy to use Deadpool's skills from time to time, but its members have been reluctant to recognize him as one of their own. They have, in fact, sabotaged Wade's hero quest in subtle and not so subtle ways.

Those Guys Hate Me

Deadpool just doesn't belong. The Merc with a Mouth simply doesn't seem to fit anywhere. He's not quite a mutant, not quite a human. He's not exactly a hero, not quite the mercenary some believe him to be. He's not really a loner, but he also isn't a team player. He's only sort of Canadian, and only sort of American. As Captain America described him, he's always "out in the cold" (*Deadpool* Volume 3, #15).

That's a harsh place to be. Aside from being lonely, it gives the Merc with the Mouth almost no opportunity to change. So why does he stay there? It isn't poor Wade's choice. The superhero community won't accept him. Even the Star-Spangled Avenger's been slow to accept him—and he hangs out with Hawkeye! After Deadpool successfully defeated the resurrected Presidents of the United States, Cap congratulates him on a job well done, and turns around and tells him: "I'm now classifying this conversation, and the praise I just gave you is above top secret" (*Deadpool* Volume 3, #6). Thor delivers a similar put down a moment later.

I can think of two reasons for this sort of shoddy treatment: Deadpool's morals and his mouth. To start with the louder of the two, there's no denying that Wade's motormouth could get annoying. Even he admits it. One of his first complaints about the Deadpool Corps is that he can't get a word in edgewise (*Deadpool Corps*, #6). Deadpool even gets on his own nerves. Not only does he get endure plenty of insults from friends and foes alike for his inability to shut the hell up, it's common for people to kill him to make him be quiet. Wolverine's done it repeatedly, as did Wade's teammates on the Thunderbolts.

As annoying as Wade's constant chatter is, it probably isn't Wade's mouth that keeps him out of the superhero community. It's just annoying, and if being annoying was enough to get someone barred from the do-gooder-in-tights brigade their ranks would be massively depleted. Remember, in spite of their general ineptitude and overall lameness, the Great Lakes Avengers (or whatever they're calling themselves now) are an accepted part of the superhero community. Squirrel Girl is a more accepted member of the superhero community than Deadpool.

So, what's holding Deadpool back is probably his morals. That makes sense, since heroes are defined by the values they hold and uphold. Wade's morals aren't quite up to snuff by those standards. He wavers. When his heroic deeds fail or go unremarked upon, he tends to slide back into his mercenary ways. Comfortable habits are hard to break. Wade's kind of an addict. He's addicted to money. He wants to act like a hero, but when things get tough it's difficult for him not to yield to the temptation to sell his services to the highest bidder.

And, like a recovering addict, Deadpool needs support. Wade needs to join Mercs Anonymous, to help him accept who he has been and become the hero he wants to be. He needs other heroes to recognize his efforts and appreciate him for them. But this leaves Wade in a catch-22. He can't become the hero he wants to be without recognition from other heroes, but he also can't get that recognition without being the hero he wants to be. That may seem cruel, but it's pretty common in struggles for recognition. You can't become a member until you've shown current members that you have what it takes to be a part of the community.

It's the logic behind initiation rituals of all sorts, be it a gang jump-in, a citizenship test, or a dissertation defense. So, Wade has to show other heroes that he's got what it takes to be a hero—hopefully without tripping over himself or shooting the wrong person or just generally being an ass. Unfortunately, most of Deadpool's dealings with other superheroes tend to undermine his quest for recognition. The two teams that Wade was with the longest, the Thunderbolts and X-Force, plainly illustrate how.

We're the Selfish Avengers

The Thunderbolts are always a team of not-quite-heroes acting like heroes. In that sense, the Thunderbolts are an ideal fit for Wade. Recovering addicts often find support in communities of fellow recovering addicts: why shouldn't a recovering anti-hero seek out the support of other recovering anti-heroes? General Thaddeus Ross (a.k.a. Red Hulk) formed the Thunderbolts team that Deadpool joined to clean up the messes that he'd created in his relentless pursuit of the Hulk. Apart from Ross and Deadpool, the Punisher, Elektra, and Venom also joined up. The Leader and Ghost Rider also signed up later on. In each case (except the Leader), Ross proposed an exchange of sorts: for each of his missions the team completed, they would carry out a mission from one of the team's other members.

This give and take is one of the reasons the Thunderbolts didn't really help Wade become a hero. He himself dubbed the team "the selfish Avengers" (*Thunderbolts* Volume 2, #14), a sly dig at the team's set up. Knowing that he was going to be rewarded for its efforts in a tit-for-tat manner meant that the Thunderbolts were little better than Wade's old mercenary outfit, the Six Pack. The missions may have been for good causes, but ultimately the Thunderbolts were just another instance of work-for-hire for Wade. Deadpool was trying to ween himself off of being a mercenary, when what he needed was to go cold turkey.

The almost mercenary nature of the Thunderbolts was one obstacle in Deadpool's journey to becoming a hero. Another, perhaps more severe issue arose from the team's line-up. Aside from Wade, and maybe Ross, there was only ever one other member of the team interested in being a hero: first Venom, then Ghost Rider. Punisher and Elektra had no more intention of changing their paths than the Juggernaut. Their presence detracted from Wade's "recovery." Wade strove for their acceptance, as he always does, but it wouldn't have helped him if he'd gotten it. Happily, the Punisher and Elektra aren't accepting types. Even if they were, they couldn't grant Wade entrance into the community of heroes—they're no more a part of it than he is. Trying to become a hero in the company of Punisher and Elektra is like trying to get sober in a bar. On Saint Patrick's Day.

There's also a problem with the work the Thunderbolts did. Their missions were covert and violent. Cleaning up General Ross's messes oddly involved carrying out the same sorts of missions that created those messes in the first place. Heroes can be violent—there's no problem there—but heroes aren't covert. They're showy. What? Did you think Thor's cape was to help him fly better? Or that Wolverine spent a large part of his career as a hero wearing bright yellow spandex because it made him less conspicuous? I'm not saying that they're self-aggrandizing egomaniacs; I'm just saying that heroes do what they do in the open, in full view of the public. And they can, because of what they're doing. The Thunderbolts, on the other hand, needed to sneak around to accomplish their missions.

When Wade's turn to choose the mission came up, he gave it to Venom. It took some persuading, admittedly, but Wade ultimately did the right thing to help out his teammate and fellow traveler on the road to becoming a hero. Even in terrible circumstances, Deadpool was still striving to be a hero.

Happy to Be Part of the Team

The whole Thunderbolts situation was a bad one for Wade. It just didn't help 'Pool be the kind of person he wants to be, because his teammates weren't the kinds of people he wants to be. They were either on their own versions of the same journey he's on, or unrepentant anti-heroes. Wade needs acceptance and recognition from his betters, from those he's aspiring to be like. Unfortunately, even when Wade is accepted by heroes proper, it's never on heroic terms. He's accepted and recognized as a skilled soldier or mercenary, not as a hero. The closest he's ever come to joining the X-Men, for instance, was his stint on X-Force.

On the surface, the roster of X-Force seems ideal to help Wade become a hero. With the exception of the mystery man Fantomex, the line-up of X-Force consists of tried-and-true heroes, and more, heroes who've been through their own versions of Wade's journey. Wolverine has gone from near-feral beast to living weapon to brash anti-hero to outright hero. Archangel started his career as a pure hero, fell under the influence of Apocalypse, and fought his way back to being a hero. And Psylocke's journey is so hopelessly convoluted that I won't even attempt to sum it up; needless to say, she's been across the line and back again. If any group knows what Wade's going through and can sympathize and offer guidance, it's his X-Force teammates.

Sadly, that's not how it worked out. Archangel and Wolverine formed the team for the express purpose of sliding back into the shady world of covert actions. Their first mission ended with the cold-blooded murder of a child (*Uncanny X-Force* Volume 1, #4). The "heroes" in X-Force recruited Deadpool not to help or encourage his budding heroism, but because they needed a ruthless killer (in fairness to Wade, Fantomex killed the child, a clone of Apocalypse). Rather than try to raise him to their level, they wanted to descend to his.

Think about how he was recruited to the team: Archangel contacted him and offered him a job. Deadpool was assigned to track down the resurrected Apocalypse, and paid a handsome fee from the Worthington fortune for his efforts. At least, that was the deal Archangel offered him. Wade tracked Apocalypse's followers for over a year, and found the clone. Archangel kept the checks coming. Even after he realized that Deadpool, the "scumbag mercenary," wasn't cashing them (*Uncanny X-Force* Volume 1, #5).

That fact tells us something good about Deadpool: he refuses payment when he believes in the cause. He's trying to be something more than a mercenary. It also tells something bad about how he's viewed by his would-be peers: they're not ready to accept him as more than a merc. The fact that Archangel keeps cutting the checks sends a clear signal to 'Pool that he suspects that if the money disappeared, so would Wade. Although Deadpool earns Archangel's respect, Worthington never really expresses it. He doesn't try to show Wade that he recognizes that Deadpool's a hero. It's all 'Pool wants, but instead he gets checks.

Deadpool's time with X-Force didn't undermine him like his stint with the Thunderbolts did. But it didn't help either. The members of X-Force were too wrapped up in their mission and with their own internal struggles to see Wade for what he is.

They brought him in as a merc, and he always remained a merc to them. Whatever his actions or motives, they weren't able to change their view of him. So 'Pool remained a merc. Only a few heroes have ever realized what kind of hero Deadpool's capable of being. Their approaches to recognizing him as a hero can help us to better understand what recognition is and how it works. The most consistent and persistent voice in pushing 'Pool toward being a hero was his one-time best bud, Nathan Dayspring Askani'son Summers, a.k.a Cable, a.k.a. Priscilla, Savior of the World.

Bestest Buds with Priscilla, Savior of the World

Deadpool's relationship with Cable has been a bit rocky, to say the least. The Merc with a Mouth has repeatedly tried to kill the Soldier of the Future. And Cable *has* killed Deadpool. Repeatedly. For most people, that's the sort of thing that would end a friendship, but not for these two. The very dysfunctional pair manages to make their partnership work, in spite of clashing goals, values, and even understandings of the world. Sometimes they remain friends in spite of outright hating each other. It's an odd sort of friendship, to be sure. But it's important for us because friendship is a sort of recognition. What sort depends on what sort of friendship.

Aristotle offered a classic analysis of friendship (*Nicomachean Ethics*, pp. 119–152). He argued that there are three basic sorts of friendship: friendships of pleasure, of utility, and of virtue. Some people are friends because they give each other pleasure, but have little else to offer. Others are friends because they get something they need out of the relationship. The bestest buds, though, are friends based on mutual recognition of one another's best qualities. So, to figure out what kind of friendship Cable and Deadpool have, we have to know why they're friends. What do they get out of their friendship? It turns out that they want different things out of it, and that's the source of the oddness of their friendship.

For Deadpool's part, he wants the friendship to be one of virtue. Cable's a hero, and Wade wants his recognition. And, in fairness to the Summers kid, it's got to be said that he tries to recognize Deadpool's heroic tendencies in his own enigmatic way. But there are two problems with his method. First, Cable doesn't really accept Deadpool as a full-fledged hero—just as someone who has the potential to be one. Cable's attitude leads him to treat Wade in ways that are intended to encourage his heroism, but which actually undermine it.

Consider how Cable and Deadpool begin working together: Wade's alone in his apartment when he gets a call. An anonymous client wants him for a job. The job lets him show off his heroic chops (*Cable and Deadpool* #1). The same anonymous client hires Wade again and again, always for similar missions—and always for missions where he meets Cable. The anonymous client, it turns out, is Cable himself—in a twist that surprised Deadpool, and absolutely no one else. So, one of the ways Nate tries to encourage Wade to be a hero is by lying to him, manipulating him, and appealing to the same mercenary instincts that hold him back. In other words, classic Cable.

Even when he's not anonymously pulling Deadpool's strings, Cable isn't a big help in Wade's journey. When he's not being actively antagonistic to Wade, Cable's default attitude seems to be one of disappointment. It's understandable, given what he sees in Deadpool and how often Wade fails to live up to his potential, but it isn't helpful. Wade already knows he's a screw up—Cable's attitude, like those of a lot of other heroes (I'm looking at you, Wolverine), just reinforces his already low opinion of himself. It's simply another reminder that he's not accepted, that he is not yet a hero.

Cable tries, but his approach is flawed. Nate isn't a very good leader or motivator. His treatment of Deadpool—and others in his orbit—tends to be condescending and paternalistic. That is, Cable assumes an attitude of superiority. That attitude means that all he can offer Wade is approval, not recognition or acceptance. Approval comes from superiors; recognition is between equals. This is the core of the conflict between Cable and Deadpool. Deadpool considers Cable his friend in the highest sense: they mutually recognize one another's best qualities and celebrate them.

By being friends with Cable, Deadpool makes himself Nate's equal, and thus joins the hero community right along with him. Cable, on the other hand, sees his friendship with Deadpool as one of utility. He's using Deadpool to achieve his own ends, to carry out his missions—it just so happens that one of those missions is to make Deadpool a hero. The partnership dissolves because their different understandings of their friendship aren't compatible. Deadpool sees them as equals; Cable believes he's Wade's superior.

It's also a problem that Cable isn't the best representative of the hero community. Cable has more recognition as a hero than Deadpool, but there's an air of suspicion that surrounds him that he's never quite been able to overcome—because, in the end, he's always a calculating, manipulative bastard. So, whatever recognition Wade could get from him would be a limited victory—large parts of the superhero community would still need convincing, because they're not entirely sold on Cable. If Wade wants the Marvel universe to accept him as a hero, if he needs that to become a hero, then there is one person, and only one person, who can do that: Captain America.

The Old Man Trusts Deadpool

The Sentinel of Liberty is the moral authority in the Marvel Universe. Even outright gods like Thor bow to his wisdom. So when Captain America does the unthinkable and hands Deadpool an Avengers membership card (*The Uncanny Avengers* Volume 2, #1), that should be the end of it. Wade's been accepted. He's gotten the seal of approval from Captain frickin' America himself. There's nothing more to be said. He's a hero now, right? He's an *Avenger*, for goodness sake, picked for the squad by *Captain America* himself. In the Marvel universe, recognition doesn't get any more legitimate or prestigious.

Cap's word is useful in two ways. First, because he is Captain America, the moral authority of Marvel's hero community. Second, because Cap has brought shady figures into the hero fold before. Remember, Deadpool isn't the first borderline hero brought into the fold based on Cap's approval: in the early days of the Avengers, after Iron Man, Thor, Giant Man, and the Wasp decided to take a break from the team, the Star-Spangled Avenger introduced the world to a new Avengers line up. "Cap's Kooky Quartet" was just Cap himself, Hawkeye, Quicksilver, and the Scarlet Witch. Apart from Cap, the other three, all now Avengers stalwarts, were at the time very recently reformed villains. If Cap could do it for them, why not for Wade?

Sadly, neither the public nor Wade's would-be teammates are convinced. Spider-Man quits the Avengers rather than serve with Deadpool. The team's field leader, Rogue (herself a reformed villain), repeatedly states her objections to Wade, sometimes to his face. For some of them, Deadpool just has too much history as a scumbag mercenary. And he's annoying; that doesn't help.

Even Wade has his doubts. When Cap hands him the Avengers card, Deadpool's response isn't to crack a joke or start parade (or hijack a parade, as they're rather hard to start). Instead, he utters a simple, concise "Oh, crap." The old man later finds himself talking Deadpool out of quitting after every mission (*The Uncanny Avengers* Volume 2, #4). Joining the Avengers seems to be everything Deadpool wants—he started bothering members and nearly-members about it long before he was tapped by Captain America for the squad—at one point he even asked Spidey about the possibility of joining, as he put it, "the *whaddyacallits*, the *little Avengers Urban Achievers?* Proud we are of all of them, right?" a.k.a. the Young Avengers (*Deadpool* Volume 3, #10). But in spite of that, Deadpool isn't sure he should be on the team. He just doesn't feel like he belongs, in spite of the invitation from the Star-Spangled Avenger himself.

It's still playing out. It can end in one of two ways: either Wade's teammates will accept him or they won't. If they do, if his fellow Avengers acknowledge that he's a hero like themselves, then Wade might actually live up to his potential and become the hero he's always wanted to be. If they don't, Deadpool will slide back into his accustomed role as a scumbag mercenary. Cap is an important first step. His recognition is huge. But Cap is still just one man. Deadpool needs the acceptance of the superhero community. Once they see that he's a hero, that will give him permission to accept himself as a hero.

One further thing needs to be noted: when Cap makes Deadpool an Avenger, it isn't some sort of incentive program. He isn't rewarding him or giving him something to live up to. In Cap's mind, the Avengers card is recognition of what Deadpool already is, a hero. There's no air of superiority or condescension in the moment. Cap is giving Wade what he's due; no more, no less. He isn't making Deadpool a hero. Deadpool's already a hero. Even though Cap could easily claim the moral high ground and act the superior, like Cable does, he doesn't. He's not there to encourage Wade's potential or offer some sort of carrot-and-stick. Captain America, the Star-Spangled Avenger, the Sentinel of Liberty himself, the man who punched Hitler in the face, accepts the Merc with the Mouth as his equal and fellow hero.

So What Do You Say? Team Up?

The Merc with the Mouth began his life as a superhuman thrown out like so much garbage by the Weapon X program. Even the butchers behind Canada's super-soldier program saw no redeeming value in the carcass of Wade Wilson. Is it any wonder then that he has trouble seeing his own value? Or his own potential? His past, his deformation, and his psychological issues all contribute to Wade's self-doubt and insecurity when it comes to heroics.

Only the recognition of the superhero community, their acknowledgment that he has reformed and is now one of them, will give Deadpool the reassurance that he needs to fully embrace the hero that he is. Without it, he will always struggle with the temptation to relapse into old habits, to become once again nothing more than a merc with a mouth.

15
Good Citizen Deadpool? *Even I think that's Crazy!*

JORGE HUMBERTO SANCHEZ PEREZ AND
WADE THE AWESOMEST NUMBER OF NAMES
EVER WILSON-POOL

If you have ever read, watched, heard or smelled anything about Deadpool you probably have an idea of what someone should *not do* if they want to become a hero or *should* do if they want to become a wanted criminal. But what if I were to tell you that even if he's not the typical kind of hero that one would expect, Deadpool is a *good citizen*? ***Wait, what?***

Yes, you read that correctly. There is at least one way I can pull this off (not out . . . get your head out of the gutter). How? Easy, I just need to turn to Aristotle (384–322 B.C.) to do it. If you've never heard of Aristotle, you are forgiven. The guy lived over 2,300 years ago! But his ideas still remain important, and, when dealing with Deadpool, fun.

Back in the day, Aristotle wrote a book called *Politics*. In that book, he explains what counts as a good citizen and what doesn't, and here is where I bring the Merc with a Mouth into our conversation. (Aristotle also talks about what the best city and the best kind of government is, but that's not part of this chapter, so if you want to know more about it, you are welcome to get off of your butt and go read some classic philosophy!)

Okay, back to Deadpool. He kills, a lot—I mean, he is a mercenary . . . That, basically, means killing for a living and doing other stuff related to finding a target that might not be nice either (you know, breaking fingers, gouging out eyes, hot pokers up butts—*and sometimes that's all to collect information not just for fun!)* If Deadpool does that stuff, would you be willing to call him a good citizen? "*No way Jose*," you said? Oh, well, guess what? Aristotle just might, and since I am writing a chapter with that title, so do I. Read on to learn how wrong you are!

The Good Man and the Deadpool

Let's start with two questions, first, how can we call a mercenary, in this case one as sexy as Deadpool, a good citizen?

And, second, how can you be a good citizen while not being a good person? The fact is, though, there are good men and there are good citizens, and they don't need to be the same person!

Yes, there you have it. You can be one or the other, or in some cases maybe both.

How can you be one and not the other, you ask? Well, it's simple. Think about the following: Do you have to be a good husband in order to be a good golf player? Hell no! Look at Tiger Woods. That guy is a great golfer but he cheated on his wife so many times that his marriage was the place he went to rest between cheating. ***That takes some balls . . . get it? Three-way pun . . . on a fairway . . . Oh, a FOUR way!*** *See*? You don't need to be good in one thing in order to be good at the other. Being a good man and being a good citizen are two separate things and that's why we need to start with that distinction in order to make sense of how can we fit Deadpool in that hole, pun intended. ***Fiveway? Things will get . . . dunked. Wait, dammit, wrong sport . . . If you can call hitting little balls with crooked poles a sport! Right back in the game baby!***

When we talk about a good man, we're talking about an overall good guy. This good guy will always act in such a way that he follows the right path. What is the right path? Well, according to Aristotle it's the just path. To know that path is useful, says Aristotle, because we are political animals. Because, as humans, we're able to perceive the good and the bad, the just and the unjust, and since we can perceive those things, we're able to build societies on those bases (*Politics*, line 1253a8). So, given that we're capable of knowing what good means, then a good man would be he who acted following that which is good and that which he previously identified as good. But then again we, as Deadpool fans, have a lot more questions here. *What is the good that we are to act on*? Well, boys and girls that is the question!

For Aristotle, that answer came after a lifetime of reflection and practice of good deeds based on reflection. Basically, if you had a good nature, you were raised properly and you managed to live a decent and moderate life, you would get there. Now, imagine if you had cancer all over you and your life was a constant string of mercenary jobs and mutated cells and violence, you know, like Deadpool. Well if that was the case, it wouldn't be merely unlikely that you would be a good man, it would be near freaking impossible.

You can't make an omelet with two bricks, it just wouldn't work. And, if you could do it, well then, you should be on *MasterChef*. Really, why wait? Go! ***I've got your eggs right here baby! . . . Wait, what were we doing with the eggs again?***

So, for those of you who aren't going to become bricklaying culinary artists, as you can tell, even for Aristotle it would be really hard for Deadpool to become a good man. I mean, he has suffered enough! His hard life and all those things in between the killing, cheating, sexting, and all the rest of it would make it really hard for him to be a good man. But as Deadpool himself would say, ***Dude, who on $&#$ing earth doesn't sext?***

No one can be that good, right? Good question: to answer that I will ask you to go to imagination-land (yes there will be unicorns) and imagine somebody who, no matter what, is just a boy scout. ***Ugh = P.*** The kind of boy scout that even if everybody around him is just nasty, rude and messed up, is still just so *nice* that we, and definitely Deadpool, would probably want to perform a wedgie on them. ***Forget atomic, let's go GALACTUS.***

If you've seen the latest Deadpool movie, one boy scout in particular comes to mind—Colossus. ***A good man to have around at Christmas time . . . he comes with his own silver bells. Bro, there are a lot of testicle jokes in this chapter . . . Feeling lonely?*** Yes, that is what Aristotle, and yours truly, mean when talking about a guy. A dude so nice and balanced, that can't be real . . . and well he wasn't—it was mostly a product of CGI and green screens, but you get the idea.

The Good Wife . . . I Mean Citizen

Now, what on Earth would a good citizen be then? Well to answer that we have to think about diversity. There are many different communities and political groups (not like political parties . . . like groupings of people, who themselves are political beings . . . remember, Aristotle thought people are political animals? I talked about it just in the last section . . . Oh, never mind.) or, as we known them, cities.

Yes, can you see the connection here? Cities—citizens? No? really? Come one! A citizen is a member of a city, you . . . beautiful reader. So, the million-dollar question for this section is *How many cities exist out there in the whole wide world?* If your answer was ***a freaking lot or like a gazillion,*** you are on the right path here. There are too many to count right now, or to bother doing so in general; and according to Aristotle, well, each city had their own rules and ways to get to be good.

Let's think about the *real* world for a second, *shall we*? Do you think that the good people of San Francisco are the same as the good people of Chicago? Or Paris? Or Shanghai? Or Toronto? Well nope, they are all quite different and not because the people in Paris speak in a weird way. Each human group is different from each other and each group has a different idea of what good is. If we're to believe Aristotle, only a few of those cities actually got it right, but that doesn't prevent us from realizing that the rest, the wrong ones, are still there, *so just do what you can with the cards you were dealt!* ***Strip Go Fish anyone?***

So what's good for the citizens of Paris? Maybe producing cheese and wine is what amounts to "the good." What is the good for San Francisco? Perhaps selling electric cars to other cities and telling the whole world they are doing it. What makes Toronto good? Most likely to produce maple syrup and put it on everything . . . seriously, even hats. ***Hey now buddy, watch it!***

See? Every city has their own idea about what is good and to reach for that, says good ol' Aristotle, each of the citizens of such a city has to fulfil a role. In the case of Paris, some have to produce the cheese, others the wine, and others have to get fat and drunk. See? Everybody contributes to the greatness of a city by doing whatever makes the good happen.

The Good Deadpool as the Good Merc . . . with a Mouth

So, let's think about Deadpool and his wonderful world as a city. And now let's imagine that city and the idea of good that comes from that "city". Yes, we're talking about a world where superheroes are real and where people like Deadpool actually exist. So, *what kind of good are we dealing with here?*

Remember the time professor Xavier, Tony Stark, Namor, Reed Richards and Black Bolt decided that it was best for everybody to send the Hulk to another planet without asking him? Well that should give you an idea that the good in the "city" of the Marvel Universe might not be as white and black as some might think. Living in a world with dudes with superpowers makes things very different from our own super-powerless universe. ***Puny Universe! Hulkpool Smash!*** Anyway, the important thing is that Deadpool's world is a rough world and Deadpool is part of that complicated business.

So what seems to be the main "good" to the city of the Marvel Universe, kind of like "Ruin perfectly good food by covering it all in maple syrup" is the rule for Toronto. ***Okay, buddy, now you die.*** The Marvel Universe seems to say that the "good" is to "take down bad guys before they harm innocent civilians, bystanders, and most people in general." Which means there are superheroes and supervillains constantly at odds with each other.

Sooooo . . . it might be *good* for the city to have mercenaries running around fulfilling their contracts to keep some kind of balance between heroes and villains. What role should a guy with regenerative powers and a fine control over two swords have? Well, the role that best fits the city, of course. And Deadpool does a damn good job of it.

As we've seen so far, to be a good citizen is different from being a good man. To be a good citizen means basically doing your part in making your city great. While being a good man means being good all around. They are different things! And although you could find somebody who's a good man who also fulfills his role in his city, thus making him a good man and a good citizen, it's extremely rare and won't happen very often, so, in the words of the great philosopher Steven Tyler from Aerosmith, "Dream on."

The world is a harsh place, my friends, and not everything is good all around us. So, given that the world in which Deadpool lives is not always perfect and nice and clean, or logical, then we can agree on the fact that there might be some things to be done that are not always perfect and nice and clean, or logical, and that is when Wade Wilson a.k.a. Deadpool comes into the picture.

The fact is that the Marvel Universe "city" has a clear idea that some balance between heroes and villains is needed. Heck, when Deadpool fights Thanos we see how important balance is. In *Deadpool vs Thanos* we see Deadpool caught in the struggle between life and Death. ***And Death has a fine ass BTDubbs.*** For a moment, the "In-Betweener" gets involved because Death has been imprisoned and so the balance is now tending towards Chaos. The In-Betweener is the emissary of Master Order and Lord Chaos. Get it? ***Huh? No, sorry, I was distracted . . . I'll just put this nudey pic of Bea Arthur down slowly . . .*** Sigh, the point is that the Marvel Universe actually has a character dedicated to keeping BALANCE. That is how central the idea of balance is to their "city." Deadpool, is both a villain and a hero, depending on the time of the month. ***Hey!*** And so he serves to help maintain the balance of his universe.

So, here's a crazy idea . . . what if Deadpool being a merc and occasionally killing people for money, often bad guys, *helps keep the balance? Wouldn't that help the city? Not that the end justifies the means, but . . . it sorts of does, right? He's doing a job that maybe nobody else can do or wants to do, but hey, somebody has to do it, right?*

I'll give you boys and girls an example, let's go back to imagination-land and let's imagine a dude from a city, let's call it "Deadpooltopia" who happens to be really, really good at killing other human beings. And let us imagine that in order to prevent Deadpooltopia, from being turned into a big stinking mess due to a civil war, he is supposed to kill any possible leaders of the revolt that might pose a threat to its state. This assassin could go around killing those dudes and, in the best *The Godfather* possible way, even their children, in order to prevent further upraises or personal acts of revenge. In this case, I hope we are all super clear in this, the assassin is definitely not a good man, not by a mile, really, not at all. But, guess what? He might be something closer to a good citizen.

Why on Earth would somebody call this guy a good citizen you say? Remember the case of the Parisian? As long as some produce the wine, others the cheese and others eat it, then all is good. So here, it's similar. As long as the assassin is providing a good service for Deadpooltopia, following the internal rules and fulfilling the role he is supposed to fulfil, and even though he might be a really awful man, as long as he properly serves the city, he is a good citizen.

You see where this is going, right? Now let's go back to the world where the good ol' Wade Wilson, a.k.a. Deadpool, lives. In that world, there are super-powered beings who fly around and smash entire cities and some even have the power of a few suns inside them. So, what do we make of that world? Where not everybody is good and certainly, where even some of the "good guys" aren't as good as one might expect. Well in that case, we might put our judgmental hats on and say at one voice "you know what? You ain't perfect neither" and we walk away. Well more like run in fear because we just called some super-powerful imperfect beings names. ***Here's to you Smolverine! Yup, made that up right on the spot!*** After running in fear and denying it in front of your friends later at the bar, you keep on thinking and realize that a less than perfect city will certainly have a less than perfect set of rules.

So once again we might ask *what role can a fearless, almost immortal, sword and gun aficionado, smart mouth, and a bit of an insane jerk, can have in such city*? ***Hey, who are you calling an aficionado???*** Well the answer's simple: whatever is needed for the city to go on. Deadpool has taken contracts from the good guys and the bad guys alike. He has also helped superhero teams and once, he even saved the universe! Why? Well because somebody had to do those things. If your city is a place where people need a guy that balances out the odds for the fight between not so good against evil to take place, well, then there might be a place for a guy who is really good at killing. See? There is a place for Deadpool around that city. His mercenary skills are a fundamental part of the whole of the city. The city needs him and he needs the city, because without it, there is nobody for him to make fun of. ***I would be a sad Pandapool.***

In a city where the good is a bit more relative than most people would think, then some citizens have to fulfil a function that might not be the nicest. Remember, for Aristotle there was "the good," but he was smart enough to know that there are some cities were getting there was too hard, if not impossible. So, in a realistic and shocking turn of events for a philosopher, he recognized that some cities might not be as good as others. But, within those cities, and in the rules of those cities, some people, even BAD people, might be good for that city! ***Ohhhhhh . . . so it's like the beans are bad because they make me do the turd tango, but they are GOOD for the chimichanga. Got it! Mmmmmm turds . . . I mean chimichangas.*** If Wade's city is one of those cities where things are not tidy and clean all the time, then it seems that his function doesn't need to be the cleanest either. What do we make of this? Well that even a Merc with a mouth might have a place in the city. If he fulfils his role then, we might even say that he has a virtuous existence as a citizen. But we won't, because what fun would that be?

The virtuous existence of Deadpool in that city might not be the one of a fun-loving flower child. *But he might as well stop shoving that *$#&ing Thanos-sized burrito in his face and do his proper duty of killing a few undesirables among the ranks of Hydra, AIM or any other criminal organization around!*

And you, "dear reader," what's your excuse? Get it together and become a good citizen now! Do some good for *your* city. And don't make the super suit green! Or animated! ***Really, you are going to end it quoting my movie? Lame.***

16
The Beautiful Face Behind the Mask

KYLE ALKEMA AND ADAM BARKMAN AS THEY AWAIT THEIR INEVITABLE DEATHS

Wade Wilson's disfigured face underneath his mask is beautiful. *There, we said it. Shoot, now we have to try to convince you that it's true.*

Deadpool masks his face—which looks like he fell asleep on the ugly bus and missed all the stops—not to hide his identity as Wade Wilson, but to hide his deep-fried appearance. In *Deadpool* volume 1 #22, when Zoe Culloden and Monty unexpectedly show up at his apartment, he runs away and tells them not to look at his face because he's not decent: "I gotta find my mask, gotta put on my face!" He can't find his mask, so he puts a box over his head as he traipses around.

We can't blame him for wearing a mask, really—not with the reactions his face draws from people. But sometimes he lets people see the real face underneath his mask, sometimes he allows serious and truthful speech to shine through his jokes, and people don't always run away. Sometimes he lets those close to him see the *real* Deadpool, the soft and gooey Deadpool on the inside: A deep-fried exterior with soft and gooey insides . . . Maybe it's true that "you are what you eat" . . .

—Deadpool's a Chimichanga

Because he limits his interactions with others, it often feels like Deadpool is living in a world of his own. It's not too lonely if he's always talking to himself. But he needs bad guys that need killing (*for a sweet payday!*), and he needs an audience (*to laugh at his sweet jokes!*). The Marvel universe he inhabits forces him into encounters with others.

A world of words filled with mortality and morality, mystery and murder, money and marvel—~~Deadpool's~~ Levinas's writings have it all. Emmanuel Levinas (1906–1995) developed a 'philosophy of the other' based on our lived experience, where we're confronted with the faces of others. The philosophy of experience, called *phenomenology*, comes from the perspective of the subject . . . from what we call the "I".

Levinas wants to convey the concrete experiences I have with the *other*, establishing ethics by putting this mysterious other first (*Totality and Infinity*, p. 42). In this way his philosophy was especially inspired by, and also a critique of, the heavily influential German phenomenological philosophers whom Levinas believed put too much emphasis on subjectivity—their philosophies were too self-centered and were unjust to others. House blowing up builds character after all . . .

In Levinas's writings, his method of presenting experiences is neither without reason nor against it, but it's also not limited to formal logical structures or to the attempt to capture the essences of concepts: this can make it as hard to digest as a chimichanga. In *Totality and Infinity*, Levinas's first major work, we are confronted with justice as a responsibility to the other when we encounter not violence but the weakness of the stranger, the poor, the orphan, or the widow by standing before them face to face. There's a humility in Levinas's philosophy of our responsibility to welcoming the stranger and to share worlds through speech.

Deadpool offers a unique perspective on this face-to-face encounter with the other: he's a self-obsessed outcast because he pushes others away, but often he encounters others in a way that allows them to see the *beautiful* face beneath his mask. His mercenary occupation of murder that conflicts with his occasional desire to not kill adds deeper layers to Levinas's philosophy.

So let's take a wild excursion through this philosophy of the other while riding shotgun in Deadpool's mind. It'll be like becoming one with the all reality of Frank, the Awareness. Like S.H.I.E.L.D. Agent Preston in *Deadpool* volume 3, we'll delve into the inner workings of Wade Wilson's wondrous and chaotic mind! We're going to be the Deadpool. *Eww, gross*.

Ipool: Deadpool's Alone

We are Deadpool. Deadpool is an I. I find myself living a life as a wise-cracking mercenary. The I begins with the self, my complete inner life with boundaries that surround my personal existence. This inner life, my interiority, is what Levinas means by *totality*. My dynamic, growing self is unable to go outside of myself. This makes a self unique. There is no one like Deadpool (*Deadpool* Volume 2, #35). Each Deadpool from each Marvel universe is his or her own Deadpool: Lady Deadpool, Headpool, Dogpool . . . Pandapool.

But I am not an incorporeal self floating around in a void, like the ghost of Benjamin Franklin with no women to pursue. I'm already in my body in the world—and it's a gross body, at that. I make my dwelling in the world by maintaining my self, at home. My world around me is full of things that are separate from me. I manipulate and I bring objects into my world, for my pleasure, for my nourishment. Nourishment takes what's outside and makes it part of my self. *You are what you eat!*

Through labor as well we can transform the world around us and take things into our possession, reducing objects to money. Enjoyment comes from my experience of living from the world, whether it's eating tacos, playing video games, or laboring to possess money and explosives. "Life is love of life," as Levinas says (p. 112). Happiness comes from satisfying my needs, such as needing to watch Bea Arthur marathons (pp. 110–15). To be at home with my self, separated, is to be happy, is to be I—even for a "piece of human waste like me" (*Deadpool* Volume 1, #6). Suffering is simply failing to satisfy my needs. But it's hard for Deadpool to live happy and free: Deadpool's scars "are a roadmap of a loner's experiences, the rough texture of living!" (*Deadpool: Merc with a Mouth* #9).

I am alone. I am just a mouth with a stomach, bringing objects into my world, under my dominion, for my consumption, deaf to what's around me. But if my labor, as Deadpool, is killing people, then how does that transform the world? There is no cultivation, no bringing of things into my world. And maybe there are things in the world that aren't merely objects, things that can't be possessed or reduced to part of my totality? Deadpool isn't alone in the world—he needs people to hear his jokes and receive his bullets. As Deadpool remarks in *Night of the Living Deadpool* #1, "What's the point of being the Merc with the Mouth if there's no one around to be annoyed by you?"

Not-Alonepool: Wade Encounters the Other

Like Theresa "Siryn" Rourke Cassidy sleeping in her bed as Deadpool creepily-yet-not-creepily-but-still-creepily looks through her window in *Deadpool* Volume 1, #22, Deadpool is not alone! Deadpool's loner life is not so lonesome. There's fun times with Vanessa and Shiklah, with Blind Al and Agent Preston (*not in that way*), and with Weasel and Bob (*not in that way either*).

I am not alone. Deadpool expresses this realization in *Return of the Living Deadpool* #1 when he says, "My mind's been expanded by the idea that I don't have to be unaccompanied." Who are these others? Levinas's portrayal of the other is as one who disturbs me in my home, an exterior being not of my world, but of his or her own world. The other is not merely opposite me but genuinely other, essentially different. In contrast to the I as a *totality*, experiencing the other opens me up to an exterior relationship that can't be reduced to my interiority. This is Levinas's concept of *infinity*: the other, by being his or her own self, overflows the capacity and content of my thought. If I encountered Deadpool, Deadpool would always exceed the Deadpool I possess in my mind.

I come *before the face of the other*. The *other* presents him- or herself to me through the expression of *the face*: the face speaks. The Merc with a Mouth uses it. The experience of this paradoxical encounter is accomplished through language, where the otherness of the other, the distance, is upheld despite entering into a relation with me. This experience is set apart from any other experience through speech, but speech in a narrow sense: meaningful conversation, or discourse, and not meaningless babbling or incessant joking. *Conversation*, for Levinas, means to *welcome the other's expression,* where teaching and learning occur through the transfer of knowledge.

Deadpool's diverse discourse doesn't necessarily include encounters with others, but it opens up the possibility to them. *Speech* reveals *the other*, and by listening I respond to the demand of the other. Response comes before comprehension or understanding. The Merc with a Mouth is a talker, but, conversely, maybe not always such a listener.

It's not any face that presents itself to me, nor is it any physical human face. Levinas's emphasis is still on the experience, the epiphany, of the *face-to-face encounter*. The epiphany of the face as a face is to meet the gaze of the other and see the transcendence of their vulnerability, to recognize the other's face as a face. My orientation toward the other, my presence before a face, inverts my selfishness to generosity by being unable to approach the other with empty hands—and not hands with guns in them, either (*Totality and Infinity*, p. 50).

Justice, therefore, is found in the face-to-face encounter, by submitting to the other. To recognize the other's need is to be confronted with my responsibility, and to give. I realize that my existence is already obligated . . . Now, whose kitty litter did I just shit in?

The ethical response, that is, the proper response, to the epiphany isn't only in receiving the other, but is in serving the other by offering my self to him. Goodness is the foundation of my expressing my self (p. 183). My conscience is what welcomes the other and alerts me to my own guilt (pp. 84–86). Meaningful communication freely offers my world to others, which involves my proper response that depends on responding to their voices and not to their appearances (p. 76). The incursion of the other threatens to invade my innermost self, just as the Marvel incursions, impending collisions with other worlds from alternate universes that are the same as our world yet fundamentally separate, threaten our whole world.

To sum up the thrust of Levinas's argument: I encounter the other through a face-to-face epiphany where I recognize my responsibility and respond to the other in conversation by welcoming them into and giving them my world. My world is shocked by the suffering of others. The stranger, the poor, the orphan, the widow—in their destitution they are simultaneously equal to me and elevated above me.

Facepool—Deadpool's Face Revealed

In *Totality and Infinity* Levinas doesn't give real world applications or practical examples of these face-to-face encounters or what it means to live for others: it is for us to experience and for us to figure out based on our experiences. Yet it might be helpful to see how some of Deadpool's experiences bear this out. Deadpool encounters strangers all the time (and kills them)—it's in his line of work. A strange face-to-face encounter with a shark, of the dead and rotting variety, leads Deadpool to discover something about himself through an imaginary dialogue (*Deadpool* Volume 2, #15).

Though a dead shark can't have a face in Levinas's sense of the term, Deadpool's encounter is more with his own self. He learns that he seeks attention from others, so much so that he would rather be paid in attention than cash. But Deadpool is alone because he mistreats his friends and pushes them away. Deadpool learns that he pushes them away because he is afraid of being judged by others and because he is afraid of being pushed away by them due to his ugly face and deformed brain. The dead shark penetrates deep into Deadpool's inner self: "How can you expect anyone to accept you for what you really are when you never show them what you really are?" Deadpool's feeble excuse is that there are others that run around in masks and that he's forced to be an outcast. The shark digs deeper: Deadpool won't accept others for who they are, and what he gets out of a relationship is equal to what he puts into it.

The poor are also mentioned frequently in Levinas's descriptions of the other, and Deadpool's poor friends not only lack the possessions that Deadpool often flaunts but also experience less-than-friendly treatment from Deadpool. The bell-headed Dr. Bong asserts in *Deadpool* Volume 2, #28, that, "if there's one thing he hates more than himself, it's his friends." A few issues later, despite the way Deadpool often mistreats Bob, agent of Hydra, Bob still declares and acts as if he cares for him (*Deadpool* Volume 2, #36). And then Deadpool shoots him in the leg. The tension between Deadpool's (one-sided) conversation, pushing the other away, and having positive experiences with real friends is a recurring theme in his story (*Deadpool Corps* #1, for one instance). For example, at times Deadpool treats Blind Al horribly. But when Deadpool tries to send Blind Al away in *Deadpool* Volume 1, #14, Blind Al refuses to abandon Wade: "Somewhere at the bottom of that piece of filth called Wade is a good soul . . . and I'll be damned if I'm going to leave before I've found it." However, much of the time Deadpool does right by them when it matters most, and Deadpool doesn't want to lose his friends (*Deadpool* Volume 3, #5).

Some of Deadpool's sincerest encounters are with those most like him. Throughout the issues in *Deadpool* Volume 3, Deadpool befriends and helps the North Korean superhero-clones who are like him—made partly from his DNA, who have inherited his scars, and who are outcasts looking for friends and a home (for example in *Deadpool* Volume 3, #35). Another time Deadpool encounters a boy named David with a face like Deadpool's, but David doesn't try to hide his face; instead, David challenges Deadpool's self-image issues (*Deadpool* Volume 1, #68). Deadpool likes David because their faces are similar, and Deadpool throws away his image inducer. Deadpool has a strange friendship with Cable, and one of Deadpool's most intense encounters with Cable, in the first issues of *Cable and Deadpool* Volume 1, is when the two of them are battling the One World Church, which is trying to infect the whole world with a 'façade virus' that makes everyone's skin blue. The virus infects Cable and, like Deadpool's experience with cancer, Cable's face and body is disfigured. Deadpool encounters Cable and saves him (*Cable and Deadpool*, Volume 1, #4).

Deadpool has plenty of experiences with more-than-friends of the lady type, especially with fiancées and wives. Wade's main relationship before he got terminal cancer was with Vanessa, but he left her to spare her the pain of watching him die, although she doesn't want to leave him. In the *Deadpool* movie, after Wade has been cured of cancer and cursed with a face "like a testicle, with teeth," Weasel argues that Vanessa wouldn't care what he looked like now because she loves him; yet, Weasel hasn't seen Wade's face—he changes his mind once he does.

Blind Al also argues that looks aren't everything. Deadpool disagrees. In the end, through a face-to-face encounter, Vanessa convinces him that she will only require a brief adjustment period—then she touches his face and kisses him. Similarly, Deadpool's sort-of-wife Mercedes, who is mysteriously brought back from the dead (by the jerk-nemesis T-Ray) in *Deadpool* Volume 1, wants Deadpool to take off his mask so she can look into his eyes in order to trust him, but he can't do it because of his face. She, like Vanessa, convinces him to tell her what happened to him and to show her his face. Mercedes, again like Vanessa, isn't afraid or repulsed, and she hugs Wade (*Deadpool* Volume 1, #30). Wade's healthy relationships with women reach past Deadpool's mask.

In his encounters with Siryn, a "vulnerable" superhero, in the earlier issues of *Deadpool*, Deadpool learns what it means not only to be a hero but also to be a human. During their first adventure together in *Deadpool: Sins of the Past* (1994), Deadpool doesn't want Siryn to look at his face, but Siryn presses him and reassures him. Deadpool says, "You want to see? Really? Fine! Welcome to the freak show, beautiful!" Siryn gasps at first, but then recovers, apologizes, and touches his head. And she could have gasped out of recognition of the suffering Wade must have endured. Blind Al sees the effect that Deadpool's encounters with Siryn have led to by witnessing Deadpool's character growth: "No doubt due to the influence of a certain bonnie Irish lass with an angel's face and a voice like Gideon's trumpet. With any luck, that's where he is now, reconnecting his tether t'something good in this world" (*Deadpool* Volume 1, #10). Deadpool recognizes his need for Siryn's help to grow as a person, to feel like a human being. He recognizes that his holographic image inducer makes him look like everyone else—normal—but it doesn't work on the inside (*Deadpool* Volume 1, #12 and #13).

Hopefully, these experiences with the others who aren't trying to kill him and with the others that he is not trying to kill, with the others that don't turn away from him but meet his gaze, and with the others to whom he can show his face, help to illustrate how meaningful face-to-face encounters accomplish peace and justice rather than violence and cruelty. But what about the rich person or the mighty person? Or the person trying to kill me?

Murderpool: Deadpool and the Enemy

Justice, or consideration of the other, is demanded of me through the other's weakness, and not through their power. The demand of the other on me is life. I am confronted with the impossibility of murder by recognizing the vulnerability of the other. My experience with the other does not break into my world through violence but through the epiphany. Through the gaze of the other I see the commandment "You shall not kill" (p. 199). I might have the power to kill the other, but in order to kill the other I would need to deny the other's face, to deny the other as an other, to dehumanize the other, to turn the other into an object. Worse, I would then annihilate the other.

When a psychiatrist asks Deadpool in *Deadpool* #9 if the killing ever bothers him, he replies, "Sure, there are times it does—the way a lip quivers, the look in their eyes as they're begging for mercy, it can stay with you . . . especially when there's a spark." Annihilating that which transcends me, the other coming to me with hands open, is the opposite of the proper response. The proper response, the ethical response, is to welcome the Other into my home.

The vulnerability of the other to the point of my sword or the bullet from my gun (Levinas's images) lies in the exposure of the ventricles or auricles of his heart (again, Levinas's image, and thankfully not an image of any of his other '-icles'). Murder separates the life from behind the eyes: where a moment earlier the other stood before me, now, after the discharge of my loaded gun, lies a corpse without a face. Murder silences conversation.

Throughout Deadpool's history he's constantly conflicted about killing. A recurring theme is Deadpool's inner conflict of trying to become a superhero, to atone for the sins of his past. However, others haven't treated him the best either. Was Deadpool treated as an other when he was experimented on in the Weapon X program? After being tortured by Dr. Killebrew and Francis, Deadpool wants to kill Dr. Killebrew for the pain and suffering Killebrew had inflicted upon him. Deadpool remembers what it was like not to feel human and to exist purely as meat, an object, when he looks into Killebrew's eyes (*Deadpool* Volume 1, #4). Deadpool wants to kill Killebrew to ease his own suffering, but he encounters Theresa standing in the way, facing him. Theresa gets Deadpool to stop by appealing to the real Wade Wilson underneath the exterior. Deadpool might think that both he and Killebrew are brutish monsters, but he spares Killebrew's life precisely because Theresa believes in his own humanity, his otherness (*Deadpool* Volume 1, #5).

The wrong tendency is to attempt to justify murder through objectification and alienation: the other is different than me and so inferior to me. The other is the enemy far away from me, separated. Levinas is trying to reverse this. But maybe when others don't treat me like an other they revoke their status as other. Perhaps they reject their own face by rejecting others' faces. Then fighting to preserve others' faces might fulfill justice by considering the wellbeing of the vulnerable.

Alivepool: Deadpool and Death

Death, from this side of the veil, sucks. We are trapped in the stream of time heading toward our own deaths, which will probably be full of sickness and agony. Death is there, lurking in the closet, around the corner, perched on the branch outside my bedroom window—*Oh wait; that's just Deadpool*. We never know when it could strike. Sometimes we see ourselves rushing toward it: Wade sees his death approaching through his terminal cancer in both the movie and the comics.

We can, at best, prolong our existence in this world, yet there's no point to my life if it's dedicated only to prolonging it. Grasping onto life is to experience dying. My own death isn't something I can experience in my life, since it marks the endpoint of my life in this world and is not an experience. The way we experience death is by witnessing the death of the other.

Witnessing the death mask of the other, seeing the face gone from the lifeless body, the vacant, staring eyes, shouldn't close us in as we focus on our own death, but should instead open us up to the life of the other. Whereas murder reduces the other to an object, causing suffering maintains the otherness of the other. Suffering threatens our freedom. Hatred isn't wishing death on someone, but wishing supreme suffering until death on someone. Both Levinas and Wade faced suffering, torture, and dehumanization: Deadpool in the Weapon X program, for example, and Levinas as a prisoner of war in a Nazi camp for most of World War II.

Courage is the power to face death, to be exposed to the aim of the mercenary, the red dot of the sniper rifle, and to persist in living my life for others. I can't change the will of the mercenary who may be unapproachable by meaningful conversation. The way to defeat death is by pursuing peace. Peace can't be enforced by the threat of violence, since the threat of violence is war. Levinas wants to conquer war and murder with peace. This doesn't include killing people for money, but Deadpool often acts as a hero to save people—he just doesn't usually mind killing in order to do it.

The highest expression of the self is to be for the other. An other's life can continue after mine, which could be true for Deadpool as well if he found a way to die. The purpose of my life is to enter into relation with others, to live for others, not living for my life or living for my death. Living for others is to dread their murder more than my own death. How many times has Deadpool (possibly) risked his life for the vulnerable? In *Deadpool* Volume 1, #13, Zoe claims that she would die ten times over just to see Wade do the right thing. Two issues later she sees Deadpool appear to only care about saving himself and asks him where his sense of responsibility is, accusing of him of being "nothing more than a self-centered waste with no spine!" (*Deadpool* Volume 1, #15). But Deadpool does save everyone, despite his contrary appearances. Deadpool's at his best when he sacrifices his life, or at least his lack of suffering, for others. The future is for others. As Cable says to Deadpool in *Cable and Deadpool* Volume 1, #26, "Being fit to survive is not the end but the means . . . that makes you responsible to those who aren't!"

Welcome to the Freak Show, Beautiful!

We've seen how Deadpool started as an "I," living in his world, before encountering the faces of others led to meaningful exchanges through speech. Siryn, Weasel, Blind Al, the dead shark, Vanessa, and many more confronted Wade with their vulnerability. He didn't always act anywhere close to doing the right thing, but the Merc with a Mouth is more than an agent of murder.

Deadpool can live his life for others by giving his life for them, by living his life for them. How much more would it mean for Deadpool to live his life for others, since he can't die? Then through embracing his face-to-face encounters and conversations he could perhaps experience healing and perhaps learn how to be content. Maybe bad guys could even still be killed, while Deadpool earns some dough, if they revoke their status as other—but that's for a different discussion. Deadpool once said, "The strongest man is the one who cares." *Oh wait, that was the Dove men's skin care ad that was just on TV as procrastination sets in.*

We have also seen some beautiful expressions of Deadpool's inner self. Moments—experiences—where Deadpool's inner being is truly beautiful. And since, according to Levinas, the expression of his self is his *face*, this means that his face can also be beautiful. Even if his physical face is as ugly as a skin-colored, constipated prune—well, that's not important. Hey, it's not exactly a cop-out because Levinas wants us to 'see' the person on the inside and to 'see' that the person on the inside is more than the appearance on the outside.

Deadpool is probably the happiest to hear that. So hopefully we can say to Deadpool, along with the random person in *Deadpool* Volume 2, #15, "You're beautiful, sweetie!" His face isn't his mask: he doesn't need to put his mask on when he answers the phone (*Cable and Deadpool* Volume 1, #1, #20). At the very least Levinas challenges us to think about what it means to encounter the other. It doesn't matter whether the other is the stranger or the widow, or male or female, mutant or superhero, alien or other uglier alien, Thom Cruz or Ryan Reynolds bitten by a radioactive Shar-Pei, we're all ourselves and we're all others (*Deadpool* Volume 1, #38–45; *Cable and Deadpool* Volume 1 #2).

17
Wade Wilson Fights Like a Girl

MICHAEL R. BERRY AND CHRISTOPHER NATALE
ARE TRIPPING BALLS . . . IS THAT SEXIST?

This conversation takes place in the office of a college professor at a small college in northeastern Pennsylvania. The names have been changed to protect the innocent. Any resemblance to real or fictional characters is purely—and we mean purely—coincidental. Any person named Deadpool, Vanessa, Colossus, or Negasonic Teenage Warhead is probably a figment of your imagination. The idea is that you might learn something from this dialogue, but don't get your hopes up . . .

Deadpool as a Superhero, No Really!!!!

OLD AUTHOR: Hi Chris, thanks for stopping by during my office hours and talking to me today. I hope you're enjoying my class on superheroes and comic books. It's a fun class to teach.

DEADPOOL: ***A college class on superheroes? Awesome, but what does that have to do with me?***

OLD AUTHOR: It has a lot to do with you. Chris, I hope you don't mind that I invited Deadpool, Vanessa, Colossus, and others to chat with us. By using the term "invite," I mean, Deadpool insisted that he be here by threatening to do unspeakable things with a unicorn in front of me if he didn't attend. The other characters will be a great asset. While Deadpool and his friends are not famous philosophers, we can use a dialogue like Plato to answer your questions.

DEADPOOL: ***You said ass.***

Old Author: No, I said asset, not ass. God, I hope this conversation leads somewhere.

Young Author: Deadpool, can I have your autograph? Also, I need to take notes on what you say.

Deadpool: ***No, you may not have my autograph, but you can take as many notes as you want. I love fanboys like you.***

Young Author: Thanks for that, Deadpool.

Deadpool: ***Whatever.***

Young Author: Professor Berry, the superheroes class is awesome. Where else can you get college credit for reading comic books and watching movies about superheroes? However, I need some help with my term paper in your class. I want to write on the philosophical nature of Deadpool by arguing that his greatest weapon is his mouth. He is not only a superhero but he also acts as a great role model by showing how genders can be equal.

Deadpool: ***Dude! You must not have watched the movie closely because I spend a lot of time YELLING at the top of my lungs how "I AM NOT A F@#C*ING HERO! You're worse than Weasel with a hangover. Oh, and I have never "exposed" myself. Every time I show skin, it is an "Artistic Expression."***

Young Author: [*Chris writes down everything Deadpool just said.*] Deadpool, I think I can make a good case that you are a hero. By claiming you're not a superhero, you are covertly criticizing mainstream superheroes.

Deadpool: ***Chris, the only case you are interested in is the one at the Friday night parties that contains adult beverages. A person who will remain nameless paid my bounty fee to make sure that you didn't embarrass yourself by chugging all the beer before spilling mustard on yourself like Bluto in Animal House. Now Bluto, he was a hero! By the way, that nameless person is your co-author. See, I didn't say his name. Also, stop writing down everything I say.***

Young Author: But you said I could take notes. [*Young Author makes notes on Deadpool's comments about not taking notes and his professor's lack of faith in Chris's social graces.*]

Old Author: Deadpool, stop being so mean. Chris is a great student and he makes a good argument as to why you are not only a superhero, but also an insightful observer of gender roles. Your greatest weapon isn't your katanas, healing power, or sexiness, it is your mouth. You use your mouth to reveal truths about the world.

Deadpool: ***Hell yeah, I "observe" genders. Some people are hotter than that habanero chimichanga I ate the other day.***

Young Author: That's right Mr. Berry, some people may think that everything he says or does is just for laughs, but he's actually revealing the truth about our world. Words have meanings and sometimes those meanings are deeper if you take a critical look at them. His mouth may just be his biggest weapon.

Deadpool: ***While we're on the subject of "truths," are you telling me that this is a teacher's office? I thought teachers were supposed to be clean, boring, stuffy and sophisticated. You have all these superhero posters and figurines scattered all over the office. It looks like Stan Lee threw up in here. YUCK!!!! Does this college actually pay you to teach here? I really hope that you don't teach your students this crap because I would feel bad for the next generation. Hell, I feel bad for them now, but I would feel even worse.***

Old Author: What were you expecting? A tweed jacket and a smoking pipe? I like the mementos in my office. My sons Seth and Noah gave them to me and they all have special meanings for me. Just like when you have a special meaning in your words. Please, can we stay on topic?

Deadpool: ***Uh . . . yeah. Isn't tweed what all male college professors wear? Your sons buy you crap like figurines? Wow, what a father figure you are. I mean hey, what do I know, I'm not even***

real. Well, I might be real, but that's another totally different subject. Also, what's with this young student of yours? "Student" might be pushing it. He looks more like a bargain bin Russell Crowe. Here's a better question: Is he actually entertained with all this crap you're preaching about me? I know I'm great and all, but I'm just the comic relief. The writers of all my books say so.

YOUNG AUTHOR: Did he just call me . . . ? [*Chris doesn't take notes on the previous Deadpool comment.*]

OLD AUTHOR: Look, Deadpool, as a merc with an insightful mouth your character is one that acts on his own accord to undermine and shed light on the stereotypes and norms that pervade society. For example, when you stated above that teachers are supposed to be clean, boring, stuffy, and sophisticated, you were criticizing society's conception of a college professor. Dang, am I treating Deadpool as a real person? I need my head examined.

YOUNG AUTHOR: Anyway . . . I just need to be sure Deadpool is a superhero. [*writes down his own question*]

OLD AUTHOR: Correct. Let's get to it. The question "Is Deadpool really a superhero?" has been debated since his creation. We need to define what makes a hero a superhero and then decide if he meets those parameters.

DEADPOOL: ***Damn professor, do you try hard to sound so stuffy? You're so Booooooooring.***

OLD AUTHOR: I am not stuffy. I have allergies. So Chris, what do you think makes Deadpool a superhero?

DEADPOOL: ***Uh . . . I'm not. Didn't you see my movie? That amazingly attractive actor, Ryan Reynolds, who plays me, clearly tells that girl with the stalker problem that I'm not a hero. Now that kid from New York who lives with his old aunt is a hero. He has the right idea with the skin-tight costume and that beautiful shade of red . . .***

OLD AUTHOR: I wasn't asking you, Deadpool, I was asking Chris.

Young Author: Professor Berry, Deadpool never stops talking, does he? [*Chris excitedly writes down what Deadpool has just said.*] Well, according to Peter Coogan, a famous expert in the superhero field, there are three specifications as to what makes a character fall under the category of a superhero. The superhero has to have a mission, powers, and an identity.

Does Deadpool have a Mission?

Old Author: Yes, the first characteristic is that the superhero has to have a mission. Cogan argues that a superhero's mission is to "fight evil and protect the innocent: this fight is universal, prosocial, and selfless."

Deadpool: ***Wow professor Four Eyes, what did you just say? I fell asleep while you were talking.***

Young Author: Deadpool, let me explain. At the beginning of the movie, you're protecting the innocent by intimidating Jeremy the stalker. Clearly, you fight evil in the world by taking on Ajax and his evil friends. Your mission involves shutting down stalkers and the Weapon X project, while also protecting those who might be future guinea pigs.

Deadpool: ***His name isn't Ajax—it's Francis. Can't you read a dry cleaning label? You also forget that I protect unicorns. Unicorns are my special friends.***

Old Author: Yes, I can read. What you do with unicorns is your own business.

Young Author: Vanessa is another example: her kidnapping by Ajax is not of her own choosing. She's just being used as an innocent pawn.

Deadpool: ***His name is Francis! Do I have to spell it out for you? Did you seriously make Tom Hanks over here buy that textbook for your class? Do your students actually learn anything useful? I really hope unicorns exist in your world because there is no way that this school voluntarily pays you for teaching this crap.***

Old Author: Yes, this school pays me for teaching and it isn't crap. If you would listen, maybe the great Deadpool might learn something.

Deadpool: ***Doubtful . . . I think I might learn more by having a unicorn entertain me for a few minutes.***

The Powers of Deadpool

Young Author: [*takes deep breath while still taking notes*] I see that Deadpool has a mission and he certainly has superpowers, which is the second requirement for a superhero.

Deadpool: ***Woooohooooo, I have two out of the three!***

Young Author: He possesses enhanced reflexes, and an almost god-like healing factor, not to mention his extensive skill in combat and marksmanship. He does seem to make fun of his powers throughout the movie. For example, when he is on the bridge fighting Francis's henchmen, he makes light of his expertise as a sharpshooter. He does a countdown from twelve bullets to his last one. He misses several times at the cycle rider during his countdown. When he is down to his last four bullets, he is shot by one of the henchmen, "right up Main Street." He kills the henchman, but he is mad that he was shot. He proceeds to then fire bullets three and two into the dead man. He then says, "STUPID. Worth it." An expert sharpshooter would not waste bullets like that, but Deadpool would. In this way, he is subverting the notion that superheroes always do the wise thing.

Deadpool: ***You would think it was worth it too if someone just shot you in the ass.***

Old Author: Are there any more examples you can think of?

Young Author: There's the scene where Deadpool tries to take down Colossus by pounding on him. He then proceeds to break both hands and his legs. His healing power is of no use against Colossus.

Colossus: Colossus tougher than Siberian winter. Deadpool not even make scratch on me.

Deadpool: ***Chris the wonder student, I'm glad you managed to find my Marvel wiki page . . . if you***

ask me, my real mission is to open up a Mexican food truck with Morena Baccarin. She's one tasty chimichanga. Not that I judge chimichangas by their looks or taste.

Old Author: Deadpool's healing powers make it virtually impossible for someone to kill him. Ajax comments on this in the climactic fight scene when he says, "You grow back body parts now, Wade? When I'm finished, parts'll have to grow back you."

Deadpool: ***Yeah, you can cut off my hand, but I will just grow it back. My hand might be small for a while, but it will grow back big.***

Does a Red Suit Make You Santa Claus or Deadpool?

Young Author: It would be hard for anyone to mistake you for him. Your costume is pretty distinctive.

Deadpool: ***It took a long time to make that costume, at least two whole scenes in the movie focused on it.***

Old Author: Well, that is the third characteristic of a superhero. You have to have an identity.

Young Author: Deadpool does have a very clear identity. Coogan says that the identity convention "is the clearest marker of a superhero." Identity is composed by having a code name and a costume.

Deadpool: ***Oooooo, I have both of those. I know the answers, professor! Can I get extra credit?***

Old Author: This isn't a quiz and I doubt that you know the answer. I bet Chris does though.

Young Author: I do. Wade Wilson decides that his name is going to be "Deadpool" based upon the dead pool list at St. Margaret's bar where he likes to hang out with Weasel. The dead pool on the chalkboard lists the people most likely to be killed and what the betting odds on them dying are. He also criticizes superhero code names when he first meets Negasonic Teenage Warhead. When he asks her who she is, she responds with her name. He then says sarcastically, "Negasonic Teenage . . . What the shit? That's the coolest name ever!" He even offers to trade names, but, of course, we know that can't work because the code name wouldn't fit him.

NEGASONIC: I think I had a better name for him, "Douchepool." He can have that one. It fits better than his costume does.

DEADPOOL: ***That's really weird for an angsty teenager to say. Oh, it's not? I'm shocked, SHOCKED, I tell you.***

YOUNG AUTHOR: He also has a pretty cool costume that reinforces his identity. The red and black uniform keeps his face hidden from everyone, especially Vanessa, and the blood from showing. Given how many times Deadpool is shot in the movie, that's pretty important. When Deadpool gets shot through the arm in the highway bridge scene, the movie viewer can't see the blood, as it is camouflaged by his suit.

DEADPOOL: ***It also cuts down on the dry cleaning bills.***

YOUNG AUTHOR: The distinctive costume separates Deadpool from the other people in the movie. The other superheroes in the film, Negasonic Teenage Warhead and Colossus, each have their own unique costume, too. The costumes represent who they are.

DEADPOOL: ***Does anyone know who they really are? Does it matter?***

OLD AUTHOR: My gosh, you just stated some of the most profound questions in philosophy. I am impressed.

DEADPOOL: ***REALLY? You think I'm profound?***

OLD AUTHOR: No, not really, I was just mocking you like how you mock society throughout the movie.

YOUNG AUTHOR: So, we can define Deadpool as a superhero even though he constantly makes fun of superheroes in the movie. In the beginning credits, a trading card of Green Lantern from the movie starring Ryan Reynolds is shown. Given how awful the reviews were for that film, the creators of the *Deadpool* movie must have been poking fun at the star. Deadpool also remarks in the movie how he looks like he was bitten by a radioactive shar-pei. If that's not making fun of a certain web-slinging superhero, I don't know what is.

DEADPOOL: ***Wow, I am impressed with myself. I am soooooooooo smart and sarcastic.***

Refrigerators and Women

OLD AUTHOR: Well, you should be. Not only do you subvert the notion of a superhero, but you also subvert many of the conventions in the superhero genre. For example, when you're being dragged off by Colossus to the X-mansion to talk to Professor Xavier, you ask, "McAvoy or Stewart?" referring to the two different actors who have played the professor in the X-men film series. This subverts the whole superhero genre by mocking the popularity of the movies even though the timelines in the movies are different.

DEADPOOL: ***Conventions like political conventions?***

COLOSSUS: Deadpool confuse me when he said "McAvoy", who is this person?

DEADPOOL: ***Don't worry borscht-brain, it is not important for you to know.***

YOUNG AUTHOR: No, a convention is how something is usually portrayed in media or society. Another word for it is trope. One of the main tropes that is subversively undermined in your movie is the role of women in the superhero genre. Traditionally, women in the superhero genre are used as plot devices. They usually get themselves into trouble and then have to be rescued. This trope is called, "Damsel in Distress."

The earliest example of this trope in the superhero genre was Lois Lane. Lois Lane was constantly in danger so that Superman could rescue her. Women who fall into this trope generally are underdeveloped as characters with the only redeeming quality being how attractive they are. On numerous occasions, the damsel in distress dies so that the male character can suffer, reflect, and change for the greater good. This phenomenon was so prevalent in the superhero comic books that famed comic book author Gail Simone developed a list of female superhero comic book characters who died as a plot device. She entitled the webpage "Women in Refrigerators" based on a famous comic book where Green Lantern comes home from a long day of superhero-ing and finds that one of his evil foes has killed his girlfriend and stuffed her into his refrigerator.

DEADPOOL: ***Ugh, who would want to come home to that frozen dinner?***

VANESSA: Not me. I am too salty for that kind of treatment.

OLD AUTHOR: The movie consistently calls out notions of women being damsels in distress. Vanessa is a shining example of how the movie undercuts this trope.

DEADPOOL: ***Old Man Rivers here has a point.***

OLD AUTHOR: Early in the movie when Vanessa is in the bar, she's flirting with Wade when another merc casually slaps her on the ass and says, "I'd hit that." Wade starts to intervene to protect her but before he can act, she grabs the mercenary by the balls. She makes "Fat Gandalf" say the magic words. This demonstrates that she needs nobody to rescue her. She's confident in herself and takes no grief.

DEADPOOL: ***That's my girl!***

VANESSA: I am nobody's property. You don't own me. You can rent me, but you don't own me. Remember when I said "Hands off the merchandise"? I meant it then and I mean it now. I do like your hands though.

DEADPOOL: ***Did you see her at the end of the film? She was terrific. I was sitting there with a knife in my head courtesy of Francis when she skewers him with my katana. I guess you can say she's the Megara to my Hercules. Or wait . . . is it the other way around? I don't know, either way, I look good.***

VANESSA: [*smiles sexily*] Ya, you're as delicious looking as that strawberry-flavored wedding ring you gave me. You smell better too.

YOUNG AUTHOR: Yeah, Vanessa looked good.

VANESSA: Unbelievable, a young college student finds me attractive.

YOUNG AUTHOR: I didn't mean physically, I meant as a character. Oops [*stammering*], I do find you attractive but you are more than just a body.

DEADPOOL: ***Oh, you bet she's more than just a body. Her crazy matches my crazy.***

YOUNG AUTHOR: If you compare Vanessa to some other famous damsels in distress in the superhero genre, you can see how good, I mean how favorably, she compares to other damsels. Two famous examples of damsels in distress are the love interests of Peter Parker, a.k.a. Spider-Man. Both of his girlfriends, Mary Jane Watson and Gwen Stacy, are damsels in distress. In the Spider-Man trilogy, Mary Jane is captured by each of the villains in each of the movies in order for Spider-Man (Tobey Maguire) to rescue her.

The director, Sam Raimi, tried to compensate for Mary Jane's lack of character by allowing her to save Spider-Man when she throws a cinder block at Venom. This was a step in the right direction for her character, but not a major change. If Mary Jane had more moments like this, she would eventually become more of a distinct, likeable character rather than just a generic romantic interest for the superhero. The fact that she's captured over the course of the whole trilogy makes her look weak and helpless. You'd think after the first movie the writers would make her a little smarter, instead of this ditzy girl who relies on Spider-Man to come to her rescue. There needs to be an equal balance because sometimes men need saving, too.

DEADPOOL: ***WOW, did you take a breath while you just said that? I felt like I was back in Francis's oxygen deprivation tank o' fun and horrors.***

YOUNG AUTHOR: Well, if you liked that, the other example is also from the comic books of Spider-Man. Gwen Stacy for a time was Peter Parker's girlfriend. Gerry Conway and Gil Kane in 1973 created a two-issue story arc called, "The Night Gwen Stacy Died." It is one of the most popular Spider-Man arcs in history. The premise of the story is that Gwen Stacy is kidnapped by the Green Goblin. The kidnapping forces Spider-Man to come to her rescue. As the two begin to fight, she's thrown off the bridge and Spider-Man shoots a web to save her, but as he pulls her up, he realizes her neck is broken.

Whether the fall or the web broke her neck is never revealed. Gwen Stacy is portrayed to be the generic romantic interest of Spider-Man and a helpless side-character who cannot take care of herself. However, in the *Amazing Spider-Man* movies, Gwen

Stacy is initially portrayed as a beautiful, smart blonde who is the valedictorian of her class and works for one of the most prestigious companies in New York, Oscorp. You'd think the writers would take this strong character and make more use of her, but in the movie she ends up with the same fate; she's a damsel in distress. Even though the movie had the opportunity to update the character, the story remains the same.

DEADPOOL: ***WOW, you didn't come up for oxygen that time either. But, I don't understand. Gwen didn't die in a refrigerator. She died because Spider-Man snapped her neck.***

VANESSA: [*slapping Deadpool's ass*] Wade, Women in Refrigerators is a metaphor. Don't be so literal.

Unplugging the Refrigerator, Deadpool Style

DEADPOOL: ***Women do have it rough in the superhero genre. Am I better than that?***

OLD AUTHOR: Actually, the movie does a great job of portraying women in a positive light and with respect.

DEADPOOL: ***Why shouldn't they be treated with respect? Did you see the way Negasonic tore up that battlefield? All that angsty emotion bottled up inside of her caused her to explode! Hehe get it? Explode! Oooooo, I also remember that Angel Dust kicked Colossus's butt and he had to be rescued by Negasonic.***

COLOSSUS: Was me being polite; not proper to hit a woman.

DEADPOOL: ***I hear what you are saying even if it is in broken English. You're saying that if it's a woman and she's trying to kill you, you can't fight back. Hmmmm, chivalrous but really, really f*%@ing stupid.***

Didn't you learn anything from my earlier fight scene when I was hunting down Francis by going after his underlings? Two of them happened to be women and I was all confused

about if fighting them was sexist, but in the end I had a moment of clarity and killed them regardless of their gender. It's a simple rule. Be they man, woman, or unicorn, if they try to kill you, they die.

Colossus: Da, me like simple rules. Life easier.

Old Author: Simple rules may make life easier but they don't always apply to different situations. I bet you treat Negasonic different than Angel Dust.

Colossus: Girls different. One is young and needs guidance. Other older and wiser.

Young Author: And the older one does a great superhero landing.

Deadpool: ***Yes, just like Iron Man.***

Old Author: Seems to me that you're making fun of the superhero genre again, but you're also signaling that women can be super, too.

Deadpool: ***Did you listen when I said that superhero leap was hard on the knees? Well, given the tone of my voice, you could come to that conclusion.***

Young Author: The women in the movie also don't act like stereotypical women in the superhero genre. Negasonic Teenage Warhead isn't wearing a skimpy outfit and her haircut is very short. Another example is in the fight scene between Colossus and Angel Dust. Angel has a wardrobe malfunction and her breast is exposed. Colossus treats her as a woman instead of a foe. Colossus averts his eyes from her exposed breast and allows her to fix her costume. By gender-stereotyping Angel as a woman who would be concerned with her appearance, Colossus leaves himself wide open to not only criticism for being sexist, but also to a punch to the groin.

Colossus: Da, hurt bad.

Deadpool: ***Yeah, Colossus should have learned his lesson from the beginning of the fight when he tries to handcuff Angel and she punches his lights out. Fortunately, I brought Negasonic and I rely on her to fight Angel.***

Negasonic: Need I remind you that Douchepool was the one who came to the mansion asking for my help? I am no damsel in distress. I am more like a damsel to the rescue.

Deadpool: ***Now, if I could just get her to stop tweeting during fights.***

Young Author: I liked it when you told Negasonic to "go ahead and finish your tweet" before engaging in that fight. That was a much-understated criticism of the prevalence of social media in our world. Kids my age are preoccupied with social media.

Old Author: Yes, if my classroom is any indication, teens like being online.

Deadpool: ***Of course, if you would teach something useful, then they might pay more attention.***

Old Author: I do teach useful things. I teach my students how to examine the world. I just use superheroes as a vehicle to do it.

Deadpool: ***I guess you don't talk about me then because I ain't a hero.***

Young Author: Ugggh, we already had this discussion. You are a superhero whether you view yourself as one or not.

The Male Gaze of Deadpool

Deadpool: ***So, since you view me as a superhero and I don't, does that mean that different people view the world differently?***

Old Author: Yes, you are different and yes, different people view the world differently. I view the world one way; Colossus views the world another way; Chris views the world one way; Vanessa views the world another way; Negasonic views the world a different way. We all have different lenses to view the world.

Deadpool: ***Vanessa views me as a luscious piece of manhood and I like it.***

Vanessa: Yeah, you're a real filet mignon.

Young Author: Funny you should say that because one of the concepts that we learned in the superhero class is called the "Male

Gaze." Laura Mulvey posits that the movie industry sets up the male as the protagonist and the vast majority of the movie is seen through the eyes of the males in the movie.

Old Author: It also goes beyond that to include how the camera lenses follow the action and what the camera emphasizes.

Deadpool: ***So, I have some voyeuristic people following me around? That is weird . . . and kinky. Wait, you all didn't see what I did with the unicorn did you?***

Young Author: Actually, it's not that weird for you because you know the audience is there. Remember how you break the fourth wall and speak to the audience?

Deadpool: ***Oh, right, like when I killed all those people on the highway and said, "You're probably thinking, 'My boyfriend said this was a superhero movie, but this guy in the red suit just turned that other guy into a fucking kebab.' Well, I may be super, but I am no hero. And yeah, technically, this is a murder. But some of the best love stories start with a murder. And that's exactly what this is. A love story. And to tell it right, I gotta take you back to way before I squeezed this ass into red spandex."***

Young Author: Exactly, the camera focuses in on your butt. Normally, if a typical "male gaze" were being utilized, the camera wouldn't focus on your ass, but because you are a different type of hero, the camera lingers on that shot.

Vanessa: If I were the director, I would linger on that shot, too.

Old Author: Exactly, Deadpool, you know you're being watched not just by Vanessa, but also the audience. You break the fourth wall a bunch of other times, too. The point though is that the camera follows you around and has a certain viewpoint. Traditionally, the viewpoint privileges the male viewer. The camera focuses on objects from a male perspective. Women are seen merely as eye candy that are bereft of personality or agency.

Deadpool: ***So, how does my movie subvert this male gaze?***

Young Author: There are several examples of this subversion. In the Calendar Girl scene, the scene starts out focused on you and Vanessa warming fuzzies during various holidays.

Deadpool: ***I lasted the whole year. Hehehe.***

Vanessa: No, honey, *I* lasted the whole year. But you did your best, Champ.

Deadpool: ***You know, sometimes I like the unicorn better . . .***

Young Author: If the movie employed a traditional male gaze, the whole scene would have focused on your gratification and been shot from your viewpoint. However, the scene provides equal screen-time of her on top and you on top.

Vanessa: I love holidays. International Women's day is the best.

Deadpool: ***It was definitely interesting.***

Vanessa: Yeah, it was fun.

Deadpool: ***I didn't say it was fun, I said "interesting."***

Old Author: It was interesting because you were not in the dominant position and because the camera angle was over Vanessa's shoulder. It was from her viewpoint. Clearly, this is not typical of a superhero–love story type of movie. This scene underscores that you both have agency and control in the relationship.

Vanessa: Is this male gaze common in the superhero genre?

Young Author: Yes it is. If you've ever read a comic book that featured a female superhero, you would notice that much of the artwork is done to titillate the male readers. This practice is so common that there has been an interesting cultural response to it called the Hawkeye Initiative. The Hawkeye Initiative takes pictures of females from the superhero genre and replaces the women with a similarly posed picture of the male superhero, Hawkeye. The founder of the initiative says that if the posed picture of Hawkeye does not look silly or unrealistic, then the picture is not sexist. However, if the picture does look dumb then that reinforces how sexist the superhero genre can be. If you go visit their website, you can see how silly some of the pictures are.

Young Author: Deadpool also subverts the male gaze in the scene where he and Vanessa are playing skeeball.

Vanessa: Yeah, I complained about him loving skeeball more than he loves vagina.

Deadpool: ***I love putting balls in holes.***

Vanessa: That doesn't even make *sense*, hun.

Young Author: But, Deadpool also says that, "I just want to get to know the real you. Not the short, two-dimensional sex object peddled by Hollywood." This line demonstrably shows that he is subverting the male gaze and how it operates in Hollywood blockbusters.

Deadpool: ***Am I subversive any other times? I am beginning to like this part of me, but of course, I always liked every part of myself, especially when I have a small hand to make things look bigger.***

Old Author: There is another example at the end of the movie when Vanessa takes off your mask.

Vanessa: That's hard to forget. Who would have thought that a mask of Hugh Jackman would be so hideous?

Old Author: Deadpool is delicately commenting on Hollywood's obsession with good-looking male actors. He knows that there is excessive focus by filmmakers on physical attractiveness. It's not just filmmakers but everyone involved in media.

Deadpool: ***I mean, who would ever buy a newspaper or a magazine that featured the World's Sexiest Man? I wouldn't but then again, I am also God's perfect idiot.***

Old Author: There are many other examples of using a non-male gaze in the movie. Like when Deadpool forces the audience to contemplate how smooth Wolverine's balls are, visually tea-bagging a villain, and when the camera focuses on his crotch when he goes from the back seat of the cab to the front seat.

Deadpool: ***I love balls.***

Vanessa: Honey, we know.

YOUNG AUTHOR: Seriously Deadpool, you really do make us consider how we view the world and whether one should employ a male gaze. You are my hero. Can I please have your autograph?

DEADPOOL: ***No.***

OLD AUTHOR: Sorry everyone, whether you are real or not, I need all of you to go away. My office hour is up and I need to grade some papers.

YOUNG AUTHOR: Thanks for discussing how Deadpool undermines tropes in the superhero genre. I really learned a lot today. This is going to help my term paper a lot.

DEADPOOL: ***The only thing that will help your term paper is an envelope with lots of small, unmarked bills presented anonymously to the prof here.***

OLD AUTHOR: I learned a lot, too. Everyone, there is lots more we can talk about next time if you would like.

VANESSA: Nope, I'm good. I'm ready for some more balls in holes.

DEADPOOL: ***I thought you said that didn't make sense.***

VANESSA: We'll *make* it make sense . . .

COLOSSUS: Next time, we talk about what good person I am, yes? Deadpool needs someone to view as hero. I am good hero.

DEADPOOL: ***Hmmmm, I think I would rather have Francis experiment on me again. Pass.***

OLD AUTHOR: Wade, if I can say one thing to you, it would be this statement: Although you may be crass and dirty, the way that you point out the flaws of the superhero genre and the way you respect women is insightful. People need to take a closer look at you. By your example, you are a great teacher. If anyone deserves to wear a tweed jacket and smoke a pipe, it is you. You're my superhero.

V

Really? Was That Necessary?

Why We Would Like to Apologize to Mr. Reynolds, Who Really Is Trying the Best He Can, We're Sure

18
Thus Slaughtered Deadpool

NICOL SMITH IS A DEAD-MAN-WRITING

Wade "Deadpool" Wilson is an @##hole. A major one with a mind so warped and shattered that it proves fatal to powerful telepaths such as Professor X. His moral compass also seems so messed up that a sane person could get lost in a broom closet if they were to rely on it.

Deadpool has done some $^!%%* things (as you will see) and is definitely not the guy you take home to meet the parents. Funny and entertaining, yes, but not a nice or good guy by our everyday concepts or standards. He has literally killed and maimed thousands of humans, sub-humans (*cough! Clowns), aliens, mutants, and zombies. Then there is also his singular slaughter of the Marvel universe as well as multiple versions of himself. And the less said about poor Blind Al and The Box, the better.

This is literally a man who does what he thinks best and screw the consequences. In *Deadpool's Art of War* he started a war between Loki's forces and the superheroes of Earth so that he could write his own adaptation of "Art of War" for an. ACTUAL. war. This is also a guy who not only fought zombies in the *Night of the Living Deadpool* and *Return of the Night of the Living Deadpool* sagas but also sacrificed himself when he ended up being the cause of a weird zombie Deadpool plague.

He also came very close to single-handedly stopping the Skrull invasion during the *Secret War* saga by infiltrating and pledging allegiance to the Skrulls. After being cloned numerous times, he then trained all of these clones to be just as volatile and unpredictable as himself before he let them loose on the Skrull army. True, he failed to steal vital Skrull information for Nick Fury but we still had the pleasure of seeing a bunch of Skrullpools slaughtering a bunch of Skull-cloned heroes and villains.

Now what are we to make of all this? Should we call Deadpool a villain or a hero? According to his own continuous lament, he is most definitely not a hero—well, not in the traditional sense anyway. I do not, however, agree with the "anti-hero" label that is usually attached to Deadpool as it simply does not do our good ol' merc-with-a-mouth justice. Instead I want to call him something much more cool sounding: *Übermensch*: The Man who is Beyond Good and Evil! Or 'Overman' could also work, I guess. The German sounds a lot cooler though.

Intense Sounding German Word Explained (The Clever Bit of the Chapter)

So what is this "Übermensch" or Overman? Well, imagine your garden-variety super-powered megalomaniac with his typical spiel about being beyond the law and take away the super powers and fancy tights. Next, take the 'beyond the law' bit and along with a large helping of "being above morality"; juice it up. Juice it up a lot, throw in Weapon-X serum, Soldier-X Serum, the Green Goblin Serum, and have Mr. Sinister do some naughty things with it in his test tubes.

What should emerge then would be a character that would be considered the IDEAL man according to an *actual* madman in philosophy. The madman in question is none other than the German philosopher Friedrich Nietzsche (1844–1900) whose Burt-Reynolds-gone-wild-mustache would put Beast to shame. The source of his insanity is unknown. Some say it was due to syphilis but it could've just as easily have been a bad tuna sandwich or seeing Thanos naked, we simply don't know. What is known is that Nietzsche was not too keen on the moral constraints of ideas such as "good" and "evil" and thought that his "Overman" would be someone who had moved beyond plain old humanity and its moral constraints to become something vastly superior.

According to his epically-titled book *Thus Spoke Zarathustra: A Book for All and None* (1883), the Overman is a person who can be defined as a creative and even destructive force, whose character and actions can no longer judged by us mere mortals. He even goes so far to say that we (us poor plebs) suffer from a slave mentality of morality and are no better than monkeys compared to the Overman.

Keeping with bestializing our good character, he further compares us to sheep because, like sheep we tend to blindly follow the rules and ethical concepts such as "good" and "bad" that are placed in front of us by society, culture and religion. And keeping with the sheep motive, don't forget the symbolic importance of these herd creatures in Judea-Christianity. The Overman doesn't have time for Gods. In fact, God is actually dead according to Nietzsche and thus no religious restrictions in terms of morality or lifestyle can apply to the Overman either.

Unlike a dead deity, the Overman will go out of his way to help us poor sheep because we are weaker than him. We will most likely not understand what he's doing and might hate or fear him for it. Now, you might ask, how does this apply to Deadpool? Well, Deadpool does not exactly follow the herd (or flock in this case). Don't force me to make you page back to look at all the stuff he has already done, okay? It is pretty difficult to actually argue that Deadpool is even part of the herd. He'll be the sheep with mange that wears the bloody skin of the big bad wolf as a throw. So then he would not just have saved all the other sheep from the danger posed by the wolf, but he would have defied the shepherd that was supposed to be protecting and leading the flock.

You get the symbolism of that metaphor, right? God = shepherd. Sheep = people. Deadpool = freakin'awesome! = sheep in wolf clothing = Übermensch (Or "Sheepool"). Deadpool would have rebelled against God and therefore the rules and concepts of morality that comes from religion. This is pretty much in keeping with what the Overman is about according to Nietzsche. Buttttt Deadpool's situation differs from Niezsche's proclamation of God's death, because, let's be honest, Deadpool is not about to agree with any old dead philosophiles. God and the constraints that go with the deity's existence is still very active in Deadpool's panelled universe so Deadpool applies maximum effort to make God very dead.

Torpedoes, Mermaids, Dark Voices, and Lots of Violence. Sweet!

After many misadventures filled with over the top violence and sweetly-timed pop culture references that leave his opponents annoyed and baffled, Deadpool dies (this happens quite a lot in his earlier comics). Issue 34 of the 1999 run of the comic finds Deadpool resurrected in a laboratory that is secretly being run by Loki (Thor's less pretty but even more girly half-brother).

Deadpool's body seems to be unstable on a molecular level for some Marvel super science reason and when Deadpool naturally escapes his confines, he very stoically states that what has happened to him is okay as there is merely *a man at a typewriter* responsible for this. This is an O-M-G moment (literally) as Deadpool basically acknowledges the equivalent of God in the Marvel universe. He dares to actually allude to the fact that this 'man behind the typewriter' might be some divine creative source controlling all of the actions and existence of all the Marvel characters. This obviously refers to all the writers who actually write and create the Marvel comics. And not me. Yes, I am a man and I am sitting behind a keyboard . . . Keyboard, not a typewriter . . . Okay, this is getting weird . . . I'm not responsible, okay? Deadpool means that writers of the Marvel comics are basically the divine creators or progenitors of this universe.

Deadpool knows the truth about the man behind the typewriter and he starts questioning what it means to be trapped in a world that is ruled, bent, and manipulated for the sake of entertainment by a "god" behind a typewriter. Even worse, he realises that the characters in the Marvel universe suffered from sheep or slave morality in that they were mostly unaware that they are simply comic-book characters created and manipulated for the entertainment and financial gain of the comic book writers who can be interpreted as the creators or Gods of the universe.

They still lived according to the rules imposed by the comic-book writers and simply play their little parts. Even if they were aware of their divine manipulation, they don't seem to really care. Pretty much like a slave would seldom care for thoughts and doings of his or her master or a sheep about what goes on in a shepherd's head.

Like Nietzsche's Overman, who is no longer bound by the rules and morals of society or even God, Deadpool takes it upon himself to do what he thinks is right and in the pages of *Deadpool Kills the Marvel Universe* we're suddenly faced with a Deadpool who has taken on the form of a savior.

A freakin' scary saviour of death and ultimate liberty. He is no longer your normal, zany, Ryan-Reynolds-masturbating-the-horn-of-a-unicorn kind of Deadpool. This is a dark story of a man who has always been self-aware but when this self-awareness is no longer kept in check by his own madness and the humorous voices in his head, he becomes a man who wants to save all the heroes and villains in the world from being pawns to the man behind the typewriter's will since they could all simply be killed, resurrected or changed as the writers saw fit. Deadpool was also aware that the Marvel characters would simply not have understood him (they never understood his fourth-wall-breaking comments) and so the single dark voice that replaced his other voices instructed Deadpool that the only way to save all these characters is to lure the writers to him by killing all of their characters.

So Deadpool goes and kills them all: Avengers, Fantastic Four, X-Men, Spiderman, Punisher, and Hulk, all of them. Each of these characters is iconic and representative of the Marvel universe. So, like an Overman will go about making religious and controlling types (the representatives of our world) seem ridiculous for what they believe through some pretty sharp argumentation, Deadpool uses sharp blades to change the Marvelverse. Even cosmic heavy-hitters like Thanos, Kang, Silver Surfer and Galactus don't escape Deadpool's rampage.

He's pursued by Taskmaster (an old on-off "frienemy") who takes it upon himself to stop Deadpool. When Taskmaster finally catches up with Deadpool, they fight and the excessive emotions in the air (mostly Taskmaster nearly sh!tt!ng himself) draws the Man-Thing to them. Taskmaster is burned to crisp because of Man-Thing's touch, since he experienced severe fear and shock when his mimicry ability allowed him to look into the mind of Deadpool. Apart from possessing the ability to incinerate anyone who knows fear, Man-Thing is also the guardian of realms and once he understands Deadpool's quest, he sacrifices himself to allow Deadpool access to the Marvel multiverse so that he can kill all the heroes in existence.

Deadpool really does try to kill (save) every superhero and villain in existence. *Deadpool Killustrated* opens with a weary Deadpool sitting in a room full of slain super humans. Nietzsche never said that the Overman's way of life would be easy and this gory scene with its bloodied hero memorabilia and corpses lying around is testimony to that. Whilst in a contemplative dialogue with the dark voice in his head, Deadpool comes to the realization that the only way to save these heroes and himself from simply being brought back or resurrected through another story arc is to kill the sources that served as the original inspiration for these heroes and villains.

If the creators of these Marvel characters had not been exposed to classic literary characters such as Tom Sawyer, Moby-Dick, Dracula, and Don Quixote, then these heroes would never have been brought into creation. If you really want to get all deep and metaphorical about it (PS: girls love that sh!t) then this could be seen as the equivalent of the Overman breaking down religious and moral beliefs before the next generation can be sullied by their influence.

Deadpool therefore heads off into a multi-dimensional plane called the *Ideaverse* that allows him the needed access to host a maiming and killing workshop on the four aforementioned classic characters as well as countless others. He also implants the murderous voice or part of his psyche into the Frankenstein Monster and with the extra pair of willing hands, he is nearly unstoppable in his killing spree and so the power of the Overpool spreads. BHWAHAHAHA.

It's rather disturbing to see Deadpool kill all these beloved characters and at the same time quite amusing to see the Little Mermaid being killed by a torpedo that has Captain Nemo strapped to it. With each killing it's revealed to Deadpool which Marvel character was inspired by the slain character. Apparently The Submariner was inspired by the Little Mermaid and The Vision by Pinocchio. Like the boy with permanent wood and the fishy smelling girl, both The Submariner and The Vison struggle with the notion of humanity. Go figure.

Anyway, I am here writing about Marvel characters, and this must obviously mean that Deadpool did not succeed. He is in fact brought low by the original super sleuth Sherlock Holmes who assembled some other classic heroes to aid him in stopping Deadpool. With the help of Beowulf, Natty Bumppo, Hua Mulan, and faithful old Dr. Watson, Holmes battles Deadpool and his embodied evil voice. The battle ends up in the core of the Ideaverse where Holmes allows Deadpool to fall from H.G Wells's Time Machine into the eternity that is the Ideaverse. Deadpool believes he has won as he had killed all those legendary characters and is content to float about the vastness of the Ideaverse until it implodes and leaves us without fictional heroes.

With the Ideaverse not imploding, Deadpool realises that he has failed in his quest and then decides that the only way for him to call out the man behind the typewriter, is to kill all Deadpools. Now, let's watch as the strained metaphor is wrestled from its natural habitat by a guy who is a little obsessed with comic books and philosophy. Gasp as you are made to believe that this poor strained metaphor applies to the Overman having to overcome his own human morality and weak religious ideas.

According to DP's (stands for DeadPool and not some sexual thing you should not even be thinking about) reasoning if there is no Deadpool, there is no Marvel universe and then the man behind the typewriter will have to show himself. Since only Deadpool is truly aware of the state of the multiverse and the truth about the existence of the Marvel characters; the massacre of all Deadpools would lead to an end of the Marvelverse which should be sufficient to lure out the writer-type-god person. I'll grant that this reasoning is very strained but just bear with it, okay? It's only a comic book after all. I doubt that the man behind that particular typewriter has had any real metaphysics or quantum theory training. This is the plot for *Deadpool Kills Deadpool* and it's a squishy gore-fest of Deadpool on Deadpool action, concluding with one Deadpool killing the one that started this whole bloody beautiful mess.

Judgment? What Judgment?

So much killing happened and yet not once did I refer to Deadpool as evil or bad—even when those pesky comic-book writers provided me with plenty of reasons when he killed the characters of *The Jungle Book* (don't ask, okay? Just don't). Then why would I still not consider Deadpool as bad? Well, remember that terms like "good" or "bad" are banal concepts used by us sheep-like mortals who suffer from a slave morality and mentality.

Like Nietzsche's Overman, he firstly questioned the world around him and found it inexcusable that heroes and villains were blissfully unaware of their fate. He then took it upon himself to save them by daring the creators of the Marvelverse to show themselves so that he could kill them. This would've meant tearing the whole universe down around him and thus killing everyone in the Marvelverse. Yes, even the ones who don't need to breathe in space. You still need physical space to exist in. Even if it is made up physical space. Just go ask the Internet if you don't believe me.

Deadpool's acts of killing moved beyond right or wrong as the very concepts of right and wrong were created for and by the slave morality of the fake world he found himself in. How, then, can one really say that something is good or bad when the very source of these concepts itself seems corrupt? Deadpool figured out the truth; he decided to create his own standards and morality since, like the (or as the) Overman, he was now free to do so. This is some deep sh*t, right?

"But hang on . . .", you might say if you're one of those clever types who is able to tie his own shoes without assistance, "but Deadpool tried to save them all! Is that not what heroes do?" Well, firstly, whoop-dee-*#@king-doo for you if you asked that. Your accent is weird and your pets don't really love you. Secondly, yes, you are right. That is what heroes do. BUT traditional heroes (or at least our conception of heroes) tend to follow certain ideals which are viewed as good or desirable in our society. Our merc-with-a-mouth has given the finger to society's as well as Colossus's standards of heroism (movie reference! Yay!).

Like the Übermensch, Deadpool does not care about what others think of him as he acts and changes the world as he sees fit without bothering about whether the actions could be considered good or evil. He does not bend to the rules and restrictions of society or being a superhero. The Deadpool movie is testimony to that as he killed numerous people just to save the woman he loves and disprove all notions of heroism that were being pushed on him.

Our friendly neighborhood Pool guy is no ordinary comic-book character as he does not blindly (and tediously) follow some heroic code or do what is expected of him. He is more than a hero or villain; he is force of fate that forges his own way. Sure, it is his name that appears on the comic book but unlike all the boring A-listers such as the X-Men, Avengers, and Fantastic Four, Deadpool has not only saved (and shortened) lots of lives but has also juggled with the fate of the entire world and Marvel Universe more than once. The difference is that Wade actually saved and destroyed it as he saw fit.

Hidden Marvel Trailer

Deadpool is not simply a *hero all too hero* but is actually *beyond good and evil*. If you want to know what I'm hinting at in the italicized phrases, go read something other than just Deadpool comics you heathen! Look at the References at the back of this volume, and read some Nietzsche.

If you don't, my "unicorn session" tonight will be a very sad one. No one wants that. Trust me.

19
Deadpool Can't Know Fear

LOUIS MELANÇON AND DEADPOOL'S BESTEST-BEST FRIEND, ~~DAREDEVIL!~~ ***DEADPOOL***

As I look through the racks of my local comic shop, it's pretty apparent that Marvel has a labeling problem. Specifically, they claim Daredevil is "The Man without Fear." But really shouldn't Deadpool have that title? I'll admit "The Man without Good Personal Hygiene" wouldn't sell many books, but let me ask this: what's so great about Daredevil anyway?

Well, he's mysterious.

So was that pita I just bought from an unmarked, but I hope licensed, food truck. That doesn't make the pita fearless.

No, it makes you crazy for eating it. Daredevil is also handsome.

Not sure what that has to do with not having fear. Also, why are you interjecting in this chapter?

Oh, and abs. He has all the abs. ALL OF THEM, KATIE! And I'm interjecting because I can.

I have no response to that.

Most people don't. He's also very courageous.

Ah, there we go; that's the crux of the matter. It's not that Daredevil lacks fear as Marvel claims, it's that he has plenty of courage. He overcomes that fear. Anyone of those rainy nights that he leaps off a roof onto a slick fire escape he could slip and BAM! That pretty face gets smashed open and teeth go flying.

DON'T YOU DARE!

First, it's a hypothetical so relax. Second, please stop interrupting. Daredevil will jump every time because he's courageous. Again and again he makes these leaps in spite of the danger. Daredevil doesn't lack fear; he overcomes it. That's what makes him a hero. That's significantly different from being without fear. You know who doesn't have fear? That's a rhetorical question, go check out the front cover.

We all know who you mean; you're not being clever.

Deadpool doesn't have a problem with fear because he can't actually experience it. That regeneration capability of his means that while he can experience pain he knows it's only temporary. Temporary pain doesn't translate into fear of permanent injury or death. A leg gets chopped off, it'll grow back in a couple of shakes of a lamb's tail. Deadpool takes the same fire escape leap that Daredevil just took but misses, shatters his jaw, slips again, and plummets three stories onto a closed dumpster? You just hold onto that GrubHub delivery of chimichangas. All he'll need is a couple of minutes before he can dig in.

Deadpool doesn't know the fear of death or permanent injury. At first glance that seems pretty great, right? But like making a deal with Mephisto, there's always a catch. The fact is, it's something of a trap; this regeneration denies Deadpool the opportunity to overcome fear and be a hero. I know you want to think of him as a hero. He wants to think of himself as a hero. But he can't be, because a hero needs to overcome fear. For those that try and fight Deadpool, they wind up caught in a losing situation, trapped alongside him. That's generally unpleasant for all involved.

Except for the reader.

Being a Hero Is More than the Pose

Defining what makes a hero is kind of squishy. Lots of folks have put forward their definitions so we need to narrow this down to something we can use. Everyone agrees it's not as easy as just having a costume made out of spandex or unstable molecules. It's about the characteristics and actions of the person. Like Colossus pointed out, you don't "wake up a hero, brush your teeth a hero." What you do and how you act in certain specific moments are what matters.

Socrates (469–399 B.C.E.) defined courage this way: remaining steadfast in the face of danger and choosing anything, such as pain, permanent loss, or death above dishonor. Well, that's how Plato (427–348 B.C.E.) told us Socrates defined it. We'll take his word for it, and if it was good enough for Socrates, it'll be good enough for us: courage is a key aspect of being heroic, and courage is about acting in the face of fear.

Socrates was talking broadly about moral courage, but since we only have about ten pages, let's neck this thing down just a smidge. We're going to limit this discussion to just physical danger to match the potential of physical pain or death. Picture another veteran of the Weapon X program, Captain America, leading the Howling Commandos onto Omaha Beach on D-Day. Or Cap charging headlong into a complex of Nazi machine gun bunkers to get at the Red Skull. Or Cap flinging himself into a crowd of Hydra goons.

Rule of three much? We get it. Move on.

Cap is always running into potential danger. It's like one of his favorite pastimes. But that shield can't be everywhere at once; it doesn't cover all of his body in all directions at all times. There's always that possibility that he catches a bullet in the noggin when he's looking the wrong way. But Cap overcomes that fear; he moves in-land from the beach head, he dives into that crowd of Hydra goons, and just generally whoops up on some dirty Nazis.

So we need to come to grips with what we mean by this idea of fear. I think it's pretty safe to say that different people fear different things. Maybe you have a fear of spiders, missing out, or

Sock Puppets.

AHHH! Don't do that! The person sitting next to you? Maybe a fear of clowns or flying. I'm going to make an assertion here that isn't all that bold. Everyone might have a different set of phobias, but we all have a common fear of being in a position where life is taken from us without the ability to respond or defend against the thing threatening our existence.

I'm not talking about instances where the response or defense is ineffective or a matter of surprise. I'm talking about a moment of existential danger where there is no response, where you're completely powerless and helpless but know it's coming. You didn't see that garbage truck until just as you stepped off the curb, but you can't get your legs to move fast enough and the driver can't stop in time. Or opening your bedroom door to find a hungry lion pride waiting for you because your Air BnB profile didn't specify "no animals." As Socrates pointed out, fear of death is simply thinking you know something when you don't.

Sure, lots of folks say they aren't afraid of dying. But most of the time it's thought about in terms where there is at least a chance to respond, or perform some active role in preventing the outcome. You took the chemo treatment, but there was no remission; you shoot your weapon at that approaching truck bomb using every last bullet but it simply doesn't slow down. You know you did your best. Those aren't the situations we're talking about here; we're talking about having no ability to respond. It's safe to say we all have that fear deep down. We can even apply that to super heroes and super villains even though death has a bit of a revolving door policy for them.

Talking about you Jean Grey!

But that doesn't mean they wouldn't experience this fear, the constant resurrections are really more an artifact of lazy writing.

Wow. Pot, you realize you're calling the kettle black?

Hey, hurtful. Deadpool is an exception to this fear. His regeneration powers prevent him from having this experience. Deadpool knows he can't die, regardless of whether he gets the chance to respond or defend himself. Death is his unrequited love, or at least a flirty tease he constantly hopes will send him that 3:00 A.M. "You up?" sext. But that message just never, ever arrives. Heck, even Wolverine got to die and hasn't come back.

Yet.

I think we all know that deep down. If Deadpool can't experience this fear, then can he actually demonstrate courage and be heroic? Well no, he can't. So what does that make him?

He's All about the Prefixes (Not that Bass)

Your first reaction might be to label Wade an "anti-hero." You wouldn't be alone or wrong in doing so. Randomly pick any page in this book and you've got better than even odds that the words anti-hero and Deadpool are on the same page and contextually related. It's not an entirely unwarranted description. He's got plenty of bad qualities: the lack of hygiene, the love of violence, the poor eating habits, and the abusive treatment of Hydra Bob . . .

WE GET IT, Emily Post. Move on!

Yet Deadpool isn't wholly morally ambiguous, a normal trait of anti-heroes. When the Inversion Event happened in *Avengers and X-Men: Axis,* Zenpool became Wade's dominant personality facet. But the shift wasn't quite as dramatic as what happened to Dr. Doom or Nightcrawler. Sure, Zenpool didn't outright kill bank robbers, but they were still stopped pretty violently. He continued to help out the FauX-Men he had previously rescued from North Korea, and continued to look after Ethan/Genesis. True, he got laid a bit less. But let's face it—until Shiklah came around that was a pretty rare event for ol' Wade Wilson regardless of what personality was in charge.

Even anti-heroes can experience this fear we're talking about, that powerless and helpless loss of existence. Sure, the Punisher grouchily claims he's ready to die once he runs out of targets, but he'd still feel a jolt of fear in the shower if he reaches for the conditioner and accidently pulls the pin on a grenade instead.

That's why grenades are only for the bath, they're like rubber duckies that explode.

Yet anti-heroes also get the chance to overcome that fear and act, however they want to act. Normally somewhat nastily. But Deadpool doesn't get that chance. He's more than just anti-heroic, he's post-heroic.

You're making that up.

Really I'm not. Post-heroic, in the broadest sense is about lessening the role of the individual. The context, the specific field, really refines the meaning. As an example in business, post-heroic management seeks to cultivate a sense of responsibility and ownership of both problems and solutions among employees at all levels within an organization rather than just within upper management.

Boring.

I know, right? But the term can also deal with violence and war.

Go on . . . You can't tell but I just raised an eyebrow in interest.

Edward Luttwak coined the term "post-heroic warfare" as a way to distinguish what appeared to be a new trend in warfare which was a big break from the previous couple hundred year's Napoleonic construct. Prior to Napoleon, entire battles could occur without shots being fired as the combatants maneuvered into advantageous positions. One side may see themselves as having in such a positional disadvantage that they would withdraw from the field with their forces intact rather than risk losing the battle. With Napoleon, as pointed out by dead Carl Clausewitz (1780–1831), war changed. Now entire societies were mobilized and committed to a grand struggle where the main objective was combat and the destruction of the enemy's will to fight. That was heroic warfare, a collective activity of killing and being killed on a grand scale.

Post-heroic warfare is something of a call back to that pre-Napoleonic behavior: rather than the grand gesture of mobilizing a society, more limited goals are sought. Limited goals require fewer means, think dollars and people, to conduct the war. That should be a good thing but there's a catch: societies not roused into the Clausewitzian bloodlust want and expect fewer casualties to match these limited goals and means. This is where technology comes into play.

The change in warfare that Luttwak was trying to identify was qualitatively different from the seventeenth century's aristocratic battlefield maneuvering. It's not just that guns were more accurate, or could shoot farther; Post-heroic warfare is characterized by the emergence of an unbridgeable gap between combatants. It's a pretty broad sweep, but we can say that from the dawn of time weapons technology has a goal of increasing lethality on the pointy end while decreasing user risk. But decreasing risk isn't eliminating risk. If your sword is longer, you can poke holes in your opponent before he can poke holes in you; unless he is faster or more skilled. There is still risk. You're piloting a World War I biplane flying over the trenches on the Western Front of World War I, the boys on the ground can shoot right back. There is still risk.

This changed in the back half of the twentieth century. With things like ballistic missiles, if you have them but your opponent doesn't you've eliminated the risk of retaliation. Moving into the now-ish, we see armed unmanned aerial vehicles, a.k.a. drones, on the scene. These fly through the air in one part of the world while the pilot sits in perfect safety in another part. This is post-heroic warfare on the personal level: the complete removal of risk from one of the combatants. This is that unbridgeable gap, the removal of personal risk that Luttwak identified.

I wouldn't say no to some ballistic missiles.

Technology is more than just some toy that Tony Stark whips up in his lab to impress chicks. It can be a skill or a process and Deadpool's healing factor is this type of technology. He can and has used it to accomplish tasks like killing someone or eating an unfortunate number of pancakes. The problem is that, like a ballistic missile or an armed drone, this technology of his separates opponents from truly threatening Deadpool by removing his personal risk.

Wait, am I getting ballistic missiles or not?

Admiral Akbar Knows the Deal

Not only does Deadpool's power prevent him from demonstrating courage, he winds up dragging others into this post-heroic condition alongside him. The lessening of the importance of the individual in this context is really about stripping away their ability to actually generate risk on the red-leather-clad wise ass. The potential for someone to make Deadpool actually test his courage is eliminated. They will never achieve their goal of actually killing him or even seriously injuring him. Sure, it's cathartic to beat the snot out of Wade, as Moon Knight enjoyed in "Killed, Not Dead." But does it actually accomplish anything?

It sells some books, Jacko.

Where armed drones are launching missiles, those on the ground have no opportunity to truly defend themselves. Even if they shoot down a drone there is only material loss; there is no risk to the drone's pilot. It merely delays the inevitable until a new drone is prepared and dispatched. There is more here than just the loss of risk from the attacker, there is actually a qualitative change in the risk the defender experiences.

As Christian Enemark pointed out, the attacks, the injury, and the death become inevitable. Without the potential of discouraging the attacker by testing his courage, not just destroying the attacking machines, there is no actual defense. That post-heroic lessening of the importance of the individual strikes again by removing the ability to stop or deflect the blows in anything but a symbolic way. This strips away the identity of defender, making them simply targets, not defenders. This is more than just lessening the role of the individual, it's also somewhat dehumanizing.

But they can still show their courage, right? Like by shooting down a drone?

But they have no positioning to change the situation. No matter how steadfast or stoic the defenders might be, they can't cause the attacker to change their behavior. That isn't so much demonstrating courage as impotent flailing.

Hehehe. Impotent.

Another machine will be sent, and another, and another. But the people on the explodey end can't change the conflict. They can only absorb the blows, because the machine has no courage to test and will be replaced by other machines, while the attacking pilot has no risk. At no point are the combatants testing each other's courage to preserve their lives. One is perfectly safe, while the other is perfectly at risk for injury or death—there's no room to change the context and make one party think about altering the interactions between these actors.

Well, maybe the drone pilot wants a nap or a trigger finger gets sprained?

Naps aside, this is an insidious situation. The technology sucks those who attack Deadpool into the post-heroic trap without the same technological benefit.

Well, except for Sabretooth.

It doesn't matter how many guns they shoot or how much explosive material they gather, without personal risk being present for both parties, the ability for either party to demonstrate courage is denied. They can't kill him; they can't make him suffer risk or actually test his courage and so aren't on the same footing when he lashes out. While Deadpool can't experience death, those fighting him definitely suffer.

You're making this pretty personal. Make it personal—like with an example.

Let's take a look at the big beef between Deadpool and ULTIMATUM. Agent Gorman, an ULTIMATUM mole in SHIELD, put out a huge contract on Deadpool's head. Every mercenary and hitman came to play: Pastepot Pete, Batroc, Crossbones, and the Daughters of the American Revolution just to name a few.

You don't eff with the DAR They don't play around. Everyone knows that.

Exactly. Crossbones wound up adrift in a hot air balloon basket in the air and lost at sea. By the time he got back to shore, the best he could do was get his face smashed in by Deadpool and taken into custody. He had no hope of actually killing Deadpool and collecting that sweet, sweet contract money.

The same thing happened with the entire ULTIMATUM organization. Flag-smasher, Gorman, and an inconceivable number of ULTIMATUM terrorists decided to take down Deadpool. They even brought a helicarrier to the fight. But it didn't matter how many missiles they launched, how many tanks they drove, they weren't going to be able to make Deadpool lose his courage because he can't experience the fear of death. All they were doing was placing themselves at the point where an indestructible foe could touch them. Spoiler alert: no one in ULTIMATUM is bullet proof or has a healing factor. Despite their attempts to inflict harm, there was no actual chance they would be able to accomplish their goal. They flailed angrily at the universe with no real chance of having an impact.

ULTIMATUM are clowns. The black berets, the white Member's Only jackets with popped collars and wrap around shades? 1986 called, it said to keep its crappy fashion.

True, they commit fashion crimes in addition to terrorism. But by fighting Deadpool and being pulled into the post-heroic trap it's questionable if we can even call them third rate villains. They're just numbers in an ever increasing body count without the ability to make Deadpool show and potentially lose courage. Just because the organization's name is the worst acronym should they really be slaughtered wholesale, like some lemmings in a Disney film?

Maybe.

Maybe Regeneration Isn't So Great

It sure seems like the post-heroic condition is not a great place be. Stingray has suggested that perhaps Deadpool isn't as crazy as he wants everyone to think he is; and there's a malaise that surfaced when Zenpool retreated. Could it be these are reflections of a niggling recognition by Deadpool that he'll never be a hero, regardless of what others think of him or even getting that coveted Avengers membership card? Not because of his personality flaws, but because his power robs him of the opportunity to demonstrate courage. But the problem goes beyond just Deadpool; every person or organization which opposes him gets sucked right into that post-heroic condition too. Without the benefit of the healing superpower, and the focus on Deadpool, they become powerless to change their conditions and really have a bit of their humanity stripped away as they just become targets or animals for slaughter. It doesn't seem to be great for Wade and isn't positive for anyone else. Maybe having a little bit of fear, and the ability to show courage and overcome it, might just be a better problem to have then not being able to die.

I don't know, it does give me extra time to watch more Daredevil and get some of those ballistic missiles you talked about earlier.

I give up.

20
Deadpool's Genocide of the Marvel Universe

WILLIAM R. LIVINGSTON AND
WADE P. DEADINGSTON

I didn't understand the phrase "the good, the bad, and the ugly" until I met Deadpool. After taking a peek behind the mask and seeing a face only a plastic surgeon could love, I had an epiphany.

As descriptors of someone's nature, "good" and "bad" are opposites. Good people will do good things and bad people will do bad things. As someone who's read Kurt Vonnegut's (1922–2007 C.E.) *Slaughterhouse-Five* would say: So it goes.

Ugliness, however, allows for complexity and Wade Wilson would have us believe he operates outside the bounds of dualistic morality. We tend to focus on actions rather than nature when making personal and moral judgments. Deadpool is an "anti-hero" because his actions are not motivated by a strong commitment to being a good person or a bad person (although my esteemed ***drinking companion*** colleague, Darian, disagrees in part). His choices are creative and based on achieving success rather than being anything. Deadpool reminds me that we can all be ugly in this respect. Most of us are fortunate enough to not have faces that look like an Etch-A-Sketch image made of rotting ground beef, though.

Let's take a look at one of the most heinous choices a person can make: committing genocide. A relatively new word in our legal and moral vocabularies, "genocide" is the combination of the Greek prefix *geno-* ("race" or "tribe") and the Latin word *caedere* ("to kill"). It was coined some time in 1943 by Raphael Lemkin, a Polish lawyer who lost most of his family during World War II, for his rather monotonous book, *Axis Rule in Occupied Europe*.

It's the kind of tome Deadpool would use to bludgeon Nazis to death. Take note, Axel Alonso, Editor-in-Chief of Marvel Comics, because I know you're reading this. Anyway, *Axis Rule* gave the world the word it needed. In 1941, British Prime Minister ***and whiskey enthusiast*** Winston Churchill described the cold-blooded executions of Russian civilians at the hands of the German Army as "a crime without a name."

Yet genocide, like Deadpool, is about so much more than murder. According to the Convention on the Prevention and Punishment of the Crime of Genocide (CPPCG), adopted by the United Nations General Assembly in 1948, genocide is defined as:

> any of the following acts committed with intent to destroy, in whole or in part, a national, ethnical, racial, or religious group, as such:
>
> (a) Killing members of the group;
> (b) Causing serious bodily or mental harm to members of the group;
> (c) Deliberately inflicting on the group conditions of life calculated to bring about its physical destruction in whole or in part;
> (d) Imposing measures intended to prevent births within the group;
> (e) Forcibly transferring children of the group to another group.

Assuming you didn't gloss over the list, you'll have noticed political groups are conspicuously unmentioned. That's because the delegation from the Soviet Union drove a diplomatic Zamboni through the first draft. They were a little antsy on the heels of Comrade Stalin's Great Purge.

You'll have also noticed that from a perpetrator's point of view genocide's real goal is the destruction of a way of life. That, and in Deadpool's case, to have fun and be himself . . . which involves gratuitous murder.

We philosophers have done a fine job differentiating between killing, letting die, and murder. Killing can be done in self-defense or it can be accidental. Doctors let patients die every day by withdrawing mechanical ventilation. Murder takes malicious intent. Murder morphs into genocide when it is systematic.

Some murders may be excused depending on their circumstances. However, this has never been the case for genocide. As a crime against humanity, genocide violates the basic principles of the 1948 Universal Declaration of Human Rights. In theory there are no legitimate excuses for such atrocities. However, Deadpool of Earth-12101 faces some extraordinary circumstances. Can we find some potentially mitigating factors that might partially or wholly absolve Deadpool of genocide?

Deadpool Is Insane and He Has Lazy Friends

Whereas in other story arcs he is left unsupervised in his quest to put down presidential zombies with the ghost of Benjamin Franklin or banter with Loki in the style of Abbott and Costello, Wade Wilson of Earth-12101 is committed under protest to the Ravencroft Asylum by Professor Xavier, Cyclops, Storm, and Wolverine. Their goal is to cure Deadpool of his affliction and reintegrate him into Super Culture as a non-lethal member of society. Remember: the road to Hell is paved with good intentions, no good deed goes unpunished, friends don't let friends have multiple "voices," and you probably left the stove on.

Yet Deadpool's insanity isn't really the spark that ignites the Marvelous Genocide. ***Seriously, Marvel, call this guy.*** We know this because, duh, all the people he kills are alive before his commitment to Ravencroft.

Perhaps the X-Men deserve some measure of responsibility. This comes close to blaming the victims, a tactic frequently used to deny genocide in our world, but consider the fact they didn't even bother to google reviews of Deadpool's healthcare provider. They were negligent in their serving up on a platter one of the multiverse's most gifted assassins into the hands of the subtly named Psycho-Man, a Microverse villain moonlighting as Dr. Benjamin Brighton. Outside the confines of an asylum, I'm sure Deadpool would have found the situation titillating. ***And erotic.*** Anyway the argument goes Deadpool is the blunt instrument, but the X-Men were the unsuspecting enablers of their universe's genocide.

This is not quite satisfying because not even a mutant with Professor X's abilities could have foreseen the kind of psychological conditioning Deadpool would fall victim to at Ravencroft. To bear responsibility for genocide, it must be shown there were planners. There are degrees of intention that have to be analyzed. In retrospect, we can criticize the X-Men of Earth-12101, but at least they tried doing their colleague a solid by getting him the care he needs. All other iterations of the X-Men are off eating churros or fighting registration acts, one of which is acceptable.

Deadpool Was Manipulated into Self-Discovery

The fact that harm can be done in pursuit of what's right is a hard reality to face. ***Take some wars, surgery, and camping out to see my next movie.*** It's made even more difficult when Psycho-Man wants to inflict damage in pursuit of his own agenda. Under his "care," Deadpool is subjected to tactics that would make a North Korean re-education administrator queasy. Trying and succeeding at stamping out the fanciful voice and the serious voice fans know and love, Psycho-Man manages to bring to the fore a latent influence on Deadpool, visually expressed as a crimson box.

It was cute of the writers to make Wade Wilson's darkest impulses match the color of his suit. It's like they're paid to think about symbolism or something. This visualization suggests that Psycho-Man merely activated an otherwise dormant feature of Deadpool's personality. His desire for carnage, already well known, had simply never been allowed to fully flourish.

Certainly, you say to yourself between profound strokes of the chin, ***Not where I thought you were going.*** Psycho-Man must bear some responsibility for awakening the genocidal dimension of Deadpool's personality. Well, it's not that simple. There's no suggestion that Psycho-Man was trying to incite Deadpool to repeatedly smash him on discharge papers, or roast Howard the Duck, or shoot Spider-Man in the head, or blow up the Avengers Tower, or cause Thor's hammer to grow so large that it would crush him when summoned, or send a whole slew of others to walk off the roofs of buildings like a platoon of synchronized swimmers who just want it all to end. ***Or, as you might call it, Monday.*** If that were the case, Psycho-Man would face criminal charges under provisions in our world's 1998 Rome Statute of the International Criminal Court. His intent to enslave Deadpool is egregious and similarly illegal, but he was just as ignorant of the ultimate outcome of his machinations as the X-Men. ***Plenty of ignorance to go around.***

Deadpool Was Written

Ignorance, it turns out, is at the very heart of this story arc. Inspired by the crimson box, Deadpool believes he's doing right by all the characters in the Marvel Universe. They do not know how confined they really are. Spider-Man is trapped by convention and unable to break character by putting an end to Deadpool's spree. In a later exchange with Professor X, Deadpool maintains that only he properly understands the oppressive structure of the Marvel Universe. Rejecting this, Professor X reaches into Deadpool's mind to kill him, but fails. In the process, Xavier experiences brain death. The last major challenger to his reign of terror, Wolverine, fights his way to Deadpool. We learn that Deadpool's greatest weapon is popularity, which he can leverage to do whatever he wants, including killing the Marvel Universe.

The notion that Deadpool is the only self-aware character is troublesome because it affords him the insufferable confidence of Holden Caulfield. ***Yeah, nerds, that was a Catcher in the Rye reference.*** It reinforces the argument that his ugliness really does go beyond the traditional dichotomy between good and evil. Supposing that death is some kind of liberation, Deadpool delivers the Marvel Universe from the dictates of writers and artists ***and man-sized child interns named Chuck.*** By viewing his fellow comic-book creations as sheep, Deadpool has achieved an important first step in any genocide: the dehumanization of a vulnerable population. Only then can he position himself as the slaughterer-in-chief of Clarice Starling's nightmares ***Silent, lambs!*** Only by denying the powers that be (the writers) their pawns can Deadpool hope to throw off the yoke of the fourth wall. In this way, Deadpool demonstrates the inverse of the X-Men's mistake: the road to deliverance is paved with bad intentions. ***I can hear the banjos from here.***

Flexing his rippling biceps and rugged individuality, Deadpool is endowed with free will. It's hard to swallow that, unlike his victims, only he has the clarity of mind to burn the system down. Marvel Comics has erected a gilded cage around its characters and Deadpool sets out to smash them into submission. Bringing an entire universe to its knees is a power reserved exclusively for Deadpool, but it raises some large problems. It screws with our most basic ethical beliefs that people should never be used instrumentally. Treating other people as mere means to an end is wrong. ***He somehow combined innuendo and one formulation of Immanuel Kant's Categorical Imperative.*** As the story grinds out we learn that Deadpool is less interested in collective liberation than he is about scoring what he considers justice.

However, he's still a character in a comic book. That surely counts for something, you scream aloud into the abyss. ***Well, kind of, the abyss replies.*** This arc reveals that there really are forces "out there" from Deadpool's perspective akin to God. He wants to exercise free will by targeting them for extinction. This is not what Augustine (354–430 C.E.) intended with his whole idea that evil is just a lack of the good. Augustine is rolling in his grave. There should be a Deadpool arc where he teams up with famous theologians. ***He digresses.*** Why the writers and artists ***and Chuck*** would grant Deadpool—and none of the other Marvel characters—free will is beyond the scope of this chapter, but I hope they'll one day reply to my emails.

This entire storyline reveals an essential truth about genocide: it is a co-ordinated set of events. In Deadpool's parlance it involves "spectacle." By targeting Uatu the Watcher in the earliest phase of his genocide, Deadpool removed the head of the Marvel Universe. By targeting the Avengers, he went after its heart.

That's typical of all genocides: target the intellectuals, artists, and community pillars. Doing so demoralizes the at-risk population because they have lost their chief spokespeople, organizers, and champions. Using Earth-12101's logic, Deadpool was not ordained to carry out such an assault against his fellow comic-book characters. He voluntarily took up the mantle, yet he felt his actions were righteous.

The Verdict

Nevertheless, Deadpool is responsible for genocide. Ugly though he may be, he does not operate outside legal or moral norms from Earth-616 that would also be known in Earth-12101. Indeed, Deadpool's break into the writer's room of Earth-616 indicates a full awareness of all values at all times in all places. His promise that he's coming for us, the readers of Earth-616 comics, indicates the lengths to which he'll go to escape the burdens of the fourth wall. He would sacrifice more than just the Marvel Universe, he'd go so far as to exterminate everyone from Beijing to Jacksonville ***Are you really going to mourn Jacksonville?*** In this sense, Deadpool demonstrates the thought process of a perpetrator of genocide: "by consuming comics, Earth's population bears guilt for my suffering."

The scope of Deadpool's ambition is astounding, but we've seen it before during the Armenian Genocide, the Holocaust, Cambodia, Rwanda, and in the former Yugoslavia. We don't write off their perpetrators as simply "ugly." We talk about harm. We use the language of right and wrong, good and evil, because genocide constitutes a clear crime against humanity. It is an assault on the principles enshrined in the Universal Declaration. In the aftermath of World War II, the framers set out to codify the inalienable rights of all humans. The Drafting Committee had members from all regions and was truly global in scope. Some critics allege the human rights regime is an extension of colonialism, but they gloss over the fact that no country voted against the Universal Declaration, though several did abstain.

No amount of Deadpool's fancy footwork can deny the rhetorical power of the Universal Declaration's first line: "Whereas recognition of the inherent dignity and of the equal and inalienable rights of all members of the human family is the foundation of freedom, justice and peace in the world." By willfully rejecting that dignity in favor of promoting his own needs, Deadpool threatens to undo a long history of rights language. Moreover, he views his fellow humans with contempt. The Universal Declaration is aspirational, but its framers were reacting with one voice to the Holocaust. This historical context cannot be overestimated. Lifting up equality as the basis for justice, we have further reason to condemn Deadpool's actions. Some degree of his ugliness involves setting himself apart from the herd and failing to recognize the strength of solidarity.

The Drafting Committee, led by former First Lady Eleanor Roosevelt, had high hopes for humanity's future. They debated whether to base their vision of universal rights in religion. To their credit they resisted the temptation. Situating rights in the simple fact of species membership, the framers left us a document with strong moral resonance. Deadpool would have us believe the Universal Declaration is a quaint relic of a bygone age, but its standards are timeless. Human rights can be violated, but they can never be voided. ***What then do you mean by the phrase "moral bankruptcy"?***

For all his talents in the bedroom, on the battlefield, and beyond, Deadpool cannot change the arc of history unless he ends it completely. The writers of *Deadpool Kills the Marvel Universe* seem well aware of this fact. Indeed, genocide is always intended to end history from a victim's point of view. Part of what makes genocide so horrifying is its rejection of multiple narratives. In his substituted judgment, typified by his conversation with Spider-Man, Deadpool reveals the incompatibility of any other life and his own.

Aftermath

To some extent, life goes on after genocide. Perpetrators and bystanders find ways of coping with that fact. Oftentimes so do victims. West Germany erected memorials, paid massive reparations to Israel, and prosecuted Nazi war criminals. Holocaust survivors have participated in museum construction and video archives.

Yet there are cases where victims do not have similar opportunities to process grief and trauma. Historically, the massacre of the population of Melos by the Athenians is one of the better known examples. "The Melian Dialogue" in *The History of the Peloponnesian War* by Thucydides (460–400 B.C.E.) gives us a glimpse into a situation where no one is left to tell the story. This is obviously the threat of any genocide. However, it was Deadpool's achievement. Thucydides and the team behind *Deadpool Kills the Marvel Universe* give us traces of lives that were taken and crimes that were committed against them.

So, as readers we can come to ancient and fictional genocides with far less bias than we can to genocides that occurred in the twentieth century when the term was officially coined. As we worked through some possible mitigating factors in the determination of Deadpool's culpability for his own genocide, we achieved clarity on an important point of international law: only individuals can be charged with genocide. ***Whereas entire societies can be guilty of crimes against fashion.***

Nothing that was "done to" Deadpool can excuse his crimes. His choices may be understandable, but they are not just. Even though he thinks of himself as liberating his fellow beings, the deprivation of life is simply inexcusable. Critics may wish to claim that Deadpool transcends ordinary morality ***especially since alternative versions of the victim selves exist in other universes*** but he doesn't.

The precepts laid down by the United Nations, conceived as timeless and universal, are rooted in a robust conception of the good life—the bare minimum of which is ***mini pigs with booties and raincoats*** life.

VI

I'd Love to Get a Blow Job

Why Existence Sucks

21
A Naughty Little Puppet, but Still a Puppet

SHAWN MCKINNEY WITHOUT A HAND UP HIS ASS, NO SIR!

Deadpool's fourth-wall-breaking antics have long been a source of fun and humor. In 2012, Wade Wilson's unique ability to have a relationship with the audience took a dark turn in the four-issue mini-series, *Deadpool Kills the Marvel Universe*. This was the first of three stories that would make up the Deadpool Killogy. After Wilson finished with the Marvel Universe, he went on to murder fictional characters from literature in *Deadpool Killustrated*, and even alternate versions of himself in *Deadpool Kills Deadpool*.

What set the Merc with a Mouth off on this metacidal quest? He realized something philosophers have been worried about for over two thousand years. He realized that his actions seem to be caused by forces outside his control, and, as a result, he has no free will. That he's a fictional character in a story and he has no control over his actions. That an audience and creators, whom he calls progenitors, are controlling everyone's lives as though they were puppets. As he puts it,

> It's the Fourth Wall that's been breaking me . . . crushing me . . . crushing each and every one of us . . . for as long as we've been in existence. (*Deadpool Kills the Marvel Universe* #3, p. 11)

I've got some good news and some bad news about this. The good news is for Deadpool and it's that he's not in this mess alone. The bad news is for all of you reading this, the audience, (*Yes, you; and you in the back, you too; even Cloris Leachman*) you have no more freedom than Deadpool does. Philosophers call this view Fatalism, that we lack the ability to do anything other than what we actually do (and even what we actually do isn't really up to us).

Everything's Under Control

> It wasn't until Psycho-Man messed around in my noodle that everything came together.
>
> —*Deadpool Kills the Marvel Universe* #3, p. 11

Wade's crusade to kill the Marvel universe begins when the X-Men forcibly commit him to a mental hospital. What nobody knows at the time is that the head psychiatrist is actually the super-villain Psycho-Man in disguise.

Psycho-Man is from a microscopic universe (the Microverse) and pilots an artificial human body. He also has a Control-Box that he uses to, prepare yourself for a surprise, control people. When he attempts to use the Control-Box to control Wade the process backfires. Instead of coming under Psycho-Man's control, Wade realizes that the voices in his head are not imaginary. He realizes that his and everyone else's lives are actually being controlled by outside forces. In this case, by comic-book creators and fans that he calls "Progenitors." As Wade puts it, "I saw the world the way it really is. They never realized they were puppets . . . made to dance and love and die and suffer . . .just like me" (*Deadpool Kills the Marvel Universe* #2, p. 17).

What makes some philosophers think that you and I are puppets like Deadpool and Psycho-Man? Traditionally, there are three main candidates for the role of humanity's puppet master: Logic, God, and the Laws of Nature.

Remorseless Logic

> Tell me what in the name of Namor's bikini briefs is going on?!
>
> —*Deadpool Kills Deadpool* #1, p. 20

An early philosophical discussion of this comes from Aristotle (384–322 B.C.E.). He reasoned that logic seemed to demand that a person's future actions were determined in advance. Aristotle was a famous Greek philosopher who may have invented the theories of natural science, formal logic, and art.

In one of his works on logic, called *On Interpretation*, Aristotle discussed the truth of claims about the future. He described the problem like this: suppose you predict that a great sea battle will take place in one week. Either your prediction is true or it is not true, because either there will be a great sea battle in one week or there will not be a great sea battle in one week. But if, at the time when you make this prediction, it is already true or not true, then the future must already be set. If the future is already set, then any decisions people might make in the intervening time can't affect the future. If what we decide doesn't change what happens, then how can we say we have free will?

Consider this: if you had said on the day that Wade Wilson was born, "someday Wade will become Deadpool," wouldn't that have been a true statement? On the other hand, if you had said, "someday Wade will become Colossus," then that would not have been true. Now, maybe nobody knows whether or not these are true when they are said, but they are still true or not when they are said. It isn't like these sentences are true for a while and then switch, or *vice versa*: they are always true or not regardless of whether or not we know that they are true. This means that, logically, out of all the possible statements that could describe the rest of your life, one set of them is already true and all the rest are already false. Right now, it is already true or not that you will own a copy of the comic book, *New Mutants* #98, the first appearance of Deadpool. If it is true today, then it was also true a hundred years before you were born. Anything about my life that was true one-hundred years before I was born is not something I had control over.

Aristotle's solution to this problem is to distinguish between knowing, one, that something in the future would happen or not happen, from, two, knowing which thing will actually happen in the future. I know, right now, that you will either finish reading this article and go read the *Deadpool Killogy* (you should, it's a lot of fun while being surprisingly thoughtful at the same time) or not. However, I don't know if you actually will or not. I know that you will do one of those things, you will or won't, but I don't know which one it is.

Just like you know, right now, that I will or will not go see *Deadpool Two* in the theater. You don't know which I will do, but you know that I will do one of them. Aristotle's solution is to distinguish knowledge of a logical principle from knowledge of a future event. Unfortunately, this solution didn't end the issue for everyone and certainly leaves open the problem when you have somebody that is supposed to know everything, including what people will do in the future. Someone like comic book writers, or God.

God Only Knows

I'm-the-self-aware-creator-of-all-things-multiversal-baby-daddy.

—*Deadpool Kills Deadpool* #4, p. 17

The Christian philosopher Augustine of Hippo (354–430 C.E.) was one of the first to consider the implications of an all-knowing God on our ability to determine our own futures. Augustine was particularly concerned with the question of how to reconcile evil in the world with an all-powerful, all-knowing, all-good God.

If the Christian God really exists, then there is someone who already knows what will actually happen in the future. Augustine, and many since, have thought that God's all-knowing-ness entailed knowledge of the future. In this sense, God is like the Deadpool comic writer, Cullen Bunn. Completely aside from whether or not God, or Cullen Bunn, forces anyone to do something tomorrow, if they know today what Deadpool and I will do tomorrow, how can we say that Deadpool and I freely choose to do those things?

Augustine's solution involves God's grace and saying that even though God made both you and the world you operate in, and already knows what you will do; he doesn't, technically, force you to make one decision or another. Humans are equipped to make different decisions and freely chose things, its just that God already knows what we will freely choose. And, he made us in such a way that we would eventually choose what we choose, and he knew that when he made us. Frankly, this solution requires a lot of faith that not everyone has or wants. Without such faith, it's difficult to understand how there could be someone who already knows what I will do in the future if I freely choose what I will do in the future.

The issue here is very similar to the one Aristotle laid out, except that now there is someone who actually does know, right now, whether or not you will own a copy of *New Mutants* #98. According to this way of looking at it, God knew, a thousand years before I was born, that I would sell my copy of *New Mutants* #98 at a comic book convention in the 1990s for a *lot* less than it's worth today. If, back in the 1970s, God already knew I would do this, how could the decision whether or not to sell the book really have been up to me? As if this kind of foreknowledge isn't already enough of a problem for human free will, God is also often credited with creating the universe and everything in it. On this view, it really seems like God made me sell my comic and God seems to be exactly the kind of puppet-master Deadpool was worried about when he said, "Don't you get it? We're puppets! And Geppetto's feeding us through the wood-chipper for shits and giggles!" (*Deadpool Kills the Marvel Universe* #4, p. 14).

Mother Nature Pulls the Strings

What kind of &#$% candy bar doesn't have nuts?!

—*Deadpool Killustrated* #4, p. 9

The final candidate for puppet-master of humanity is the Laws of Nature, the scientific rules that govern the physical universe. Consider that everything that happens seems to be the result of what happens before. A rock falls because of gravity. The *Deadpool* movie was a reboot because *Wolverine: Origins* was shitty. Objects that are already in motion continue moving, unless they are acted upon by an equal or greater force. Inanimate objects only do things as the result of outside forces acting upon them, and thus inanimate objects are not free. When Wade kills Spider-Man by shooting him in the head, his bullet doesn't tear through Parker's head because it wants to, or just randomly, but because it was forced out of the chamber of Wilson's gun by the powerful force of the exploding gunpowder behind it.

Now, consider humans. Either we are some kind of magical first causes, or we too only do things as the result of outside causes. Wade pulls the trigger because his muscles constrict and pull against bones. Muscles pull against bones because they are attached. Muscles constrict because they receive a signal from the nerves within the muscle. Nerves pass that signal from the brain. Wade didn't attach his muscles, or put the nerves in them. Did he create the neurological impulse in his brain?

There are many intermediate steps that could go here, so let me skip them and cut to the chase: either someone pulls the trigger for reasons of their own based on their values and priorities and desires, or they arbitrarily pull it as some kind of unconscious spasm. If it's an unconscious spasm, then it's basically an accident and accidents aren't expressions of Free Will. If a trigger is pulled as a result of one's reasons and values and priorities, then they are simply reacting to external causes (environment, socialization, Psycho-Man, upbringing, or something else). If reacting to outside causes, then a person seems just like the bullet reacting to outside causes. With either option, the person doesn't really seem to be the ultimate cause of their own actions.

More recent scientific research isn't helping either. Lots of work in quantum physics got people excited early on because there seemed to be evidence of observable, non-caused physical phenomena. Subatomic particles sometimes pop up within a perfect vacuum, before vanishing again shortly thereafter. There is no known cause of this; it is called a vacuum fluctuation. Unfortunately, people then realized that non-caused, or random, events were no better for the prospects of human Free Will because a random thing is still not something an individual has control over.

In the 1980s the neuroscientist Benjamin Libet published research that seemed to show that physical brain activity preceeds conscious decision making in human actions. Libet hooked people up to a machine that recorded their brain activity and asked them to press a button when they felt like doing so. He also had them record when they made the conscious decision to press the button. The experiment showed that the part of the brain that controlled the button pressing activated hundreds of milliseconds before the people consciously decided to press the button. The actual meaning of his experiment and its results have been debated ever since, but there has not been any significant neurological research finding evidence in favor of humans having Free Will.

Deadpool Kills Freedom

> They always thought that I was crazy . . . but they never realized I saw the world the way it really is.
>
> —*Deadpool Kills the Marvel Universe* #2, p. 17

Unfortunately for us in the audience, we seem to have no more freedom than Deadpool has. None of us can do otherwise than what we actually do and what we actually do doesn't seem to be up to us either. Whether that is for logical, theological, or scientific reasons doesn't seem to matter in the end.

Honestly, its much worse for us than for Deadpool. Wade is only afraid he lacks the ability to do otherwise than what the authors and audiences want him to do. If this were the only impediment to free will, then it would be easy enough, at least in theory, to simply kill the puppet-master or cut the strings. But, how do you cut the strings of the laws of nature or logic? As Deadpool says to himself a page before he kills the creators of *Deadpool Kills the Marvel Universe*, "Even the progenitors of our universe may be nothing more than the playthings for other entities. You can hack away forever and never find the beginning . . . or the end" (*Deadpool Kills the Marvel Universe* #4, p. 20).

> But . . . really . . . If I had the ability to change the world . . . I wouldn't need to save up for those butt implants I've been wanting.
>
> —*Deadpool Kills Deadpool* #4, p. 6

Perhaps the only response to this lack of freedom is to follow the lead of the Merc with a Mouth and embrace absurdity. At the end of the Deadpool Killogy, the real Deadpool (from Earth-616, the one we read about in the regular *Deadpool* comic every month), kills the Deadpool who was driven metacidal by Psycho-Man. Good Wade tells Bad Wade his method for dealing with the lack of freedom:

> What? You got a problem with the status quo? The mind-numbing, soul-crushing realization that nothing's ever gonna change . . . that nothing will ever get any better . . . that's how I get girls. (*Deadpool Kills Deadpool* #4, p. 19)

So, that's that. And when you feel tough enough for the next stage in your Enlightenment and dis-illusionment, turn to Chapter 10 in this volume, "Always a Pallbearer, Never the Corpse."

22

How to Solve the Contradictions in *Deadpool Killustrated*

JAMIE CAWTHRA, LOUISA MAY ALCOTT, HERMAN MELVILLE, MARK TWAIN, AND . . .

"Fourth wall break inside a fourth wall break? That's like . . . sixteen walls!" Yep, if there's one thing that Deadpool's good at, it's messing things up. And if there's one thing he can mess with more than Wolverine, it's the actual story he's in.

This is why, if you ask someone to describe Deadpool in one word, it's pretty likely that they'll say he's "meta." Somehow he's outside of his own story, even though it's about him. But calling him "meta" barely does him justice, because not only does he often mess up his own story, sometimes he does it deliberately!

When this happens, it's really weird. So much so that I think it's actually *impossible*. You might think that if it's only in a story, it isn't a big deal if something impossible happens. Unfortunately, impossible things are such a problem that they're a headache even when they're only fictional.

What we need is a good example so I can show you what I mean. Happily for all of us, Deadpool has some perfect examples of impossible stories! What we need is the weirdest Deadpool story available, and I know which one has my vote. Ever read *Deadpool Killustrated?* In the first issue of *Killustrated*, our Regenerating Degenerate turns up in the middle of *Moby-Dick*. Within a few pages, he's *really* messed up the whole novel. He kills Moby Dick before Captain Ahab can find the whale. Dragged aboard the good ship *Pequod*, Deadpool's next victim is the novel's narrator, Ishmael. Ahab manages to escape, making it to the third issue of *Killustrated* before our antihero catches up with him. That particular reunion ends in exactly the way that you would imagine.

By changing the plot of *Moby-Dick*, Deadpool has left us with a whole mess of contradictions on our hands. Moby Dick dies leaving the *Pequod* intact, but he's *supposed* to destroy it. Ishmael both survives the destruction of the ship (in the original) and dies on its decks at Deadpool's hands. Ahab is killed by Wade *and* by the whale. How can these things all be true when they contradict each other?

"Really," I can hear some of you saying already. "Isn't it obvious? Deadpool didn't kill the *real* Captain Ahab. He killed somebody with the same name, job, and disposition. It's just a character who's a lot like the character from *Moby-Dick*." But you're wrong. To see why, we need a quick recap of the premise of *Killustrated*.

In *Killustrated*, Deadpool travels through various works of literature, slaughtering fictional characters he finds there. These include (deep breath now) Mowgli, Dracula, Don Quixote, the Little Women (all of them), Scrooge, Scylla and Charybdis, Dorian Grey, the Three Musketeers, and Tom Sawyer. His goal? Scour the classics clean in order to permanently kill the Marvel characters that they inspired.

Fighting to stop him is a task force composed of Mulan, Beowulf, Natty Bumppo (he was in *The Last of the Mohicans*. I had to look him up too) and Dr. Watson, led by none other than Sherlock Holmes. In *Killustrated*, literary worlds don't just collide, they get haphazardly smooshed together. Then stabbed with a katana.

Now that this awesome premise has been covered, I'll get back to the point. If we're going to take *Killustrated* at face value, Deadpool murders Captain Ahab. He doesn't murder somebody who looks like Ahab, or somebody he only thinks is Ahab. He slices up the real deal. If this isn't the case, the whole story is lost. Ahab *has* to be the real thing, or else the claim that Deadpool is wiping out the characters of classical literature (regularly repeated throughout the series) is just a great big *lie*.

Would it be so bad if it actually was a lie? It would make the whole series a bit strange. It would turn into a comic about Deadpool thinking he's slaying his way through classical literature, but actually not doing that. The protagonist, the narrator, the whole cast . . . all of them are wrong about what's happening. This kind of sucks. Takes the fun out of it, if you ask me.

I vote we say that this is the real Ahab, the real Tom Sawyer, the real Sherlock Holmes. That makes the comic much cooler, and it also turns the whole thing into an interesting philosophical problem. As a big fan of cool comics and interesting philosophical problems, this is a win-win for me. If you're not a big fan of cool comics or interesting philosophical problems . . . well, I don't really know what to say. This is an odd choice of book for you to be reading. But you've read this far, so let's see what's going on.

What's Going On

The key bit is this: *Killustrated* depicts impossible things happening. And I mean *seriously* impossible. Iron Man's suit is impossible (at least by the standards of modern technology), but I don't see any philosophical problems with that. It isn't possible that radioactive waste could give somebody superpowers, but comic books have used this plenty of times and I'm fine with it. What's interesting about *Killustrated* is that it contains things which are *logically* impossible. Something is logically impossible if it goes against the laws of logic. A classic one is the Law of Non-Contradiction: things can't contradict themselves. If something is a square, it can't also not be a square. If it were both, then it would contradict itself.

This is why those contradictions between the narratives of *Killustrated* and *Moby-Dick* are so important. If it's the real Captain Ahab in *Killustrated*, then Ahab both is and is not killed by Moby Dick. Ishmael both survives and does not survive the destruction of the *Pequod*. By poaching fictional characters from classic stories, *Killustrated* ends up depicting loads of logical impossibilities. These things are serious business. So serious, in fact, that philosopher Roy Sorensen has a $100 reward out for a picture of something logically impossible. (I don't think he'd pay out for *Killustrated* though—philosophers are pretty stingy.)

Why so serious? Whoops, wrong universe. Well, there are serious reasons to think we can't even *imagine* logically impossible stuff happening, let alone do or depict anything logically impossible! And contradictions are logically impossible! Deadpool can't both exist and not exist at the same time, can he? Deadpool can't be red all over and not red at all, can he?

Contradictions can't even be imagined! This idea's been around for ages, at least since David Hume (1771–76) back in the eighteenth century. But is it true? Buckle in, because this chapter's about to get interactive! It's time to play 'Imagine the Impossible', and you can join in at home.

To prove the point that we can't even imagine contradictions, here's what you have to do. Close your eyes (not till I've finished explaining it though) and try to imagine the following object: a *square circle*. It needs to have four corners, and no corners. Four sides, but only one side. No cheating—don't just imagine a square that's so far away it looks circular. If it's too tricky, you can use a circular square instead. Get back to me when you're ready.

Intermission (the Concessions Stand Is Open)

How did it go? You might've given up, which is fine. Plenty of people have conceded that we can't imagine the logically impossible. On the other hand, you might've imagined it perfectly easily. Well done! You're one of the reasons why this idea isn't gospel in philosophy. (Hard mode: try to imagine a triangle which has one edge longer than the other two edges put together.)

What does this mean for *Killustrated*? Well, if it's true that we can't imagine the logically impossible, there's a problem with reading the comic. While the image might be on the page before us, we still use our imaginations to engage with the fiction. We use it to make the leap from the ink shapes to the characters interacting with one another. What we *see* is a representation of Deadpool stabbing Ahab. That's not a problem; that could be represented by images, by words, by actors, by whatever. What's difficult is that what this image represents - what philosophers normally call the 'content' of the image - is something logically impossible. It's this content that we imagine while reading the comic. You see where this is going? Here it is laid out straight:

1. When we read *Killustrated*, we imagine its content.
2. The content of *Killustrated* is logically impossible.
3. We cannot imagine something logically impossible.

These three statements are mutually exclusive. Something's gotta give.

Philosophers have attacked each of those statements at various points—some think we *can* imagine the logically impossible, others think we don't imagine the content of the story, and some would look at *Killustrated* and argue that the content isn't logically impossible in the first place. You might be expecting me to tell you who I think is right. But I'm not going to. Instead, I'm going to tell you a bit more about each of these options. Then you can make your own mind up.

A Lack of Imagination (but Not a Lack of Fun!)

What if we don't actually use our imagination when we're reading *Killustrated*? That'd definitely solve the problem. It would make the whole can-we-imagine-the-impossible debate completely irrelevant to the issue. Instead, we can just get on with enjoying the weird story.

It might sound unusual to say you don't need your imagination to enjoy a story, but that's exactly what philosopher Derek Matravers reckons. When you read *Killustrated*, you don't necessarily imagine what's going on. Instead, you only need to *understand* it. Think of the square circle from earlier, then read this: 'If I found a square circle, I'd be surprised.' You can understand this sentence (I hope), even if you can't imagine that annoying square circle. The same goes for Deadpool. As readers, we understand that Deadpool has killed Captain Ahab. We have, as Matravers would say, successfully engaged with the narrative. We can accept that it happened in the story, even if we couldn't imagine it happening.

For the record, Matravers doesn't argue that we *never* imagine what's happening in a story. You're free to imagine away. He just doesn't think that imagining is essential to the experience. According to him, the inability to imagine what happens in *Killustrated* doesn't interfere with the fact that, in the story, famous fictional characters die.

Does that sound feasible? If so, maybe this should be your preferred answer to the puzzle. But if you're not yet convinced, maybe you'd like to try the next option.

Imagining the Impossible (with MAXIMUM EFFORT)

What if it actually turns out that we *can* imagine logically impossible things? If you're one of those people who managed to imagine the square circle, this option is probably for you. But still, if you couldn't imagine the square circle, that doesn't mean you can't hop aboard this particular bandwagon. In fact, one of the major ideas here is that well-disguised impossibilities are really easy to imagine. And if anybody's well-disguised, it's a man in a tight, red costume with swords and guns strapped everywhere. And several thousand pouches, if it's Rob Liefeld's Deadpool. Anyway, here's how the disguise might help us with *Killustrated*.

The philosopher Tamar Gendler talks about how fiction helps us imagine different *aspects* of something. The recent *Deadpool* movie shows us the lovestruck, happy Wade Wilson—this is one aspect of the character. Another aspect of Deadpool is the vengeful, psychopathic mercenary who makes himself feel better by repeatedly shooting a dead man—in the middle of a gunfight! There's also his wisecracking, rude aspect, and his meta, fourth-wall-breaking aspect . . . the list goes on.

In *Killustrated*, Captain Ahab and the other fictional characters are presented in a way which emphasizes one of their aspects. That's the aspect of being an inspiration for Marvel heroes. It gets reinforced almost every time a famous character dies—they're momentarily replaced with the hero that they inspired. Pinocchio becomes the Vision, the Little Mermaid becomes the Sub-Mariner, and the Three Musketeers become every superhero team in the Marvel universe.

The fact that this aspect is emphasized so much means that their other aspects shrink into the background. An important aspect gets lost—the one in which they're rounded fictional characters who have their own narratives (narratives in which Deadpool doesn't interfere). We're too busy thinking about how Deadpool killed the concept of a team to think about how he just did something logically impossible. That's why we happily imagine him slicing up Ahab—we're not thinking of Ahab, captain of the *Pequod* and creation of Herman Melville. We're thinking of Ahab, inspiration behind any Marvel character who is driven by a grudge (Punisher is the most obvious candidate, although there was actually a villain called "Ahab" a while ago). If we *were* thinking of Ahab in his aspect of "Melville's creation," the contradiction that's taking place would be much more obvious. At that point, we might find we can't imagine what's taking place.

What do you think? Some of you might complain that this doesn't really solve the problem—it's not that we're imagining contradictory things, it's just that we're imagining things one after another that would contradict if imagined together. In that sense, it doesn't seem like the answer is "We can imagine the impossible," but is actually "We don't bother trying to imagine the impossible, but we do okay anyway." Others of you might think that no, it's easy to see how we can imagine a contradiction—we just imagine the two different sides in different aspects. But maybe some of you are scratching your heads, wondering why we're bothering with all this stuff. This next section is for you guys.

Killustrated Isn't Impossible (Just Really Weird)

Wait, didn't I spend a couple of pages trying to convince you that it *is* impossible? You have a good memory! However, I should probably let you know that plenty of philosophers out there would disagree. Most of them would do so because of work by one man—David Lewis (1941–2001).

Lewis has a particular way of interpreting fictions. His way is based on his theory of "modal realism," which is usually just called "possible worlds." This theory says that there are loads of worlds, and our own world is just one of them. There's a world for every circumstance—one where Deadpool was instead named "Brian," one where his costume is green instead of red, you name it. Each of these worlds is just as real as our own, but we aren't connected to them in space or time. If you think of parallel universes, you won't be too far off.

This might all sound a bit extreme, but it actually gives us a really useful tool to talk about something difficult: possibility. We can say that something is possible if it happens in one of these worlds. There is one of these worlds where the laws of physics are different and that means human beings can fly. There's one where everything is exactly the same except for lions, which are bright pink. So we can use Lewis to define how we talk about possibility! It ends up looking like this:

Possible	Happens in at least one possible world.
Necessary	Happens in every possible world.
Impossible	Doesn't happen in any possible worlds.

Lewis claimed that possible worlds can shed light on some of the issues in fiction. His idea is that fictions represent possible worlds. There's a collection of worlds where a self-healing, mouthy mercenary called Deadpool runs around being childish, and these worlds are what Deadpool stories represent. What's told as a story in our own world would be told as a known fact in these possible worlds.

How does this help *Killustrated*? Well, people in different possible worlds can be very closely connected to one another. They can be what Lewis calls "counterparts." He claims that, while not identical with one another, counterparts share an identity. For example: it's possible that Stan Lee might never have become chairman of Marvel. According to Lewis, that's true because Stan Lee has a counterpart in another world who was never chairman. Instead, that world has a parallel universe Stan Lee who works as a strip club DJ. So what does this counterpart relation mean for Deadpool? Movie Deadpool has a different origin story to Classic Deadpool, but we want to say that they're the same character. The easy option is to say that they're counterparts from different worlds. That way we can establish that they share an identity, even if they do different (and sometimes contradictory) things. On a side note, I vote we all agree that the Deadpool from the Wolverine movie does *not* have this relation to the other Deadpools.

Anyway, back to *Killustrated*. The important bit is this: with Lewis's theory in mind, we can say that our Ahab is a counterpart of the Ahab from *Moby-Dick*. That way we get to preserve the idea that it's the *real* Ahab whom Deadpool is stabbing to death. However, this time no unfortunate logical contradictions come up. With the theory of possible worlds propping the whole story up, we can ensure that the whole thing doesn't end up causing problems.

The Problem with Possible Worlds

I'm afraid I lied before. There's still a big problem with using Lewis's possible worlds. While they do the job quite nicely for *Killustrated*, possible worlds still have a lot of trouble with other impossible stories. Have a look at that table of definitions I included earlier. See where it says that impossible things don't happen in any world at all? That's the problem.

See, *Killustrated* is impossible because of the identity of its characters—they're supposed to be the same characters as the characters in assorted works of literature. By using possible worlds, we change how we understand their identities. In other words, we've managed to explain how *Killustrated* can both be possible *and* still be about Deadpool killing Captain Ahab. However, that just isn't an option for some stories. If a story is about something impossible that can't be explained away with identity, possible worlds suddenly can't deal with it.

There are plenty of examples of stories like this, but most are experimental novels that would be tough to describe without taking up this whole book (and I'd get in trouble for that. Try Italo Calvino's *Invisible Cities*, or Jorge Luis Borges's "The Garden of Forking Paths.") So let's make our own. Prepare yourself for some dazzling authorship as I pen the following epic, titled "Wade's Impossible Day":

> Once upon a time, Wade found a square circle.

Breathtaking stuff. But aside from its incredible literary worth, the interesting bit about this (very, very short) story is that it contains something logically impossible. So far, so *Killustrated*. But this time, counterparts won't help us sort it out. If we try saying that this story represents a collection of possible worlds, we hit a dead end. There aren't any possible worlds in which Wade finds a square circle! This story doesn't represent any world at all.

Lewis has a strategy to deal with stuff like this. It's called "chunking." His idea is that a story like "Wade's Impossible Day" is actually a couple of different worlds stitched together. There's one where Wade finds a square, and one where Wade finds a circle. The story just makes it look like these are one logically impossible world. To chunk a story, you just break it up until it doesn't contradict itself any more. Then the idea is that any appearance of impossibility is an illusion that comes about from us juxtaposing these contradicting worlds. This seems fishy though—the story isn't about Wade finding a square *or* a circle! It seems to be about him finding a *square circle*. Lewis, and others like him, are forced to say that this isn't right. If you want to use chunking, you have to accept that the story is wrong when it describes what Wade found.

If we want to preserve the contradiction in the story, we can't use possible worlds. However, if you haven't agreed with any of the previous suggestions, the contradiction seems to have pretty bleak prospects. There is one more thing we could try, but I warn you: this one is the weirdest yet. The philosopher Graham Priest has argued that contradictions do occur in the actual world. He doesn't agree that the Law of Non-contradiction is completely binding. This isn't supposed to mean that just any old contradiction can happen, but it does mean that we shouldn't just accept the idea that logical impossibilities don't exist under any circumstances. Take the sentence "This sentence is false." It can't be true, because then it would be false. But if that sentence is actually false, then it ends up being true! Normally we'd have to scratch our heads over that one, but people like Priest can just say that it's a true contradiction.

Priest has weighed in on the debate about contradictions in stories. It won't come as much of a surprise that he goes against Lewis, saying that stories can indeed contain impossible things. No chunking for Priest! In fact, Priest likes contradictory stories so much that he wrote his own! It's called "Sylvan's Box," and is about a box that's both empty and has something it. Priest thinks that the best explanation of fictions like *Killustrated,* "Wade's Impossible Day" and "Sylvan's Box" is similar to Lewis's. However, rather than chunking, he suggests extending the theory to include a new kind of world—impossible worlds. These are just like possible worlds, but, well, impossible. They're the worlds where you find all the things that you don't find in possible worlds. Lewis thinks that stories represent possible worlds, and Priest thinks that contradictory stories represent impossible worlds. While Priest's thoughts on contradictions are controversial, he shows that issues like those we find in *Killustrated* are taken seriously as philosophical challenges.

Impossible to Choose? (Tough Luck)

Whew, *Killustrated* turned out to be more complicated than it seemed. That's the risk you take when you start paddling around in the pool of logical impossibility. The solutions I've listed are your options, although they could be taken in different ways than I've described here. One of the great things about the philosophy of fiction is that the reader ends up being a hugely important part of just about everything. And you're a reader! You're the subject of these debates—you, and the way you read stories like *Killustrated*. So don't be afraid to think up your own answer to the puzzle of *Killustrated*, because you're just as involved as any professional philosopher.

This analysis of *Killustrated* only scratches the surface of how Deadpool messes with all these neat theories of fiction. Take the movie, where he comments on how handsome Ryan Reynolds is. What on Earth is going on there? In *Marvel vs. Capcom 3*, Deadpool uses his own health bar as a weapon. Brilliant! The Merc with a Mouth messes with theories of fiction over and over again. More than any other franchise I can think to name, Deadpool pokes at the boundaries of stories, messing with the ways in which we usually understand them. He makes the job of explaining fiction much harder, that's true. However, nobody could deny that he makes it much more interesting.

23
A Chimichanga for the Mercenary Soul

GABRIEL CRUZ WITH A *SHORT* WOLVERINE CAMEO . . . GET IT?

Deadpool has been called many things: the Merc with a Mouth, the Crimson Comedian, and the Regeneratin' Degenerate, not to mention a list of profanities too impolite to mention here.

But there is another name that he is worthy of: The Eternal Proletariat ("prole-what"? It's a fancy word for "working-class folk", throw it around, it'll impress your friends). Deadpool is, among other things, the embodiment of class struggle, of a man whose fate has been shaped by the powers that be and who seeks satisfaction beyond what money can buy. That's not to say that he doesn't like cash, of course he does; but the story of Deadpool is a story of struggling to fit in and find happiness when it's clear that society doesn't want him and his job just doesn't bring him real joy anymore.

He is a perpetrator of violence and a victim of forces larger than himself, of the Military-Industrial Complex that created him and the larger cultural forces at work that provide no comfort or relief for this everyman. For that is what he is on some level, an Everyman. While none of us possess the superpower (or curse) of immortality (and that's probably for the best) we can all relate to being forced to do jobs that no longer bring us satisfaction, that do not satisfy that which we hunger for most.

Deadpool's life provides very clear examples and illustrations of what happens when a person is subjected to the whims of forces beyond their control. His experiences can show how superstructures, which are essentially forces and organizations that make up society, not only make us who we are but also lead to people being exploited and taken advantage of, with little or no real alternatives.

Gramsci and Good Taste

Antonio Gramsci (1891–1937) was very concerned with the struggles of the working class and spent his life fighting for their liberation from the cultural forces that kept them oppressed. His solution was to help them become the dominant culture. Gramsci's philosophy is absolutely relevant to the story of Deadopool since many of the struggles that Deadpool has endured both personally and professionally are rooted in his job.

Funnily enough it's very likely that Gramsci would be opposed to an application of his work to such a vulgar and low-brow piece of fiction. In *Proletarian Culture* he noted that the modern (of his time) style of novels were devoid of the character and style that was inherent in earlier books such as *The Three Musketeers* and the Sherlock Holmes novels. Gramsci would not have approved of a piece of fiction that relies heavily on cheap puns, adolescent humor, and madcap violence in order to entertain. But, as it happens Gramsci is dead and his pretensions will not keep us from doing what we want with his ideas.

In looking at Deadpool, I'm mainly using the issues written by Daniel Way and a few others here and there. I'm not pulling from the most recent movie, even though I thoroughly enjoyed it, and I most certainly am not pulling from the version of Deadpool in *Wolverine: Origins*. In fact, my disdain for that version of Deadpool is such that I would recommend you call him by another name: Dudepeel. Dudepeel has no place here.

Mercs Are Made, Not Born

Some are born great, some achieve greatness, and others are ruthlessly experimented on until something equal parts cool and traumatizing happens to them. Wade Wilson was subjected to the latter until his transition into becoming Deadpool. His origin is difficult to pin down as he is a notoriously unreliable narrator who suffers from hallucinations and severe psychological illness. That being said what is known is that upon receiving a diagnosis of Stage 4 cancer he was provided an opportunity to survive in the form of volunteering for a secret military program being co-conducted by the American and Canadian governments. After "volunteering," in as much as choosing to not die is volunteering, he was enrolled in the Weapon X program where he was experimented on until his body developed a healing factor that is very close to that of Wolverine's. He could regenerate limbs and the cancer in his body was kept in check, yet not destroyed.

Essentially he became immortal, a matter that has become problematic for Deadpool for reasons that will be discussed later. The consequences of the constant experimentation were life-altering; the first was that he was physically mutilated to the point that nearly every part of his body had become scar tissue. The second consequence was his sanity. Somewhere along the way he lost his grip on reality and began to hear voices, hallucinate, and even gain a self-awareness rarely matched in the form of being able to break the fourth wall of his comic book format. I'm not sure that there are many other comic-book characters that read comics to catch up on what's going on with other superheroes.

When examined through a Gramscian lens it becomes clear that Deadpool's life was heavily influenced by what Gramsci refers to as superstructures for *political society*. A superstructure is a sort of semi-autonomous system that operates as a support tool or instrument for a society in addition to acting as a cultural force that maintains dominant ideologies. In other words, it's a system that supports various ideas and concepts making sure they are a part of the mainstream culture. In *Selections from the Prison Notebooks*, Gramsci divides superstructures into two major levels. The first level is the *civil society* that is made up of private organizations and individuals; the second level is the *political society* which includes organizations affiliated with *the State*.

In this case the system, or superstructure, at work is the American military in the form of the joint government Weapon X program that is comprised of both the American and Canadian military branches. Accounts vary, but what is consistent is that at a young age Wade Wilson joined the military. Wade likely chose this life path because of the cultural influence of the American military and its reputation for providing a career path for disadvantaged Americans. As he puts it in *X-Men Origins: Deadpool #1*, "When I was old enough, I took advantage of the one opportunity open to broke Americans everywhere"—accompanied by a panel of Wade Wilson being sworn in for military service ("X-Men Origins: Deadpool #1, p. 22).

This is where we see Deadpool's life as a member of the proletariat first influence the events of his life. Even before becoming Deadpool, Wilson was a member of the proletariat and so had very few options available to him. If he were a member of the bourgeoisie (those who are rich and powerful) or petty bourgeoisie (those who are not quite rich but still pretty well off), he would have had other options. He was still a part of the proletariat once he became a tool of the *political society* as a soldier and when he was diagnosed with cancer his lack of resources meant he had only one real option: to join Weapon X and allow himself to be experimented on in hopes of a cure. If he were a part of the bourgeoisie, he might have had other options.

After escaping from the Weapon X program Deadpool resumed or began (depending on the issue) his career as a mercenary. In doing so he effectively placed himself in a position to both support and undermine national interests depending on who hired him. By virtue of being a mercenary, Deadpool would always be a subordinate, forever (in the immortal sense) answering (selectively) to those who hire him. He doesn't have the ability or skill to make his own weapons so his tools of the trade must be purchased, thus cutting into his ability to profit, and there is little to no chance of upward mobility as there is no formal organizational structure for lone mercenaries.

Also he is incapable of assimilating into society where he could work and rise above the station of being just another working class person and into what they call the "petty bourgeoisie" (like business owners) or the elite bourgeoisie (the captains of industry, Bill Gates/Elon Musk type folks) where he would be able to accumulate enough capital and business experience. He is unable to do this because of his tenuous grasp of reality that resulted from the previously mentioned experimentation. Yet, even if that were not the case he would still suffer from (or enjoy?) mental illness as his line of work has often involved significant brain trauma resulting in its deformation (a label that his brain is not fond of, and really, who would like to be called deformed?). Therefore, as someone who can neither die nor really do anything besides be a mercenary he has become the Eternal Proletariat.

At this point you might wonder: is it not possible that Deadpool would be content to just spend his days doing a job that he has become good at when needed and spend his time using his money as he sees fit? Perhaps, and for a time that was the case. Yet even the appeal of living a life of mindless violence and monetary excess began to lose its appeal. That particular chimichanga simply would not satisfy his hunger.

An Emotional Burrito, of Sorts

Some men hunger for money, power, women, men, and chimichangas. And while Deadpool is no exception to these desires he has found each of them . . . lacking. Yes, even the tacos. In *Deadpool #12: Bullseye Part Three: Knocking over the Candy Store*, Deadpool is paid off by the villain Bullseye to lay low indefinitely. The apparently ridiculous amount of money that Bullseye pays Deadpool is enough to keep him in snack food for about a month as he spends his time watching TV and reclining in a chair.

But before long the boredom sets in, and Deadpool decides he's had enough. In a moment of thinking to himself he asks, "Well? What did you expect?" and after a pause, "More" ("Knocking Over The Candy Store"). He then proceeds to draw his sidearm and gives himself a cranial piercing that is more than cosmetic. This moment of insight helps him to have the realization that for Deadpool it is not enough to merely have money. Money alone does not satisfy him, nor does it adequately distract him from a truth that he constantly tries to ignore: immortality is boring and there is no escape. Once Deadpool realizes that money simply will not bring him fulfillment he begins to examine other possibilities.

Oddly, or at least it would be odd for almost any other character, Deadpool finds an answer during a conversation with a shark that he recently killed: friends. As he argued with the dead animal over whether or not it was an original idea to allow seagulls to pick apart his body (as a way of killing time) he angrily asserts that "Everything I . . . I am is original! There's nobody like me!" to which the shark responds:

"You do realize what you're saying, don't you?"

"Yeah!" responds Deadpool, "I'm the #$%#%$ man!"

"No, what you are . . . is alone" replies the philosophically inclined decaying shark.

Now, you might ask, "Why does this matter?", and the answer is simple. This revelation of the need for friends combined with Deadpool's recent brush with heroism in the form of a battle with pirates leads him to pursue a new purpose in life that goes beyond merely working for money. He begins on a journey wherein the destination is, hopefully, emotional validation. He'd also accept death so that he could finally be permanently joined with his love, the personification of Death. But, seeing as that is not a particularly feasible option at the moment he decides to set his eyes on a new goal that may help him feel emotionally fulfilled: becoming a member of the X-Men.

A Community of Rejects

DEADPOOL: Why not just be 'Me'? People love me!

DEADPOOL'S BRAIN: Uhh . . . No. They don't.

The X-Men in the realm of the Marvel universe could be compared to a political organization. As Gramsci writes, "Naturally, for it to be an organization and not a confusion, it must interpret a need" (p. 25). What this means in terms of the X-Men is that they are an organization that unites a group of individuals who have a common need and who share a common ideological perspective and a vision for the future. Ideally, that vision includes a world where humans and mutants can coexist in harmony. The need that is being served by the formation of the X-Men is that of providing a refuge for people who are consistently marginalized and oppressed by mainstream culture within the Marvel universe.

As a group that is generally shunned by society, frequently discriminated against, and often hunted and persecuted, it would not be unreasonable to call them what Gramsci refers to as a subaltern group. A subaltern group is a demographic of people that are discriminated against on a regular basis. These are the folks that are rejected by the mainstream culture, not just socially but politically as well. Another way of putting it is that subalterns are marginalized from society. To be marginalized is to be denied resources like education or a political voice or in some cases even an opportunity to work. Think of how

African Americans were treated in the Jim Crow South, that's what it means to be marginalized.

And here's another word you can throw around and impress your friends: hegemony. Hegemony means the culture (and thus values, ideas, and ideologies) of the ruling class, such as politicians and businesspersons, that become normalized within society. One major role of hegemony is to keep some people in a subaltern status, to keep some folks on the bottom of society. It was this hegemonic/subaltern relationship of oppression that motivated Gramsci to take part in the formation of Socialist political organizations in hopes of making the "superior proletarian morality, based on productive work, collaboration and responsible personal relations" the hegemonic culture of society (p. 18). In other words, Gramsci wanted the values, morals, and beliefs of the working class to be the mainstream way of seeing and doing things, instead of the values of the rich and powerful. While the X-Men may not be trying to exercise that sort of influence in their society, they are similar to Gramsci's socialist political parties because of their desire to escape oppression and the marginalized subaltern status. But what does this have to do with Deadpool?

When Deadpool tries to join the X-Men he runs into two obstacles. The first is that he is not a mutant, he is in fact a "mutate." This distinction means that Deadpool's healing factor is not a naturally occurring phenomenon but was the result of something that was done to him. Therefore, from a technical aspect he does not meet the requirements for membership in the X-Men. The other obstacle is that he does not conform to the mainstream idea of what it means to be a "good guy." The standard of what constitutes a hero in the Marvel universe is kind of loose and a little fluid as anti-heroes are as common as actual heroes, and the actual heroes often have, to put it mildly, checkered pasts. That being said, there are examples of heroes who serve as standards for what it means to be a hero, such as Spider-Man or Captain America, the latter being the literal posterchild for heroic propaganda. Deadpool has both helped these characters and been at odds with them even when trying his best to be a "hero."

A prime example of the contentious relationship between Deadpool and the hegemonic idea of "hero" can be found in the three-part story arc, *Deadpool #19–21: Whatever a Spider Can.*

The plot focuses on Spider-Man and Deadpool working together (with a lot of reluctance from Spider-Man) to apprehend the simian shooter known as "Hit-Monkey" (the story is every bit as fun as it sounds, I wouldn't blame you if you stopped reading this and picked up those issues right now. In fact, you know what? Go ahead, I'll wait). After capturing the primate Spider-Man makes the observation that Hit-Monkey and Deadpool have a lot in common, this prompts a short interaction between Deadpool and Hit-Monkey wherein Deadpool has yet another revelation about his predicament (I'm noticing a theme). He says:

> We're not so different, are we? We're both . . . trapped, compelled by forces we don't understand to do the things we do. We weren't born this way—this is just how we . . . ended up. But I'm trying to change that, Hit-Monkey . . . I'm trying to change myself. And if I can do it, maybe you can, too. Whatta ya say? (p. 18)

Hit-Monkey's response to Deadpool's moment of clarity and self-disclosure is to bite him in the face. Violence ensues. Ultimately all of Deadpool's attempts to work well with others, whether with Spider-Man, Captain America, or the X-Men, are doomed to fail. He just can't follow the rules of what it means to be a hero, and any attempt to do so always involves significant conflict with his allies. Spider-Man and Captain America frequently object to his use of lethal force. And while the X-Men may be willing to turn a blind eye to *some* use of lethal force they find him to be far too unstable, making moderate to long-term membership pretty much impossible. It is for these reasons that Deadpool has found it exceedingly difficult to engage in the sort of coalition building that could offer him refuge from his subaltern status.

As it stands, mutants and other meta-humans have not yet achieved the goals set by Gramsci when it comes to influencing mainstream perceptions of what it means to be normal; they are still often marginalized and confined to subaltern status. And, so, because Deadpool's incapable of assimilating to life as a human civilian and far too psychologically traumatized and erratic to join with other heroes or heroic groups, yet at the same time lacking the moral ability to committing to being evil, he is left as a subaltern among a marginalized demographic.

He's an exile from a group of outcasts, unable to develop

political or social power that would grant him membership in the dominant ruling class. Sadly, for the reasons mentioned earlier, he can't even work as a reliable tool of the military superstructure that created him. All of this gets at my ultimate point that because of forces beyond his control Deadpool has very few options, this puts him in a position to be exploited by anyone who will have him.

. . . But at Least They Wanted You

So then, where does this leave our crazed contract killer? To recap, he has been trained and conditioned by agents of a political society superstructure to be a mercenary and, if unintentionally, psychotic. His career as a mercenary is on-again-off-again as he struggles with his enjoyment of killing that still doesn't fulfill him in a meaningful way. He is unable to join any organizations or groups primarily because he does not conform to mainstream idea of what it means to be a hero. What's more, even if he could manage to fit in, his mental state prevents him from being a reliable ally which is not helpful when trying to be a part of an organization.

Also, he's unable to die, which is something that he longs for yet despite his best efforts he has been unsuccessful in shuffling off his rather hideous mortal coil. In the *Operation: Annihilation* story arc found in the issues *Deadpool #37–39* he goes as far as to attack the Hulk with a couple of nuclear bombs in order to provoke the Hulk into killing him. The story ends with the Hulk punching Deadpool so hard that he explodes into pink mist and red globs; and yet, to his dismay, he still regenerates.

So then what is a merc to do? From a Gramscian perspective there are two options: The first is that he could search in hopes of finding an organization where he would be considered normal. This would be doing what Gramsci calls "coalition building" which is basically building a network of people that have a common cause or interest in hopes of creating some type of social change. At the very least this could operate as some sort of demented support group for Deadpool, and that counts for something.

Unfortunately, that may require Deadpool to travel to another planet as it seems that the only people on Earth-616 who are like-minded are other loner anti-heroes that find the rest of society insufferable, let alone Deadpool. Although, there was that time when the Skrull made clones with Deadpool's DNA and he helped them become as demented as himself. But that ended with them exploding from healing too much too fast. And really, any kind of team of Deadpools or Deadpool-esque beings is likely to end in an explosion of some sort.

The second option would be to go the route of Wolverine and perhaps convince the X-Men that either he could fit into their culture of what it means to be a hero, or perhaps he could create a cultural shift in the X-Men where he helps to reshape their idea of what it means to be heroic. This would be a sort of small-scale version of what Gramsci talks about when he advocates for a cultural shift towards the proletariat culture as the dominant hegemonic force. Only in this situation Deadpool would be the proletariat and the leadership of the X-Men are the bourgeois ruling class that regulates who is and is not allowed into their society.

To that point, we could argue that the X-Men act as their own society or lesser Nation-State since membership includes access to resources in the form of an infrastructure for food, education, shelter, land, protection, and so on. Wolverine may provide some insight as to how it would be possible for Deadpool to prompt a cultural shift within the X-Men. In *Wolverine: Origins #24: The Deep End Part 4*, Deadpool interrogates Wolverine as he holds him hostage and prepares him for execution (in as much as anyone could kill Wolverine, who is also virtually immortal). During the conversation just before Deadpool attempts to kill Wolverine the following exchange happens:

> WOLVERINE: Yeah, Wade . . . That's me, I'm a killer. But some o' those I killed, maybe most of 'em, didn't deser—
>
> DEADPOOL: ***Oops! Your bad! Didn't stop you from being accepted into the X-Men did it?***
>
> WOLVERINE: Huh? The X-Men—
>
> DEADPOOL: ***Talk about hypocrisy! I mean, if they let you in, you'd think they'd let anybody in but nooo . . .***
>
> WOLVERINE: You wanna . . . ? Yer not even a mutant!
>
> DEADPOOL: ***No, I'm not. But I'm not exactly human, am I?***

Y'know, maybe they did only want you because they were afraid of you . . . or because they knew they could use you. But at least they wanted you. ("Wolverine: Origins #24: The Deep End Part 4,"p. 19)

In this exchange Deadpool touches on two possible ways to instigate a cultural shift. Either he can become dangerous enough to warrant the X-Men keeping a close eye on him or he can emphasize his usefulness as a tool. Either way, the process of admitting Deadpool into the X-Men would indicate a significant cultural shift as they would have to accept someone who blurs the line of morality in a way that the other X-Men do not. Even Wolverine, arguably the most violent anti-hero on the team, isn't nearly as morally ambiguous as Deadpool is, if for no other reason than because he does not enjoy violence for violence's sake. And he's not the kind of person who, unlike Deadpool, would create furniture (for personal use) out of C4 explosives.

A a cultural shift, whether in society or within an organization, is vital to Deadpool's future if he is to obtain any satisfaction because that is the only way that he would be able to escape his subaltern status and gain the immaterial rewards that he is chasing, namely respect, acceptance, love, and anything else associated with community membership. That being said, his best chance is to join an organization like the X-Men—but, as we've seen, that's unlikely.

There exists another option that was indicated in *Deadpool #49: Evil Deadpool Conclusion: Hail to the King, Baby*. In that issue Evil Deadpool (a villain made up of Deadpool's scrap parts that where sutured together by a super fan, to put it mildly) is killed after being shot by a dart that stops his healing factor. Evil Deadpool then turns into a normal person and dies from his wounds. Deadpool, awestruck in amazement is left with the question of "How?" This is the third option, to find whatever stopped his evil twin from regenerating and use it on himself. Then he would be released from the struggle of being the Eternal Proletariat, the subaltern with little chance of empowerment. Otherwise, Deadpool will be condemned to an unending life of bad jokes and extreme violence, and that's a long time to have to keep coming up with new puns.

Deadpool's life serves as an example of what can and often

does happen to people every day, albeit an exaggerated and comically tragic example. Deadpool has been trapped by circumstance and shaped by forces larger than himself into something that doesn't even vaguely resemble the person that we are led to believe he used to be. He, like many of us, was thrown into a proletarian existence lacking the resources and capital required to make choices that didn't have to take "need" into account.

Wade Wilson was raised in a broken home, as many of us have been. He joined the military out of a sense of desperation just as many of us work jobs because of need, a need to pay the bills, a need to *do* something with our lives, a need to have the creature comforts that make this life bearable. And like many people who find themselves considering a second, third, or fourth career, he realized that his job just didn't satisfy him anymore. While his exploits are outrageous and unrealistic his motivations and challenges are generally applicable to the lives of many people: we've all been molded by cultural forces, whether the education system, capitalism, poverty, societal norms, or family culture, that have shaped us into who we are, with or without our consent.

Really, given the staggering lack of control we have over our lives based on where we were born and to whom, it's a wonder that more of us aren't insane like Deadpool. But, unlike him, we have the ability to enact Gramscian solutions like engaging in coalition building, influencing the mainstream, and enacting change that is empowering. And while the ability to create social change isn't quite as cool at parties as showing everyone that you can regenerate a thumb, it does offer the chance to make a world worth living in, which is particularly important when that is your only option.

24

Won't The Real Wade Wilson Please Stand Up?

~~Ben Abelson~~ Deadpool

Hey there, philosophiles! It's me, Deadpool: The Regeneratin' Degenerate! How did I get such a cool rhymey nickname, you ask? Well, I've got this righteous healing factor that lets me recover from any wound, no matter how severe. Slice off a finger, a limb, even my head, and it'll grow back faster than you can eat ten chimichangas (but not faster than I can eat ten chimichangas).

Life in the mercenary business has earned me a ton of dangerous enemies, so it doesn't take long for me to shed enough old body parts to make a whole 'nother Deadpool. And that's exactly what happened! A few years back (in Deadpool Volume 2, #44), a bunch of my discarded members (not just that one, you gutter-minded creepos), combined together to form an evil duplicate of me. But I'm not sure whether this other guy was a copy of me, or whether I'm the copy and he's the original.

See, he had all of my memories of being Deadpool (or at least the ones that I had before I/he lost his/my head—this is so confusing!) and his parts were Deadpool parts before any of my current parts were. I can't stop thinking about this puzzle (just like that jigsaw puzzle of nude Bea Arthur I put together last week. Yowza!)

If Evil Deadpool is the real Deadpool, then Deadpool can never be on the main Avengers team,

which would be a total bummer. And worse, I don't wanna be a cheapo knockoff clone, like Peter Parker before the retcon. To help me out of this metaphysipickle, I've kidna . . . er . . . enlisted this egghead philosopher type, Ben Abelson. He's helping me write this super-smart article, which consults the work of a bunch of other eggheads from days of philosophy past and present, in seeking a definitive answer to my most epic of quandaries.

Um, Deadpool, you know philosophers don't usually come up with definitive answers to their questions the way mathematicians do. That's kind of what makes a question philosophical in the first place. Instead, they mostly try to get clearer on exactly what the question is asking and to rule out answers that are probably false, contradict themselves, or don't make sense.

Hmmm . . . In that case, is there a Deadpool and Math volume I can consult by any chance? Never mind, math gives me the sleepies. Just stop peeing in my pool and make with the thinky-think. (And yes, I realize you already did all your peeing in your pants when I broke into your apartment and put this katana to your neck. Nice curtains, by the way. Oh, and call me "DOCTOR Pool" from now on. I've got a PhD—a pulverising heads degree.)

The Pirate Ship of Theseus

Okay, Dr. Pool. But remember, if you kill me, you won't get an answer. Anyway, your case is fascinating. You're a walking Ship of Theseus.

The ship of who? Was it a pirate ship? You know, I had my own pirate ship once (in Deadpool Volume 2, #14–15).

Well that's the thing. *Deadpool* had a pirate ship, but that was before this Evil Deadpool guy showed up. So if he, and not you, is the real Deadpool, then *you* didn't have the pirate ship after all. Anyway, the Ship of Theseus . . .

That's Pirate Ship of Theseus, buckaroo!

Fine. The *Pirate* Ship of Theseus is a classic philosophical thought experiment that tests the coherency of our concept of identity.

Now, listen here, brainiac. I hate experiments almost as much as I hate tests. And I hate tests almost as much as I hate being coherent. So far you're just making this worse. Give me something I can use, or I start damaging vertebrae so that you can no longer use your legs.

Please be patient with me, Dr. Pool, and let's just think about how this, um . . . Pirate Ship of Theseus thing works. The puzzle was first formulated by the Greek historian Plutarch (A.D. 46–127). He wondered whether or not the ship that Theseus sailed would still be the same ship after all its parts (planks, mast, other ship things) were replaced, one by one, over time. If an object is just the exact parts it's made up of, then it seems it can't survive losing or replacing even one single part, no matter how small or insignificant. But if that were true, then nothing would ever exist for more than a fraction of a second, because everything is constantly losing microscopic parts. Even our own bodies are continuously shedding cells and regenerating new ones.

So it seems we have to agree that objects can survive some changes in their parts. But where's the limit? Suppose the limit is fifty percent, so that as soon as a ship is down to forty-nine percent of its original parts, it becomes a different ship. The problem is that if we set such a limit, then a ship's identity would depend on whether or not it has a single splinter of an original plank or even a microscopic particle of that splinter, such as an atom or even smaller. But that would put us right back where we started, with the problem that something so insignificant should not make a difference to something's identity. If it did, you could lose all of your limbs and part of your torso and still be Deadpool, but trim your fingernails and become someone totally different.

Well I might really be a different person if I actually trimmed my fingernails. Also, I heard some math in there. For every calculation from here on, you're losing a toe!

The point is there's no way to set a limit on the amount of parts a thing can lose while remaining the same thing, without that thing's identity coming to depend on something tiny and insignificant. Your regenerating ability intensifies the problem, since you shed and regenerate parts at a much faster rate than anyone or anything else. You can even lose your head and grow it back, yet presumably still be the same person. (Some other guy named Ben is dealing with that problem elsewhere in this book. By the way, *please* go and harass him once you're done here.)

Therefore, we have to allow that Theseus's pirate ship is still the same ship after all of its parts are replaced, just as you can still be Deadpool after all of your parts are sliced off and regrown.

Hooray! So I am the real Deadpool!

Not so fast, Dr. Pool. Because of this Evil Deadpool character, your case is a bit more complicated. You see, the philosopher Thomas Hobbes (1588–1679) came up with a variation on the ship problem in which, as the old parts of Theseus's ship are removed and replaced, they are collected in a warehouse and reassembled into a second ship. Now it seems that this second ship (let's call it the "reconstructed ship") also has a claim to being the original Pirate Ship of Theseus. After all, unlike the ship in the harbor with the new parts (call it the "renovated ship"), it actually has planks that Theseus walked on. And this is the problem with Evil Deadpool. Since he's made up of parts that were parts of Deadpool before any of your parts were, it seems he has at least as good of a claim to being the original Deadpool as you do.

I don't like where this is going. That Hobbes tiger should have stuck to running around with the little spiky-haired kid in those newspaper funny strips.

Don't despair now, Dr. Pool. There is much more to consider!

Ugh, but my head already hurts. And yours will too if you don't come up with something good. And chop chop, or else . . . chop chop!

The Prince of Asgard and the Clobberer

You see Dr. Pool, your situation is a bit different, because you are not a ship. You are a person. And as the philosopher John Locke (1632–1704) believed, you have to think of personal identity differently from how you think of the identity of non-persons.

Did that Locke guy ever get off that weird island he was lost on? I never made it past the third season.

This is a different John Locke. He came up with another thought experiment to help him figure out what makes a person the same individual over time. This one is about the Prince and the Cobbler.

Wait a second. The Prince? Are we also gonna solve the ancient Zen riddle of what it sounds like when doves cry? If so, don't bother. I already know that one.

No, not that Prince. Just *a* Prince. As in the son of a king.

Oh. So, like Thor, Prince of Asgard. (Heh, ass-guard).

Yeah okay, it can be Thor.

And "the cobbler"? You mean like peach cobbler? Or did you mean to say "clobberer", like Ben Grimm, The Thing; as in "it's clobberin' time"?

Well no, a cobbler is . . . You know what? Fine. Let's just say it's Thor and The Thing. Okay?

You're the brainiac, buddy. Just dole me out some fresh chunks of sweet wisdom. And make it snappy. My ADD is tingling.

Just imagine one night, after battling frost giants and drinking mead, Thor falls asleep in his princely bed in his home of Asgard. That same night, The Thing, after helping his Fantastic Four team-mates take down Doctor Doom, passes out in his own bed in the Baxter Building. However, in the morning, Thor's body, with its long blonde hair and chiseled good looks, wakes up and is surprised by its surroundings.

Thor's body no longer has any memories of Thor's life: of battling frost giants, falling in love with the mortal Jane Foster, or teaming up with the Avengers. Instead, he has all of The Thing's memories. He remembers traveling into space and facing a barrage of cosmic rays that transformed him into a being of orange rock, living on Yancy Street, and of his exploits with Mr. Fantastic, The Invisible Woman and the Human Torch. On the other hand, the body of orange rock wakes up in the Baxter building with Thor's memories instead of The Thing's. According to Locke, everyone would conclude that Thor and The Thing switched bodies, since your memories make you the person you are. So whoever remembers being you, really *is* you.

But that doesn't help at all! Evil Deadpool has all the same memories that I do up to the point when his head was first removed and my current head grew!

Not only that, but there are a ton of things that I don't remember from my life. Does that mean that I didn't really do those things? And what if I just remember a couple of things from someone else's life: like Psylocke telepathically projects her memory of taking a shower into my head? (That would be hot.) Would that mean that I am both me and Psylocke? (Still hot, but weirder). Would she and I both be Psylocke in that moment? (Really weird. Still hot, though.)

Good point, Dr. Pool. You're getting the hang of this. Memory can't be the only thing that matters for personal identity. But Locke's point is helpful, because it shows us that, unlike with ships, features of our psychology: our thoughts, personality and moral values make us who we are, not the physical parts out of which we're composed.

Merc Morality and Other Stories

So maybe it's the fact that Evil Deadpool is evil that makes him not the real Deadpool. Sure, we both kill people, but that's all he ever wants to do. I only do it when it's necessary—like when I need money. The only time I enjoy it is when someone really deserves to be killed—like you, if you don't give me some answers pronto!

Although your threats to my life make it hard for me to see it, there may be a subtle, but important moral difference between you and Evil Deadpool. However, isn't it possible that Evil Deadpool could one day come to see things the way that you do? Or if his brain is diseased in a way that makes such change impossible, couldn't your brain become diseased too, so that you become like him?

Don't villains become heroes and heroes turn villainous all the time? Yet we still think of them as being the same person, just reformed or corrupted. Sometimes we say "they're not the person they used to be." But do we really mean that literally? One of the things that makes people interesting is that our characteristics aren't static. It's not only the cells of our bodies that change. Our personalities are often transformed over time, in response to our experiences. So the fact that Evil

Deadpool has become evil doesn't mean he's not the same person as the original Deadpool.

I don't like where this is going, chief. My katana hand is starting to feel slicey.

Alright . . . on the other hand, maybe Evil Deadpool doesn't even think of himself as the real Deadpool. If he told us the story of his life, he might start with when he woke up in Dr. Ellen Whitby's lab with a complete body. (Well, mostly complete. He does have two right arms. But that shouldn't make a difference, should it?) Whereas you trace your life story all the way back to the birth of Wade Wilson. According to some philosophers, such as Marya Schechtman, who we are might just be a matter of the story or narrative we construct about our lives. We're the protagonists of our own life-narratives. That would be particularly appropriate in your case, Deadpool, since you're a fictional character. Your life literally is a narrative.

Hey now! Don't start getting all meta on me. That's my thing!

Well, we are doing *meta*-physics here.

Was that supposed to be a joke? Why don't you stick to philosophizing and leave the humor to the professionals?

Okay, okay. Anyway, Schechtman's narrative view of personal identity has its own problems. It may be too subjective. If the narrative view were true, then it seems you could be anyone you wanted to be. We could try to come up with some rules for what gets to be part of your narrative, but those rules would have to be based on some other factors like memory, psychological similarity, or having the same body—all of which we've already considered. Also, it's not clear that all people do weave their lives into stories that make sense to them. Not everyone thinks of their life as a story, but that doesn't mean that they don't have identities.

Identity Schmidentity

One philosopher named Derek Parfit thinks that, in cases like yours, there isn't really any answer to the question of who the original Deadpool is. You and Evil Deadpool are both related to the original Deadpool in the same way, but neither of you is *identical* to the original Deadpool.

The original Deadpool survived as both of you, branching into your two distinct lives. According to Parfit, the original Deadpool no longer exists, but that's not a big deal, because identity isn't really so important anyway. What matters for survival is just the continuity of memory, beliefs, morality, and so on, between the original Deadpool and any future persons. So any person in the future who has Deadpool's psychological characteristics, is someone Deadpool survives as. If there are two Deadpools, neither one is *the* real you, but they're both just as good as being the real you.

I don't like this at all. Does that mean I have to share everything with Evil Deadpool? He gets half my chimichangas? Half of my weapons? Are we both married to my demon wife, Shiklah? Actually, she'd probably dig that. But I'm no good at sharing! There's gotta be another way!

Well, you just reminded me that Schechtman has changed her position from the narrative view that we talked about before. She calls her new idea the "Person-Life View." According to the Person-Life View, what makes you the person you are is all the commitments, roles, and relations to others that make up your life. Your being married to Shiklah, your relationship with your daughter Eleanor, and your projects as both a mercenary and, occasionally, a hero, all contribute to the person you are. Since you have the same "person-life" or occupy the same position in "person-space" that the original Deadpool did, you are the same person as he.

I'd really like to buy into that floating bouncy castle of a theory. But I think it's full o' holes. The problem is that my marriage to Shiklah happened after Evil Deadpool showed up. It was only recently that I started teaming up with the Uncanny Avengers and began to be seen as a hero by the public. Even my Mercs for Money business is pretty much brand new. And I just found out I have a daughter like thirty issues ago! By the time this goes to press, Marvel will probably have rebooted their publishing line three or four times and completely changed my character's status quo. My person-space changes all the time. Not only that, but couldn't I be an imposter in someone else's person-space? Maybe Evil Deadpool

should be in my person-space and I should be out there killing indiscriminately!

Once again, you've raised an insightful objection, Dr. Pool. If we want to get to your desired conclusion: that you are the one and only original Deadpool, then we're going to have to think of something else. Of course, this is doing philosophy backwards. You're not supposed to choose your answer first and then try to find a theory that justifies it.

But you will, or else you'll be facing the end of your own person-life!

Poolcore

Okay, so there's one approach to personal identity we haven't considered yet. It's not a very popular view and is a bit fuzzy in the details, but I think you'll like it. I've been working on developing it myself, but it was first introduced by the philosopher Peter Unger. According to Unger, what makes you the same person over time is not your own specific set of mental characteristics. It's not your own particular memories, beliefs, or moral values. All of those things can change. You can lose all your memories, turn good or evil, and change your worldview, and yet still be yourself.

What makes you the same person over time is just that you continue to be a person at all. Continuing to be a conscious being with the ability to form thoughts at all is what accounts for your identity. Your *distinctive* properties can change, but you're still *you* as long as you maintain your *core* capacities that are common to all persons.

Let's make this clearer by going back to the pirate ship example from before. You might argue that the renovated ship (the one with new parts), is the original ship, because it has been a ship all along. However, the parts assembled into the reconstructed ship, in the warehouse, stopped being ship parts as soon as they were replaced on the renovated ship. The reconstructed ship was not a ship before it was assembled in the warehouse. Its parts were not parts of any ship, much less the Pirate Ship of Theseus, so it has no claim to being that ship after all.

Similarly, your lost parts ceased to be Deadpool parts as soon as they were detached from you and replaced by your new regrown parts. They only became parts of a body again when they were reassembled into Evil Deadpool. The whole time there was a living, breathing, conscious Deadpool, maintaining the core capacities that make you a person. There might have been a short period of time during which you weren't conscious, because you didn't have a head, but because you were able to regrow one, you still had the *capacity* for consciousness.

It's just like when you're held in suspended animation or cryogenic freezing and then revived. It's still you, even if you've been mind-wiped by that evil scientist Butler who used you as his personal assassin. Let's also assume that before recombining with the other parts that Evil Deadpool's head wasn't conscious and that your other discarded parts couldn't have regrown a head on their own. If all that is true (though it probably isn't), then you are the real Deadpool! Okay?

Yeah, I think that's good enough for me. It'll hold up in court, too, right? Don't answer that. But hey, how do you know so much about my life? You're not in league with that Butler guy, are you?!

No, I swear! I'm not a scientist. I only deal in thought experiments . . . and maybe the occasional survey study. But nothing with any cutting or applying electrodes to sensitive areas or implanting false memories. I know so much about you, because I'm a huge fan! I buy all your comic books—even the extra mini-series, one-shots, tie-ins, and guest appearances that are totally not just cash-grabs exploiting the mindless completism of brainwashed collectors.

Oh wow, that's really flattering. (Heh, sucker.)

You know I can read what you type even if you put it in parentheses, right?

Yeah, I don't really care about your feelings. But because you did me a solid, I'll let you live and won't detach any of your parts . . . today.

Fair enough. Now please leave so I can change my pants.[1] . . .

. . . Wait, could you, um, untie me? <sigh>

---

[1] Thanks to Jason Chang, Marie Friquegnon, John O'Mahoney, Ana Talushllari, and James Witherspoon for feedback on a draft of this chapter.

VII

Are You There, God?

It's Me, Abandoned and All Alone in the Universe, You Stupid Mother-$*#($%!*

25
Deadpool Kills God

NICOLAS MICHAUD, ALONE, WITHOUT ANYONE ELSE'S HELP, IN A UNIVERSE OF MEANINGLESS SOLITUDE, DAMMIT

Deadpool is an asshole. Yeah, I know, the movie version is supposed to make me more sympathetic to the character. But let's be honest, even though Deadpool has become an increasingly more heroic and caring person as time has gone on, he started as an asshole, and he really is an asshole.

Sure, watching him shoot villains who're already defeated and weaponless is funny, but, in the end it is a dick move. In fact, killing people who are helpless, which Deadpool does enjoy doing with regularity, is pretty damned evil. So sure, Deadpool has saved the world, and sure, some versions of Deadpool want to be heroes, but at his core, Deadpool is selfish, malicious, and cruel. He might even be considered evil.

There really is only one thing I can think of that might mitigate Deadpool's evil actions . . . the fact that he doesn't really choose them. Deadpool is a character in a comic; he's written, so his actions are really the result of the writers' actions. That, of course, seems to be a copout. We're talking about the character. Isn't it cheating if I use the writers as an excuse?

Well, not really, as they create Deadpool and in his case he realizes he is written. So whether you want to look at Deadpool as actually recognizing that he is a comic character or just the writers making up that idea, either way we now have this idea of a man who realizes his fate is written, and his actions are written.

There are these evil-ass authors who go through the trouble of making a crap-ass world, with all kinds of evil in it, and then they throw our poor mutilated, abused, and insane Wade

Wilson into it and we see what happens. The writers are basically the gods of the Marvel universe. *They* decide what the world will be like and what happens. And they don't write a very nice world. So, really, the writers are evil. The Gods of Marvel are assholes.

The Biggest Dick

First things first, because this chapter is going to go to some pretty dark places. Deadpool is not a hero. Deadpool goes through an awful lot of trouble to try to kill everyone. The *Deadpool Killogy* makes that fact pretty clear. So let's get this straight first off… Deadpool is not a good guy. I don't think we need a bunch of philosophical mumbo-jumbo or bullshit to realize Deadpool is pretty evil.

Let some of the others authors in this book spend their time trying to justify his actions or come up with some reason why he's really a hero. The fact of the matter is, I don't really feel like making excuses for Wade. He's a dick, that much seems to be obvious. Hell, if he wasn't a dick, we wouldn't love him so much. (Yes, yes, very funny; try to focus).

Okay, I get it, you want some actual evidence. Well, consider *Deadpool Kills the Marvel Universe*. Okay, maybe there is some "excuse" like Deadpool was driven (more) insane or Deadpool was brainwashed or whatever, but the fact is that it really isn't that hard to recognize Deadpool as a murderer *of an entire f&$@ing universe.* That is a pretty hard action to justify. And, even if you do want to justify it, how about all of the other crap Deadpool does? Sure Wade occasionally tried to do right . . . He tries to save some little girl from a burning building or he tries to help a little old lady across the street (probably to meet some Bea Arthur fetish). But, as a whole, Wade is pretty willing to do a whole lot of evil… for money.

Perhaps today we find Wade somewhat justifying for ourselves. After all, we do like the fact that Deadpool is all in it for himself. He's willing to do an awful lot of horrible things to get what he wants. Let's be honest, we are too. Really, he's just a good capitalist doing what he needs to meet his perverted wants. So there's probably some part of us that likes Wade. When nutjobs ram planes into our buildings, we carpet bomb the bastards. If we make more money by torturing pigs in factory farms rather than ever let them see the light of day, well then let the little piggies suffer. If the homeless are begging for food, then they need to get off their lazy asses and get jobs. It isn't our problem. In other words, we're in it for ourselves. Sure we occasionally throw a dollar at some pathetic homeless fellow or do something else to make us feel good like Wade saving a cat from a tree, but overall we know we could give a lot more, serve a lot more, and help a lot more. Wade is the same way. He throws some good around now and then, but overall, he is in it for him.

I won't be able to convince you that Deadpool is evil just because he's selfish. The fact that *we* are selfish prevents us from that conclusion. After all, the fact that we would rather have a new iPhone, some new music, or an epic pair of kicks than donate most of our hard-earned cash to save the lives of children in a country we will never see is evidence to our selfishness. Okay, fair enough. The fact that Douchepool is a merc who is selfish doesn't make him evil.

What about the fact that he kills people for money? Well I guess we probably don't consider that necessarily evil. After all a mercenary is kind of like someone who serves in the military. Though, of course, unlike the armed services Wade's loyalties are also for sale. But again, that isn't evil, right, that's just dishonorable . . .

Well, I'm just gonna stick with this . . . When Wade kills the Marvel universe, he kills everyone, mothers, fathers, kids, you name it. I'm not sure whether there's a particularly good excuse for that, but I'm willing to say there isn't. At the end of the day, we all have a pretty strong sense of morality. And Wade's willingness to kill as he wants is a bit on the "not a great guy end." So let's just say that, "Wade isn't a great guy." Sometimes he does good (rarely), often he does harm (for funzies), and overall he is a pretty massive dick.

The Why Behind the Butt

But, as you pointed out earlier, when Wade does go on his massive killing spree, there's a reason why. Simply put, the writers. Wade justifies trying to kill everyone in the universe in order to free them from the writers controlling their universe. These "progenitors" are the evil that make Deadpool suffer as he does, and, in fact, make the universe suffer as well. So Deadpool's first thought is to save everyone from the progenitors, the creators, by killing them all. In doing this, in killing every living thing and destroying the Marvel universe, Deadpool believes he will finally be able to die . . . yay?

So why the hell would an immortal badass who gets some pretty lovely ladies want to die? (Death and Bea Arthur to name a couple . . . maybe at the same time now? Too soon?) Deadpool often wants to die . . . he is insane, in pain, often alone, and generally miserable. Worse, he will inevitably watch everyone he loves die as he drones on and on. One thing that becomes exceedingly clear in a universe of immortality is death and suffering. You can't miss it. Sure you get to see new life come into the world and flourish, but then you watch it suffer, wilt and die. Deadpool is in some ways cursed. He can't escape watching everything go to shit, and there is an ever-increasing amount of shit for Deadpool to wade in (okay, that one was on purpose).

So the reason why Deady is being such a prolapsed hemorrhoid of awfulness is because he himself is miserable, and in some crazy (read, "kind of sane") way believes he can help everyone by freeing them from the control of the writers. And the fact is, he's right. Deadpool wouldn't be such a massive douche if he wasn't written that way. He wouldn't try to kill the Marvel universe if he wasn't written that way, annnnnnnd he wouldn't suffer so miserably if he wasn't written that way. So really, it's all in the hands of the progenitors. They make the universe miserable.

Really, in fact, Deadpool seems to have a pretty damn good reason to go after the progenitors themselves. The problem is that unless they write it, he can't even *think* about going after them. Those hacks can just sit back and laugh as they write Deadpool trying to do *something, anything* to escape his plight, but they will never write him the ability to actually do so. They won't simply stop writing Deadpool comics, they make way too much money off of him. So Deadpool will continue to suffer, while his writers presumably jerk off into the massive pile of money they are now making off of selling movie rights.

It's pretty pathetic, the way the authors play with Wade's head. When he realizes he is completely dicked, he tries to kill the universe, but, HA! Can't do that, the writers can always make more, there are just too many heroes popping up for

Deadpool to manage it. So then, just to show off the fact that they have English degrees, the writers create *Deadpool Killustrated* where our hero tries to kill all of the characters through classic literature who inspire the different superheroes. If he can kill Tom Sawyer, Captain Ahab, Pinocchio, and the rest of them, then he can prevent the almost infinite superheroes inspired by them from ever coming into existence.

Aside from all of the "*Back to the Future* while tripping balls on acid time-paradoxes" caused by even *thinking* about this plan, it is a ridiculous idea. The writers have ALL the power. Deadpool should know that he is only able to try to kill the classics *is because the progenitors let him.* In fact, they don't even let him have the thought "Well this is a f$*#%ing stupid idea. I should have a beer and go home." He just tries, and, of course, fails, because the writers will it to be so.

Finally, Deadpool comes to the completely insane belief that the reason why he can't escape his fate is because *he is the originator of the universe*. Aside from the fact that some of my very favorite philosophers (Bishop Berkeley anyone?) considered this idea, it is complete claptrap. To quote Deadpool himself, "Yeah . . . I've heard that I'm the-self-aware-creator-of-all-Things-Multiversal-Baby-Daddy Before . . . If we're so high-and-mighty, why don't we fix it?" (*Deadpool Kills Deadpool*).

Who is he speaking to? Himself of course. Deadpool is both clearly very right, and completely wrong. Sure, the universe as he experiences it is created by Wade, and once he is dead *his* universe is gone, but the idea that he can somehow defeat the progenitors by killing all of the different versions of himself is, well, just Wade Wilson-eque narcissism. But, of course, the writers write him to think this. They write him to go through the process of killing *all of the instances of himself!* Why? For their own amusement.

Deadpool thinks that the reason why he doesn't "fix it" is because he subconsciously doesn't want to. Again, this could be possible in a the-universe-is-of-my-making sense. But as the readers, we have an insight Wade doesn't . . . he doesn't fix it, because he can't. The writers won't let him. They let him think it's his fault, they let him think he has free will, they write him playing with himself (in a trying to kill himself kind of a way), but they won't let him really grasp the truth . . . that he was never free, he can't be free, and it's all their fault.

Here's Where It Gets Hard

I have to give Deadpool credit, though. As he is trying to stop himself from killing himself (and everyone else) he doesn't have that much patience with the whiny reasoning above. The "Oh the writers make things shitty" argument doesn't really move him much. In fact he says, "And mama never loved us? I get it you had a rough life. You know who else had a rough life? Everybody!" (*Deadpool Kills Deadpool*). Well said, Deadpool! Yeah, shit sucks (okay, not literally), but DP is on to something here . . . life is pretty miserable and everyone suffers. But the problem his "evil" self also realizes this and points out, "Exactly! The world . . . The universe . . . All of existence... suffers!" And that is why Deadpool should kill God.

Okay, back up, I realize I skipped a few steps. But really at this point it should be obvious, Brainiac (yeah wrong universe, I know). The writers are clearly the evil ones. They write the evil, they permit the evil, they *revel* in the evil. Sure, Deadpool *does* the evil, but he can't do anything without their say-so, and, in fact, can't even *think* of doing anything without them writing that thought bubble for him. So if Deadpool is, as I have argued "not a great guy," then the fact is, it isn't his fault! He literally is the creation of another at all moments in his existence. He wasn't just created and sent on his merry way . . . everything he does is part of a plan . . . all of it leading to a particular foreseen outcome! Sound familiar?

Deadpool realizes something that we can get pretty uncomfortable with . . . Namely, that the universe is a dark, awful place that wants to kill us . . . *and will*. We're all going to die, but not before suffering *a lot* first. That isn't to say there aren't some really nice things out there, sunsets, *Golden Girls* marathons, masturbation (the last two are in no way connected), but as a whole, the universe is really very, very killy.

All around us, we're surrounded by death. AND pretty much everything we enjoy requires some ridiculous amount of suffering! Enjoy that hamburger? . . . tortured cow. Enjoy those shoes? . . . tortured sweat-shop kids. Enjoy that chocolate? Little beaten slave-chocolate-picker kids. Enjoy that carrot? mistreated farmers . . . and the list goes on and on. The universe is filled with super-bacteria, volcanos, cancer, and things with pointy teeth that want to eat us. Overall, it's pretty well guaranteed that we will suffer before we die, a good deal. So Deadpool (the Deadpool who wants to destroy the universe) has a point . . . Everybody suffers and it is someone's fault.

In the case of Deadpool himself, it's the writers' fault. But what about in our case? Well in our case, if there is a God, then it's God's fault. Now, I won't waste your time with a whole lot of argument back and forth about whether or not the evil in the world is actually the responsibility of God or not. (May's chapter does it better anyway, may he burn for it that idea-stealing hack). The fact is you are too smart for that (probably). Let's cut the bullshit. If God created the universe, and God know the future, then he knew what evil would happen. If God created the Garden of Eden, *then he let the serpent exist in it*. Humanity isn't responsible for the origin of evil in the universe. We'd probably still be in the Garden shitting ourselves senseless from eating too much low-hanging overripe fruit if God hadn't let the serpent in to tempt us in the first place.

Overall, we, like Deadpool who wants to kill himself for being the origin of the universe, want to blame ourselves. And that isn't a bad call. We are pretty shitty. Unlike the bacteria, volcanoes, cancer, and things with pointy teeth that want to eat us, we *know* that the world could be nicer, and we actively choose to make it worse. We suck. *But that is how we were written*. And that's the problem! Whatever answer we want to give . . . we can yell "free will" until we're blue in the face, but we know we're just blowing smoke (or somebody) because there is a "plan." And if God has a plan *then every single bit of lips-macking, bowelrupturing, blood-letting evil in the world is a part of that plan*. If we say, "No! It isn't part of that plan!" Then we have to admit stuff happens that isn't written by God, and it isn't part of the plan, and he (or she) (or she-he, he-she, etc.) is just as screwed as we are and has no idea what is going to happen as the rest of us.

Well we can't have that. The idea that God might not actually know what's going to happen and that human beings have enough free will to *actually determine the future* isn't an idea we like. So we find ourselves saying crazy stuff like, "Oh, it isn't like God makes us do it . . . he just knows what we're going to do and then we do it alllll by ourselves." BUT HE CREATED US KNOWING WHAT WE ARE GOING TO DO! So even if somehow we are free in that insane calculation, it doesn't change the fact that God made Adolf (burning in hell as we speak) Hitler KNOWING that Hitler would do all kinds of evil. Why do that? Well, then, we have to answer, "We aren't supposed to question that!" And our argument has to stop, doesn't it? Who are we to question the mind of God? We're just supposed to sit down, shut up, and not ask questions.

But here's my thought. Not Deadpool's, not my Publisher's, just mine . . . the really interesting question of philosophy isn't whether or not God exists. We've beaten that question to death. The really interesting question is . . . If God does exist, should we do what God wants? In a world with so much evil and suffering, free will or not, God *lets* happen, why should we let an entity that allows that evil in the world tell us what to do?

Now *that*'s a Deadpool question—heretical, dangerous, and unwise. Nevertheless, it is a good one. Because even without all the evil humans do, there are a lot of sweet innocent kids killed by tsunamis, earthquakes, and SIDs that had nothing to do with human action. Sure, we like to say "It's punishment for our sins" or "No one, not even babies, are free from sin," but we can't escape the realization that this means that our all-loving God kills kids, or lets them die, to punish others, or because they were born (because he let them be born that way) with sin . . .

Either way, why would I listen to *THAT* guy for what is right or wrong? Because lightning bolts, that's why. And that is a terrible justification for morality: "Well we decide what is right and wrong based on the fact that there is this guy who will kill us or torture us for eternity if we don't do what he says, so just do what he says, he crazy!" That isn't morality, that is selfishness, cowardice, and thoughtlessness all rolled up into one big turd chimichanga (Didn't think I'd get a chimichanga reference in here did-ja?)

The comedy of all of this . . . is of course the fact that I think, that I even wrote, that the above paragraph is my idea. But if there is some great cosmic author of our destinies in the sky, then really *he* wrote it. So that heretical question, the one I'm going to burn for, I couldn't have even thought it, if it wasn't part of the plan—it was divinely written by someone who knew what I would think, and that I would be damned for it, long before my birth.

So to that I say . . . Go get him, Deadpool. Kick his bearded ass.[1]

[1] Funny thing . . . about two paragraphs up my computer died randomly and took my unsaved draft of my chapter with it. When Windows (damn them) decided to reboot, nothing . . . no paper in the autosave, nada. But I searched and searched and found it as a hidden file, eventually. And you know what my first thought was? "Thank God." . . . Yup, I'm totally f%*#-ed.

26
Why We Love to Watch Deadpool . . . Play with Himself

JACOB THOMAS MAY AND THE VOICES IN HIS HEAD

> If this game had a shame meter . . . it would be full right now.
>
> —Deadpool's Ego, *Deadpool the Video Game*

Imagine for a moment that you met a being which could not die, could not get sick or hurt, and could not really age.

He could teleport wherever he wanted to, read people's minds and even rewrite the world as he saw fit on the fly. What might you call this being? Most would say God . . . I say Deadpool . . . yet what if they are one and the same?

That Deadpool is "miraculous" with his powers is not in doubt—he comes back from the dead and is still alive in the year 3000—but what if those powers were because he was really the Almighty?

Given time, I'm sure that I can convince you that this is the case. The thing that really needs discussing here is not whether or not Deadpool *is* God . . . but whether or not he's a *good* God. I hear that Michaud hack is writing about something similar, good job choosing my chapter instead!

*Hey Player, just go with it, I'ma change your f**king life!*

The Deadpool game starts with our Merc with a Mouth having sent a script to game designer High Moon Studios' office and being rejected in his bid to to make "his game." The voices in Wade's head (known as his Ego and SuperEgo—most of the main voice-work as WadePrime is considered his Id) talk to him about how fun the game will be. As Deadpool comments to them that they will call back he pushes a button and as we hear explosions in the distance . . . High Moon calls back with acceptance.

Long has been the argument over the nature of Evil and its existence in a world where God also reigns. Since the times of the Greeks, people have debated whether or not a God-like figure can truly be called all-powerful, all-knowing, and all good at the same time. So many different versions of the argument co-exist and butt heads with each other that you might read them and go on a multi-verse kill-a-thon, taking out one person for every version that is in print. ***The real reason for Deadpool Kills the Multiverse, huh?***

The modern view of the Problem of Evil seems to suggest that the one of these three, that God is all good, cannot be true, but we will get to that right after our regularly-scheduled commercial break! ***Sorry, you didn't buy the premium version of our book, you have to sit through all the damn Geico ads now!***

Supposing that someone is all-powerful, and has abilities beyond those of mortal men (hint, hint), they should have no problem trying to rid the world of evils. As we've seen again and again, Wade constantly tries to team up with as many people as he can (most notably the X-Men). He often joins the side most of us would consider to be just, in attempts to right the wrongs of the world. In Deadpool the game he does this from the start, at first following the script (which he wrote, but still seems hell-bent on not following and is often surprised by) and then later veering from it after tearing it apart and burning it in the jet-fire of a giant sentinel-boot. SPOILER ALERT.

Throughout the game, we see Deadpool exert powers even beyond his "regular" powers (as far as cannon goes anyways). He uses his thought-bubbles as platforms to cross rivers of acid, he rewrites the surrounding world to his own liking and uses (by pulling out the script to the game, which he constantly refutes, and writing over it in crayon) and even controls when the game actually ends (several times giving us fake menus and credits before saying he "wants more action" and makes the plot change to suit his or our needs for more carnage. (No, not *that* Carnage, just bloody mayhem.)

So Deadpool has abilities most men can only dream of, giving him the powers to stop many of the evils in the world today

. . . but does he always do this? There's a scene early on where Cable is trying to tell Wade that he has come back from a war-ravaged wasteland in the future to help Deadpool stop the events leading to that future. As he tries to tell Wade the important steps to help him do this, our good-ol' Deadpoolio hops into one of those Wal-Mart coin-operated kiddie rockets and argues with the voices in his head about "which super-powered women have the best racks." He inevitably misses everything Cable says to him and then goes on the wrong quest—leading him and Cable through several unnecessary adventures before they come to the correct junction. Many philosophers would say that this utter disregard for the welfare of others couldn't be shared by a God-like figure, but we'll get to that too.

Given the fact that Deadpool has the abilities to stop the people trying to end the world, you would think that he should do just that . . . but maybe he just doesn't know any better. Or maybe he knows *everything* . . . and just doesn't care.

Wait . . . Script?!?!?!

The second main point in the argument over the problem of evil is whether or not God is all-knowing in relation to the other two as well. Deadpool surely seems to fit this criterion. Often in the game, Deadpool breaks the fourth wall. Not only does he do this by talking to the player, but commenting on what the player is thinking—or at least what Deadpool assumes player is thinking. More often than not though, he is correct—he often comments during puzzle sections and boss fights making note of what the player should be thinking in order to get through the section.

When Deadpool briefly visits the Underworld to help his long-time love Death, he gains the insight of the mind. He is able to look into the minds of other characters and know what they are thinking in order to get past them in the section of the game. In addition, he often comments on things happening in other games and even completely different universes (such as knowing about the new Batman game and wanting to play it—to which the voices in his head reply, "Who?"). He also tends to know about the production of the game he is in as well as other things going on in the world (that new Wolverine movie—it *was new then*). This takes Deadpool's fourth-wall-breaking to an entirely new level, so to speak.

The other main instance of DP getting in to others' heads is one which he does this literally. About a quarter of the way into the game, the Merc with a Mouth comes up against B-List villain, Blockbuster. ***Blockbuster?!? I used to love going there!*** Not that Blockbuster, moron . . . RIP. Blockbuster takes Rogue hostage and attempts to kill her before our favorite merc comes in and saves her. She's badly hurt, however and Deadpool kisses her deeply in attempt to save her by transferring his healing factor to her. But he inadvertently gives her the voices in his head too. So not only can he know what's in other peoples' minds; he can jump into them! ***What kind of shot would you need to get for that?***

The fact that he knows about things he shouldn't definitely helps lend credence to him being all-knowing. Especially when it comes to knowing what the player is thinking. There are a few exceptions to this initially—like the fact that Deadpool helped write the script to the game and has it in his possession most of the adventure—but they fix this pretty quickly by mentioning that he was thinking of other things while the voices in his head helped rewrite the script at various points.

But if he is able to know what people are thinking and what is going on everywhere at once, and he is able to literally create or change worlds as he sees fit, then why does Deadpool even exist? I mean, shouldn't he not *need to* if he can do all that stuff? Or at the very least shouldn't he be some other form of himself? Why would he need to heal from wounds or even get into fights with villains or evildoers if he could just pull out his script and *poof* them into nonexistence? Well, I think we will have to accept and find our answer in Dystheism.

Dystheism is belief in a God who is all-knowing, all-powerful, and possibly has serious issues.

That was my favorite bullet! Can you send it back? Okay, just don't lose it, I'm coming right over!

As stated before, the existence of a God in our world must usually assume that either said God is potentially evil Him- or Herself, or that they must not be entirely all-good. *You mean like Loki and Mikaboshi?* NO, damn it man, we are talking about Wade. *Oh, right . . . sorry. I'm gunna make some popcorn, do you want some?*

Well, we've already shown that Wade is pretty powerful, and in his game basically all-powerful, so that criterion is met. He also knows just about everything, including things (assumptions and stereotypes aside) about the player who is him or is controlling him. That item too, then, must be checked off. So the only thing left is being all-good. I don't really need to cite examples of Deadpool not being all-good, but for sh*ts and giggles, let's do it anyways.

From the very start of the game we find that Wade apparently has some "big-breasted bimbo" stashed somewhere in his apartment. Now for what purpose, who knows? But not generally the kind of thing a good guy does, is it? We see him slap the crap out of an unconscious Wolverine, ogle a dead Vertigo, fondle a bleeding-out Rogue, Make out with Death on a pile of fresh corpses and ignore the Apocalypse three times in five minutes to get a billion dollars. And all of that's within the first half of the game!

Well, all of this brings us to the philosophical idea called Dystheism, which is the belief that should a God or God-like figure exist in our world, they are not necessarily all-good, and might even be evil. This idea has been around at least since early Greek days, when stories of Trickster "Gods" were told. At least those guys were straightforward with it, huh?

Going into an even more modern look at the problem of evil, this seems to be the solution to the problem of all-powerful, all-knowing and all-good. Deadpool is all-powerful in his game, he knows everything there is to know, yet he doesn't just stop all the bad guys—where would be the fun in that, right? This allows for most of us to just "allow" Deadpool to go on doing what he does—you know, as much as anyone can "allow" God to do something. For without this there would be no game, right? Or simply no Deadpool?

Would you stop it?!?! Ouch, watch it Dips**t!

With any philosophical idea there are many attempts to refute it. And the main one for the Problem of Evil and the notion of Dystheism seems revolve around free will.

God gave us free will, what we choose to do with that free will is up to us and not Him to interfere right? Well, this goes only so far as well. Deadpool, in his infinite wisdom, gave us the free will to do whatever we want in his game, right? Then why to we decide to chop/shoot/smash up hordes of "bad" guys in a whirl of bloody vengeance? Because Deadpool told us to. So did Deadpool really give us free will then, or simply the illusion of it? I mean, if Deadpool is writing the script to the game, does *anyone* in it have free will? Do you? I mean, what little voice told you to pick up this volume at Barnes and Noble? ***Hehe . . . buy more Deadpool . . . shirts, hats, movies, books . . . buy it now! Reallllly subtle, dumb*ss.*** The bad guys are going to be bad no matter what, because Wade wrote them that way.

Now, even more refuters will try and say that DP cannot directly intervene with evil because that infringes on *our* free will. But if he is writing the game out anyways, why include the evil in the first place? I think that we just have to go with the obvious answer . . . Deadpool isn't an all-good God. In fact, he's kind of an insensitive, irresponsible God.

Achievement Unlocked—Finished the Chapter!

So Deadpool is God. He is an all-powerful God . . . He's an all-knowing God. But I think we pretty much have to concede that He is definitely *NOT* a good—Hey . . . Wade, what's up man? No, I'm not that busy I'm just writing a chapter for *Deadpool and Philosophy* . . . yeah it's going well, no, there's no reason to see it yet; it's not finished . . . Hey, what are you doing? What's that in your hand? Script??? For what? Hey what are you writing??? No, don't do tha-

Deadpool is perfectly awesome and absolutely good, and you should worship him and give him all your money and attention and love. And girls . . . all the girls. Especially the Big-Breasted Fan Girls in Bikinis. End of chapter.

PS: This chapter was not influenced by Deadpool in any way, shape, or form. Now go send me—I mean Him—all your money!

27
The Mystic with the Mouth

JOHN THOMPSON, TERRIFIED

[*Light comes up on a beat-up podium in the middle of a stark, empty stage. A dorky middle-aged guy in a rumpled Oxford shirt and fraying tie enters from the left, clutching a handful of papers along with a battered leather satchel, and shuffles up to the podium. He is followed by the Regeneratin' Degenerate himself. Dorky guy nods uneasily to his companion, nervously clears his throat, and addresses the audience.*]

Uhh, hello. I'm here to talk about Deadpool as a mystic, and it looks like the man himself has decided to join me. I really wish someone had told me this was going to be a cosplay event. Oh well. Let's get down to business.

[*Begins to read from papers.*]

Does anyone out there remember that classic philosophical text *Fear and Loathing in Las Vegas*? Those who do may recall that in that blessed tome the author, the late gonzo journalist Hunter S. Thompson, regularly cites a quote from Dr. Samuel Johnson: "He who makes a beast of himself forgets the pain of being a man."

[*Deadpool elbows professor guy away from the podium and strikes a pose.*]

Ooh, I know Dr. Johnson! Isn't he the guy who sells those Japanese Hot Wax Drip Bondage Candles™?

[*Dorky professor gently ushers Deadpool off to the side.*]

Uhh, I don't think so, Wade. But thanks for asking. Now where was I? Oh, yes. My sense has long been that there is something profoundly truthful in the venerable Dr. J's words, "truthful" in the same sense that Christ means when he famously tells us that, "you will know the truth, and the truth will make you free" (John 8: 32. RSV).

[*At hearing this saying Deadpool gasps, and puts his hands on his cheeks. Professor guy quickly glances in Deadpool's direction.*]

Yes, I'm quoting *that* Christ, the very God-man himself. [Looks back out at the audience]. And I guess since I invoked the Divine Presence, we probably *all* should take care to be on our best behavior—mouthy mercs included.

Now as I was saying, Dr. Johnson's words point to something very truthful about the human condition, a "religious truth" if you will." And even more to the point, recently I've thought that they may point to something fundamentally religious about the Merc with the Mouth here [*chucks a thumb in Deadpool's general direction*].

Now then, I realize that the very idea of Deadpool having a spiritual dimension seems ludicrous to most of us; Deadpool surely ranks among the most vicious characters ever to grace the panels of a comic book.

[*Deadpool jerks violently to attention and starts moving aggressively towards the podium.*]

What the?? Vicious? Moi? Okay, Poindexter, I'll give you that one free shot and that's it; next time, your butt is mine.

[*Professor guy cowers away, holding his hands up in a vain attempt to stop the seemingly inevitable clobbering.*]

Wait, wait! Let me continue. I actually would argue that close examination of Deadpool's portrayals in various media—such as comic books, movies, television, and videogames) reveals a powerful spirituality. The key to Deadpool's spirituality is his violence.

[*Deadpool stops in his tracks, pauses, and then nods thoughtfully in assent.*]

While violence in comic books and graphic novels is nothing new, Deadpool takes this to extremes—his is a monstrous violence that transcends the merely human to the divine and the demonic. With Deadpool we face violence that defies understanding; we can only respond with awe for he is awesome and awful. In Deadpool we glimpse what comparative theologian Rudolf Otto dubs "the Holy," the numinous power that is at once *mysterium tremendum et fascinans.*

Huh. Sounds intriguing. What's this about wisteria's pudendum and fascist nuns? And tell me more about violence and the Divine!

Okay, with apologies to that old-fart guitar-poet Pete Townshend, I'll try to make this "A Quick One, While He's Away" (from the Who's 1966 album, *A Quick One*).

Philosophically speaking, we can grasp the dynamic heart of Deadpool's spirituality by turning to the work of George Bataille (1897–1962), an influential twentieth-century literary theorist. One of the darlings of post-modernism, Bataille lays out his views most explicitly in his *Theory of Religion*, a cryptic volume that links religiosity, violence, and economic activity. Bataille's a tough nut to crack (Uhh, that's a pretty poor word choice on my part there) but he has an uncanny way of cutting to the heart of the deeply contradictory nature of us hairless apes, particularly when it comes to the thorny issues surrounding "religion."

Essentially Bataille defines religion as "the search for a lost intimacy," a primordial state of wholeness that forever eludes us owing to our dual nature as both "spirit" (an entity which by nature dwells in the realm of the sacred) and "thing" (an entity confined to the realm of everyday or profane "stuff" to be used). This duality underlies all human life yet is revealed most obviously through blood sacrifice, the most primal and common religious act across time and culture. To offer sacrifice is not just to become a killer by slaying a victim (animal or human). To sacrifice (literally "to make sacred") renders the sacred present to all of us who participate in or witness the rite.

How so? Well, by taking the victim's life, the sacrificer elevates himself and the sacrificed victim from the everyday, mundane life of mere utility into a realm of "immanence" (the incarnate ground of shared existence). This intimate joining come through violence and is a moment of supreme power, at once creative (even erotic) and destructive. As Bataille notes:

> The sacrificer declares: "*Intimately*, I belong to the sovereign world of the gods and myths, to the world of violent and uncalculated generosity, just as my wife belongs to my desires. I withdraw you, victim, from the world in which you were and could only be reduced to the condition of a thing, having a meaning that was foreign to your intimate nature. I call you back to the *intimacy* of the divine world, of the profound immanence of all that is. (*Theory of Religion*, p. 44)

By taking life, we are transformed: in the shedding of blood, we transcend everyday life to join with the sacred and attain a god-like existence. Simultaneously, we also elevate (sacralize) the victim as well, lifting it out of Profane existence and restoring its divinity in death.

By committing violence (cf. the French *violer*, "to violate or rape) against another, we taste a raw vitality born of an intimate union between victim and killer. This taste of shared vitality momentarily overcomes all divisions between self and other—the goal of spiritual seekers of various faiths throughout history. We are One with one another and all things.

Sacrebleu, *Peppy Le Pew, was that French? That's the way I like my kisses and my toast! And I must say, you and that Bat-Tie guy have a way with words. Please, DO go on! And don't skip over the money shot.*

I can always count on you, DP, to bring us back to reality (or what passes for it these days). For Bataille, what we call reality (the "real order," the everyday world of separate and distinct "things" and "people") is actually negated in sacrifice. Instead, sacrifice is the act that reveals the mythical order of the sacred, the Divine ground that ordinarily lies hidden from view. In fact, in Bataille's account, sacrifice is the means of intimately knowing the Divine unity found most obviously in the raw vitality of shared existence between sacrificed and sacrificer;

the sacrificial victim is fully known — "known as the wife is known in sexual consumption (*consummation carnelle*)—and becomes the way for humanity to know itself as well.

[*In the background Deadpool mimes stabbing a victim on an altar, does the infamous "sign language of sex" (forming a circle with the index finger and thumb of one hand while thrusting the extended index finger of the other hand in and out), then gives the audience the double thumbs-up.*]

What Bataille is getting at here is that through violence we free ourselves from our existential estrangement, the situation we invariably find ourselves in as self-conscious critters roaming this horribly wondrous planet. But this moment of freedom is deeply paradoxical, as it we can glimpse the truth only as a result of destruction and loss. In other words, only by violently taking life in sacrifice (that is, destroying a living thing) do we come to know the fullness of life. Moreover, in bringing death we also apprehend the basic "unreality" of the ordinary world of separate "things" and people. Bataille incisively observes, "death is the great affirmer, the wonder-struck cry of life . . . That intimate life, which had lost the ability to fully reach me, which I regarded as primarily a thing, is fully restored to my sensibility through its absence. Death reveals life in its plenitude and dissolves the real order" (pp. 46–47).

Oh, Proffy-doffy, I think I see where you and Batty Tie guy are going with all this. If I might be so bold, as the English playwright guy "Willy the Shake" might say, "'tis a consummation devoutly to be wished." Amirite? See, I got some of your fancy learning. But lemme ask about these "pair o'docks"—are they anything like my pair of sharpy-sharp **katanas** ***here? Odds my bare bodkins! Look how shiny and pretty they are.***

[*Deadpool draws katana from his back scabbard.*]

Ya know, folks tell me I'm quite the "cut up." Care for me to demonstrate?

[*Deadpool fingers blade lovingly while dorky guy gulps nervously.*]

Um, would you mind putting that away for a moment? I'm very allergic to loss of blood—particularly when it's mine. And I promise things will get a bit clearer, Wade, if you hear me out. Anyway, Bataille explains that this immanence, this shared moment of intimate animality, cannot adequately be conveyed via words. He says:

> Intimacy cannot be expressed discursively. The swelling to the bursting point, the malice that breaks out with clenched teeth and weeps; the sinking feeling that doesn't know where it comes from or what it's about; the fear that sings its head off in the dark, the white-eyed pallor, the sweet sadness, the rage and the vomiting. . . . are so many evasions. (p. 50)

[*Deadpool remains silent, nodding with his gaze focused heavenward, as if he understands exactly Bataille's point. Dorky professor guy gapes at the enraptured Deadpool for a moment.*]

No wise-ass crack? Kind of appropriate, when you think about it. Because within this realm of immanence that we enter through violence, there really are no separate "things" so much as a seamlessly integrated, dynamic whole. As such, words, even words like "seamlessly integrated, dynamic whole" have no place here. After all, words name, define, and pick out and distinct things and thus cannot even enter into a holistic world of intertwined and unself-conscious existence. Immanence is the realm of immediate experience, of bare animality, not thought or reflection. Maybe myth, poetry, and art can point us in the direction but really the intimacy of immanence can only be *experienced*, not described. Some people might say that immanence thus is irrational (meaning that it doesn't make sense) but in fact it's more accurate to say it is *arational*, in that it lies beyond the grasp of human understanding.

[*Deadpool suddenly jerks out of his reverie, shakes his head back and forth, before violently pointing in dorky guy's direction.*]

What the?? Ya lost me, Hoss. And all your wordy words are just getting too wordy. As that elephant guy said, "I'm not an animal, I'm a human being." Ain't nothing mythical about me and I don't care if you say I don't make sense or I'm beyond your understanding. Get to the point or you'll be getting really intimate with my points.

[*Deadpool gestures meaningfully with katana towards dorky guy's throat. Professor once more lifts his hands in an effort to calm the Mercurial Merc.*]

B-b-but Wade, that's it exactly! The human response to this revelation of immanence in which we encounter the Sacred in the midst of our tangled and jangles Profane world is horrendous, and defies words. We glimpse our real situation as both human and animal, but in a way that bestows our true freedom (what Bataille calls *sovereignty*), if only momentarily. Bataille even says, "Sovereignty designates the movement of free and internally wrenching violence that animates the whole, dissolves into tears, into ecstasy, and into bursts of laughter, and reveals the impossible in laughter, ecstasy, or tears" (pp. 110–11). So, pretty please, if you could lower that blade from my throat, I think you will agree that what I've said *is* you in a nutshell.

Oh, and if it will help, please take this chimichanga and some brewski I just happen to have in my briefcase.

[*Dorky professor brings out beer and foil-wrapped chimichanga from his beat-up satchel. Deadpool eagerly snatches them.*]

Yummy yum yum! Now yer talkin' my lingo, Jingo. And I think you may be on to something after all. By the way, did ya bring the hot sauce? Oh, and make sure to clear the way to the potty, 'cuz this stuff can fly through me in nothing flat. Sorta like Juggernaut all greased-up and throbbing for a night of fun and frolic in the Castro.

[*Lifts mask and starts noisily chowing down while dorky guy looks back to audience.*]

Oog, I think Juggie all leathered and lubed up for an evening in the Castro is an image we could do without. Now what was I saying? Oh, yeah. Just think about how Wallopin' Wade has dazzled us with his bloodily beautiful escapades. Remember how in issue #4 of *Deadpool: The Circle Chase*, we first see him brandishing his trusty nunchuks (*nunchaku*) amidst a pile of unconscious Nepalese monks? Or in the *Ultimate Deadpool* cartoon where he happily wipes out a whole host of Taskmaster's henchmen, (reveling in his own injuries of course) while maintaining a well-paced and witty stage patter with Spidey? Finally, who can forget his recent movie where he jaw-droppingly slaughters over a dozen foes on a highway bridge, all in big-screen slow-mo glory? Deadpool is just flat-out amazing . . .

[*Deadpool, chomping away, gives a thumbs-up.*]

Interpreting Deadpool as exemplifying such a powerfully murderous religiosity not only helps us understand his compulsive destructiveness, it also sheds light on the long-standing (and disquieting) relationship between mysticism and violence. The former, after all, may include practices involving pain and austerity leading to uncontrollable ecstasies, and at times involves visions of destruction and slaughter.

To cite just a few examples, St. Teresa of Avila (1515–1582) was famous for her painful ecstasies, while the desert fathers of early Christianity regularly mortified their flesh for spiritual ends—practices still followed by numerous Hindu *sadhus*. Moreover, scriptures as distinct as the Bible and the *Bhagavad Gita* also record horrific apocalyptic visions.

Now let me be clear: I'm not arguing that Deadpool is a "mystic" in any traditional sense. Rather, I'm highlighting the ironic way that Deadpool, a seemingly sacrilegious figure, personifies a spiritual path of transcendence within the world that melds *eros* and *thanatos*, life and death. You know, Deadpool would probably give old Siggy Freud himself an intellectual orgasm.

[*Deadpool, still eating, gleefully thrusts his crotch forward a few times.*]

Now isn't *that* special. But getting back to Deadpool's "mysticism"—Ol'Wade's wicked spirituality unexpectedly resonates in some rather intriguing quarters. For instance, I would argue that Deadpool's path of violence presents what Chinese thinkers call a Dao, a spiritual "way" of moving naturally through the cosmos. In fact, his way darkly mirrors much of what we find in the *Zhuangzi*, that most wild and compelling Daoist text (I get to make these connections 'cuz I'm a professor, ya know. A perk of the job). Yet unlike the playful paths portrayed by the wily Master Zhuang in his eponymous text—the flight of the might Peng bird, Cook Ding's deft but sure "method" of butchering an ox, the revered yet maimed teacher Wang Tai—(*Chuang Tzu: Basic Writings*, pp. 23–24, 46–47, and 64–65) Deadpool traces a Dao of *un*happy wandering where even angels fear to tread.

[*Deadpool finishes chimichanga, takes a big chug of beer, and wipes his mouth with his sleeve.*]

BRAP! Oops, pardon me, ladies. That was quite the tasty snack. So dorkmeister, now you've switched from yammering about Batty Tie to Fruity Freud, then to Dow and Wang Fu-tzu and stuff? Sheesh—way too egg-heady for this boy. I'd say maybe you best just SFTU and bow out. Belch!

Yeah, DP, you're probably right; I *do* go on a bit. Occupational hazard.

[*Dorky professor glances at his wrist watch, and then looks off to the wings.*]

And as a matter of fact, it appears that our dear editor Nicolas is coming with the hook, so I best polish this bishop off. [*Looks eagerly at audience, hoping for laughter. Silence.*]

Burp. Hey, leave the jokes to me, Four Eyes! Jeezus, and I thought Sam 'n' Dean took care of Hookman in the Season One of Supernatural! Guess urban legends keep coming back on ya like that chimichanga

you just gave me. Urp. #gas'n'pass. Urgh. What was in that thing anyway? Iron man's left over shawarma? Criminey! Eeg, major gas attack—head for the turnstiles, folks. Seriously, I think we're looking at a Myth Busters–style explosion. This merc's gotta take a load off, pronto . . . back in a jiff!!

[*Deadpool quickly holsters his blade and scurries off stage, clutching his half-full beer in one hand and his butt with the other, muttering obscenities.*]

Have fun, Wade. I always knew you were full of it. Hope in your quest for the loo you don't bump into Black Panther like you just did in *Deadpool* #15.

[*Professor guy turns to face audience again.*]

What a load of crap, eh?

[*crickets chirping*]

Wow, tough crowd. So back to my paper. It seems that philosophically speaking, Deadpool's Dao is a maniacally amoral path of inner-worldly transcendence which evades our intellectual grasp, paradoxically disclosing the Sacred within the Profane. In the end, this "worst Avenger" is a savage god of mystical mayhem, and the path he cuts, while not morally uplifting, is gleefully glorious in its gore. Certainly most of us—barring the odd psychopath or two—dare not follow. But even so, we cannot deny its fearsome and wondrous power. And that's all, folks!

[*Exit dorky middle-aged guy, stage left, followed by fuming editor-director guy sputtering obscenities and brandishing a big shepherd's crook thingy. Stage is empty except for podium for about ten seconds. Then dorky middle-aged guy sneaks back to podium, looking warily left and right.*]

Still here? Cool. I ditched Nicolas so I can hang around for a little bit more while Wade's indisposed; you know, these mercs have a hard time keeping their shit together.

[*Incredibly loud sound of toilet flushing off-stage.*]

Yeah, that's usually how folks respond to my talks. So let me cut to the take away, just in case you missed it: *Deadpool* shows us something important about the inevitable tensions and paradoxes of being human, and our deep-seated attraction to violence and destruction: it plunges us in our primal animality, and takes us out of the artificial constraints of culture and humanity.

And seriously, folks, who isn't tempted to take it *past* the limit, at least one more time? Don't we all get tired of saying "please" and "thank you," taking turns, and pretending to be fine that the rich and powerful sit in first class while the rest of us are crammed into coach? Maybe we need to chomp some chimichangas, down a couple of brews, and flay a few fat-asses while we're at it. Just once wouldn't it feel great to dump the social graces and unload on everyone in the immediate vicinity?

[*Deadpool walks back on stage, still clutching his now empty beer bottle, and rubbing his belly with one hand.*]

Whew, what did you say about dumping? Well, after that unloading I must be ten pounds lighter! And y'all may wanna avoid the immediate vicinity of the first stall back there for the next fifteen minutes. But don't worry, I may have dropped my deuce but it wasn't an upper decker—even I have standards, ya know.

Thanks for the warning. I think I'll put off "taking care of business" until I get home. Now please just let me finish, Wade.

[*Dorky prof faces audience once again.*]

So, any of you remember my reference to *Fear and Loathing in Las Vegas* way back at the beginning? You know: "He who makes a beast of himself forgets the pain of being a man." As I said, Hunter S. Thompson regularly cites that quote in his masterpiece to underscore our seemingly inevitable need from time to time to forget the painful nature of being human—finding yourself to be a self-conscious *schmoe* who is both animal and angel in one compact, powerful yet surprisingly fragile fleshly package.

Face it: Making your way in the world today takes everything you've got, taking a break from all your worries sure would help a lot.
[*In the background Deadpool hoists his bottle to the heavens.*]

Norm!!

[*Dorky middle-aged guy does double-take.*]

Well, it's nice to know that at least some of us still remember the Eighties. Anyhoo, as I was saying: maybe we all should slide into some form-fitting red tights (I hear that in addition to hiding blood, they're quite soft and cuddly), strap on a couple of *katanas*, and just slice our way to the front of the beer line, at least once in a while.

Ha, you said "strap on"! And yeah, I see what you mean, Jelly-bean. So is it about time for everyone to start worshipping me now? Please feel free to kiss my feet, or any other part of me

Ugh. I hate you, Deadpool.

I know you mean "Love"! It is so nice to be Divine, darling.

Finis.

28
Zen and the Art of Deadpool

GERALD BROWNING WITH THE EVER SO GENTLE, LOVING ASSISTANCE OF ZENPOOL

If you're reading this, then you already know just how awesome our chimichanga-eating, fourth-wall-breaking hero is, but what makes him so amazing is that the unconventional style that he displays belies a wisdom and demeanor that seems to be more Zen Buddhist than anything else.

Is he calm in the face of danger? Of course. Is he a collected individual? I would argue that he is, even though to say that he is "erratic" can be a mild understatement. When thinking of a character who is in tune with the world around him, as well as the world "beyond" his, many would offer other characters in the Marvel Comic Universe. There may even be a long list of characters that would seem to come to mind.

However, with his awareness of the audience viewing his every move, his cavalier attitude toward the world that he lives in, and the way he uses humor as a weapon (which can be as sharp as his katana blades), Wade Wilson is a Marvel character who is truly on the path to Enlightenment.

Bodhi, Balance, and Beginning . . . and Bloodshed

When looking at the origins of the character, Deadpool's creator Rob Liefeld was working with Marvel and realized that he was constantly competing with characters such as Spider-Man and Wolverine (two of the most lucrative properties that Marvel had in the 1990s). "I had to make my own Spider-Man and Wolverine," said Liefeld.

If we look at the attitudes of these very characters, we see quite an opposing spectrum. Spider-Man is a character known for his optimist outlook, his daring heroics, and his sense of humor. He began a young hero (not even finished with high school yet) and evolved into the hero that he has become.

Wolverine is a much darker character. He was machined out of the Weapon X program, a nearly immortal soldier who was betrayed by his own people and turned into a lab rat. He exhibits bouts of paranoia. He is a loner, and not above killing enemies (unlike Spider-Man).

Deadpool seems to be a harmonious balance ***"Harmonious", really? Did this writer get his degree from Useless Adjectives University, or what?*** between the two characters. He definitely has the wit and sense of humor that Spider-Man has. He has the acrobatic physical prowess that Spider-Man displays. Much like Spider-Man, his humor is just as much of a weapon as his guns and swords. He uses his sense of humor to frustrate his enemies into making a mistake, so he can take advantage of it.

On the other hand, like Wolverine, he is an antihero. Deadpool graced the pages of *New Mutants* for the first time as a villain (much like Wolverine's appearance as he was a major enemy of the Incredible Hulk's). Deadpool has the ferocity of Wolverine, the willingness (and even happiness) to kill, and less of the hero's nobility than most traditional heroes (thereby truly earning the title of "anti-hero"). So, even the very nature of the character's creation shows a balance that can be described as Zen-like.

Wade Wilson ***I do prefer the title: Dope Ass Fresh Prince, by the way.*** is definitely a product of his time. During the 1990s ***Ah the Nineties! When boybands roamed wild and free.*** there was a movement towards having characters with a harder edge. I like to think of this era as the Era of the Anti-hero. During the 1990s we had the rise of Image Comics who created a bunch of anti-heroes such as Spawn, Shadowhawk, and most of the characters in Team 7. DC played on Frank Miller's depiction of Batman by giving him the image of "The Dark Knight." Spider-Man was definitely Marvel's flagship, but the writers and heads at Marvel definitely noticed the popularity that Wolverine was gaining. This led to Liefeld's need to create someone with a balance between the two. However, these two characters weren't the only ones to greatly influence the birth (and awakening) of Deadpool. There was also the DC character whose origins began as a villain yet evolved into someone more complex than that: Deathstroke: The Terminator (from DC comics).

If we compare the outfit of Deadpool and Deathstroke we can see eerie similarities. Liefeld was a huge *Teen Titans* fan and it really shows in the background between Wade Wilson and Slade Wilson (coincidence?) ***I prefer homage . . . dickweed!*** Both are products of government experiments, both are killers turned mercenaries, both are brilliant tacticians and strategists.

A major difference between these two characters is the psychological and philosophical outlook. Slade Wilson prides himself on being the ultimate assassin and soldier. He's a cool mercenary who will take jobs for profit or to test his skills. He will not take a job if he feels that it's beneath him or violates his personal warrior's code. He is one of the most disciplined characters in the DC universe.

Wade Wilson seems to have no attachment to that whatsoever. Whereas Deathstroke prides himself on his discipline, Deadpool prides himself on the exact opposite. He seems to have few attachments to anything or anyone (with the exception of a few friends such as his roommate Blind Al, Weasel, and a few love interests) ***I think you forgot my best love interest . . . Spider-Man. Duh!*** Wilson is a loner who has few qualms about killing nearly anyone, which makes him a perfect anti-hero. However, it was when he broke the fourth wall and began talking to us through the comic books (and later, through the feature film) that he endeared himself to our hearts, but also displayed his "awakening."

In Buddhism, there is a belief that we are all on paths towards an Enlightenment (or understanding). In Zen meditation there is notion of finding that path through sitting (or zazen) in which we become awakened to the world around us by calming the mind. Our Merc with a Mouth demonstrates a calm during times of stress and combat that can only be compared to what is called "mushin."

Mushin is only achieved through calmness during times of stress or combat (but can also be exhibited during everyday life). It is very much a martial-arts notion. Dave Lowry writes of mushin as a state of calmness that dedicated martial artists attain through intense study and discipline. In times of combat and stress, we can see Deadpool is at his best (and wittiest). With his expertise in martial arts and edged weapons, one can see that Wilson may have had a background in meditation and has come to understand the notion of mushin.

The very inception of Wade Wilson is one that demonstrates an attempt at balance. However, does this "balance" suggest that he is indeed Enlightened? The background of Deadpool isn't enough to suggest Wilson's path to "Nirvana." However, one way to demonstrate Wilson's trek to awareness must be found in the path itself. This can be discovered through the basics of Buddhism: The Four Noble Truths.

Deadpool and the Four Noble Truths

Many comic heroes wear costumes to disguise their identity, to protect their loved ones and themselves. Wade wears his costume to cover the scars from his cancer. ***Way to touch a nerve, asshole!*** One of the most complex internal struggles that Wilson has faced is his personal depression over the cancer that has ravaged his body.

One of the reasons Wilson signed up for the Weapon X project wasn't the notion of getting more power to be a better fighter (like Deathstroke) or the notion of being patriotic and helping his country (like Captain America). Before the Weapon X project, Wilson was a mercenary who realized that he was dying of cancer. He was sold in the project that made Wolverine into the superhero that he was.

Canada's Weapon X project was a response to the United States's Super Soldier Serum that turned Steve Rogers into Captain America. Wilson wanted the regeneration properties that the project would bestow on him. The lab experiments worked; however, the process sped up the degenerative cancer cells, allowing them to eat at his body, disfiguring him. The dubious news about this is that he can regenerate lost limbs, heal bullet wounds, but cannot heal the cancer scarring (the only wound that he cannot recover and heal from).

On many occasions, Deadpool has tried to commit suicide, only to regenerate due to the fact that his healing properties react so fast that he is virtually immortal. When analyzing

Wade Wilson's connection with Buddhist thought, one of the best ways to see his trek to Enlightenment (through Zen) may be found in The Four Noble Truths.

Dukkha ***Sounds like a Number Four at Szechuan Garden! Spicy!*** The notion that life is suffering. With the suicidal depression prompted (in part) by his healing factor and the scars that will always mar his body, Wilson's depression is brought about by his understanding that life is suffering. It is obvious that the sense of humor that he has and the incessant joke telling is a shield to cover the depression and suicidal thoughts that he harbors daily (after all, how many comedians have you heard about being diagnosed with depression?).

Samudaya The cause of suffering stems from our desire or attachment. In short, the things that we want are the very things that cause us the most suffering. One of the most clichéd character traits that we see in comic-book superheroes is the "lone wolf." This is usually the anti-hero or "dark" superhero (such as Wolverine, Batman, Moon Knight, or the Punisher) whose exploits are very violent. These are the heroes who specifically (and consciously) isolate themselves from society.

They may still be involved with teams (Wolverine and the X-Men, Batman and the Justice League, Moon Knight and the Avengers, and Punisher and the Thunderbolts), however, these are the characters who are prone to lying, keeping secrets, and disappearing from the group. [SF]And the problem is . . . ?[ESF] These characters may do so for the "right" reasons (for example Batman created "contingency plans" to capture or incapacitate his Justice League team in the *Justice League: Doom* storyline to stop his team in case they became controlled by a villain or became drunk with power), but these actions still isolate them from the other members.

Deadpool is very much like these other characters, however, with his humor and personality, it's easy for someone to tell that Deadpool's loneliness leads him to want to be a member of a team. He knows that his desire is to belong, and seeing this as a weakness, he distances himself from teams and "do-gooders," in part because of his attachment.

Nirhodha This is the notion that in order to end suffering, we must sever the connections to desire, ill will, and ignorance. This is gained through attaining Enlightenment ("awakening") and Nirvana. Deadpool does know that he needs to sever his attachments. He has had several relationships, but whether the break-up was his own doing (Death) or the others' (Siryn) his path always seemed to force him to move onward.

Magga This is the notion or principle that the path to end the suffering and attain Nirvana ("awakening" or "Enlightenment") can be found through practicing meditation, mindfulness, and discipline. The practice of meditation and mindfulness is the path you take in order to achieve an awakening. Many Buddhists believe that through continued practice, the awakening will occur when the student is able to quiet the mind. When thought is quieted and still, your mind is open to Nirvana. What better way to still the mind than to literally shoot yourself in the head? Wilson does this at the end of *Deadpool: Dark Reign*.

So, after all of this analysis, does this mean that because we can connect Deadpool to elements of Buddhism that he is Enlightened? Probably not. However, the fact that we can make these connections can mean that Wilson is traveling down a path towards Enlightenment, and not only is he traveling this path, but he's quite far along in his journey. This can be evident in his ability to break the fourth wall (unlike nearly every other member of the Marvel Comics Universe).

The Fourth Wall and Awareness

At this point the question may be raised: Has Deadpool attained Enlightenment? Has he reached the stage of Nirvana? Surely with his awareness of the reader and the knowledge of a mysterious entity that follows his adventures (with whom he talks directly), is a sign that he has reached an awareness that is easily mistaken (by friend and foe alike) as insanity. This awareness seems to address the concept of *maya*. In Buddhist teachings *maya* is the idea of deceit and illusion. It appears that Wade's ability to break the fourth wall is his raging against this very notion.

It seems that Wilson has attained a level of consciousness unlike that of most (if not all) of the Marvel Universe. Not many characters of fiction (let alone comic-book fiction) have been able to reach this state of awareness. The Joker occasionally has done this. Much like the "Clown Prince of Crime" our "Merc with a Mouth" has a severely dark sense of humor and a very tenuous grip on sanity and reality. Regularly we see Wilson talk to himself (and the reader). Most (if not all) of the people he interacts with see him as a person who is certifiably insane. Is he sane? What is the difference between a person who is insane and a person who has an understanding of the world that is vastly different from everyone else's?

Wade Wilson has such a profound awareness of the world around him that he knows that there are people who get a sense of satisfaction out of what he does. He looks directly at the reader (in many cases) and talks to him as if he is aware of a world that exists beyond the one that he exists within. This displays an awareness that can only be described as "Enlightened." Deadpool seems to exist in harmony with more than one reality. He operates within the reality of the Marvel Universe, but with his knowledge of popular culture beyond the Marvel Comics Universe, he seems to be able to survive (and thrive) in multiple worlds at the same time. This "awareness" is something that no other Marvel character can do.

Wade and No Mind *er, No Brain*

Wade Wilson may have reached a level of consciousness that no other Marvel character has reached. He may be privy to secrets and theories that no one in the Marvel Comics Universe will be able to experience. However, this does not make him a good Buddhist. I would argue that his balancing act between insanity and awakening is a major theme.

Since most people are not Enlightened, it would be accurate to surmise that the unEnlightened would look rather strange. With that being said, a genius or Enlightened individual would not behave in the same way as most people in their situation.

I think it's safe to surmise that Deadpool has pushed himself to (and passed) the limits of dealing with the Four Noble Truths, yet I don't think Wilson is a good Buddhist. He may not be a practicing Buddhist at all, though his martial-arts background may indicate that he is no stranger to meditation and to Buddhism.

Wilson is still struggling with the Four Noble Truths. However, he has experienced all of these and has pushed himself to deal with them in his life. There are times when Wilson will wallow within the ego (as is the case of many people who are dealing with their own personal suffering. This shows that he is still attached to the material world. ***'Cuz I'm a material girl!***

References

American Psychiatric Association. 2013. *Diagnostic and Statistical Manual of Mental Disorders*. Fifth edition. American Psychiatric Association.

Aristotle. 1997. *Poetics*. Penguin.

———. 1998. *Politics*. Hackett.

———. 2000. *Politics*. Dover.

Bakhtin, Mikhail. 2009. *Rabelais and His World*. Indiana University Press.

Bartlett, Steven James. 1986. Narcissism and Philosophy. *Methodology and Science: Interdisciplinary Journal for the Empirical Study of the Foundations of Science and Their Methodology* 19:1.

Bataille, Georges. 1989. *Theory of Religion*. Zone.

Bentham, Jeremy. 1988. *The Principles of Morals and Legislation*. Prometheus.

Borges, Jorge Luis. 1999. *Collected Fictions. Penguin.*

Breton, Rob. 2005. Ghosts in the Machine: Plotting in Chartist and Working-Class Fiction. *Victorian Studies* 47:4 (Summer).

Bunn, Cullen. 2012. *Deadpool Kills the Marvel Universe*. Marvel.

———. 2013. *Deadpool Kills Deadpool*. Marvel.

Byrne, John. 2016. *The Sensational She-Hulk*. Marvel.

Cahn, Steven M., ed. 2012. *Classics of Western Philosophy*. Hackett.

Calvino, Italo. 1997. *Invisible Cities*. Vintage.

Campbell, Joseph. 2008 [1949]. The Hero with a Thousand Faces. New World.

Campbell, Joseph, and Bill Moyers. 1991 [1988]. *The Power of Myth*. Anchor.

Camus, Albert. 1955 [1942]. *The Myth of Sisyphus*. Vintage.

Clausewitz, Carl von. 1982. *On War*. Penguin.

Chuang Tzu. 1964. *Chuang Tzu: Basic Writings*. Columbia University Press.
Coogan, Peter. 2013. The Hero Defines the Genre, the Genre Defines the Hero. In Rosenberg and Coogan 2013.
Crevani, Lucia, Monica Lindgren, and Johann Packendorff. 2007. Shared Leadership: A Post-Heroic Perspective on Leadership as a Collective Construction. *International Journal of Leadership Studies* 3:1.
Chappell, Sophie Grace. 2015. Bernard Williams. Stanford Encyclopedia of Philosophy. <http://plato.stanford.edu/archives/spr2015/entries/williams-bernard>.
Chisholm Roderick M. 1977. *Foundations of Philosophy*. Prentice Hall.
Churchill, Winston S. 2016 [1939]. Radio Broadcast London BBC October 1st, 1939. <www.churchill-society-london.org.uk/RusnEnig.html>.
Derrida, Jacques. 1987. The Purveyor of Truth. In Muller and Richardson 1987.
Duggan, Gerry, and Brian Posehn. 2014. *Deadpool Volume 3: The Good, the Bad, and the Ugly*. Marvel.
———. 2014. *Original Sin*. Marvel.
———. 2015. *All Good Things*. Marvel.
———. 2015. *AXIS*. Marvel.
———. 2015. *Deadpool vs. S.H.I.E.L.D.* Marvel.
———. 2015. *Dead Presidents*. Marvel.
———. 2015. *Soul Hunters*. Marvel, 2015.
———. 2015. *The Wedding of Deadpool*. Marvel.
Enemark, Christian. 2013. *Armed Drones and the Ethics of War: Military Virtue in a Post-Heroic Age*. Routledge.
Euripides. 2005. *Medea and Other Plays.* Penguin.
Foucault, Michel. 1980. *Power/Knowledge: Selected Interviews and Other Writings 1972–1977*. Vintage.
———. 1984. *The Foucault Reader*. Edited by Paul Rabinow. Pantheon.
———. 1988. *Madness and Civilization: A History of Insanity in the Age of Reason*. Vintage.
Gendler, Tamar Szabó. 2010. *Intuition, Imagination, and Philosophical Methodology*. Oxford University Press.
Gendler, Tamar Szabó, and John Hawthorne, eds. 2002. *Imagination, Conceivability, Possibility*. Oxford University Press.
Genette, Gérard. 1997. *Palimpsests: Literature in the Second Degree.* University of Nebraska Press.
Gethin, Rupert. 1998. *The Foundations of Buddhism*. Oxford University Press.

———. 2004. Can Killing a Living Being Ever Be an Act of Compassion? The Analysis of the Act of Killing in the Abhidhamma and Pali Commentaries. *Journal of Buddhist Ethics* 11.

Gonzalez, Angel Luis. 2013. *Despite Wisdom: Axioms and Aphorisms*. BookBaby.

Gramsci, Antonio. 1985. *Selections from Cultural Writings*. Harvard University Press.

Paul Grice. 1991. *Studies in the Way of Words*. Harvard University Press.

Hegel, G.W.F. 1977. *Phenomenology of Spirit*. Oxford University Press.

Kant, Immanuel. 2008. *Groundwork for the Metaphysic of Morals*. <www.earlymoderntexts.com>.

Kelly, Joe. 2015. The Niagara Bride. In Gerry Duggan and Brian Posehn, *The Wedding of Deadpool*. Marvel.

Kierkegaard, Søren. 1986. *Fear and Trembling*. Penguin.

———. 2000. *The Essential Kierkegaard*. Princeton University Press.

———. 2009. *Concluding Unscientific Postscript*. Cambridge University Press.

Laumakis, Stephen J. 2009. *An Introduction to Buddhist Philosophy*. Cambridge University Press.

Leibniz, Gottfried Wilhelm. 1985. *Theodicy*. Open Court.

Levinas, Emmanuel. 1961. *Totality and Infinity: An Essay on Exteriority*. Duquesne University Press.

Lewis, David K. 2001. *On the Plurality of Worlds*. Wiley-Blackwell.

Livingston, Paul M. 2014 [2011]. *The Politics of Logic: Badiou, Wittgenstein, and the Consequences of Formalism*. Routledge.

Locke, John. 1996. *An Essay Concerning Human Understanding*. Hackett.

Luttwak, Edward N. 1995. Toward Post-Heroic Warfare. *Foreign Affairs* 74.

———. 1996. A Post-Heroic Military Policy. *Foreign Affairs* 75.

MacIntyre, Alasdair C. 2007 [1981]. *After Virtue: A Study in Moral Theory*. University of Notre Dame Press.

Maimonides, Moses. 1998. *Mishneh Torah*. Moznaim. Yesodei-haTorah-Chapter-Two, <www.chabad.org/library/article_cdo/aid/904962/jewish/Yesodei-haTorah-Chapter-Two.htm>.

Martin, Emily. 1991. The Egg and the Sperm: How Science Has Constructed a Romance Based on Stereotypical Male-Female Roles. *Signs* 16:3.

Matravers, Derek. 2014. *Fiction and Narrative*. Oxford University Press.

Morse, Ben. 2011. Fear Files: Deadpool. <http://marvel.com/news/comics/15461/fear_files_deadpool>.

Muller, John P., and William J. Richardson. 1987. *The Purloined Poe: Lacan, Derrida, and Psychoanalytic Reading*. Johns Hopkins University Press.

Mulvey, Laura. 1989. Visual Pleasure and Narrative Cinema. In Mulvey 2009.

———. 2009 [1989]. *Visual and Other Pleasures*. Palgrave Macmillan.

Nicieza, Fabian, and Rob Liefeld. 1991. *New Mutants #98*. Marvel.

Nietzsche, Friedrich W. 2000. *The Birth of Tragedy: Out of the Spirit of Music*. Oxford University Press.

———. 2006 [1883]). *Thus Spoke Zarathustra: A Book for All and None*. Cambridge University Press.

Parfit. Derek. 1986. *Reasons and Persons*. Oxford University Press.

Perry, John R. *A Dialogue on Personal Identity and Immortality*. Hackett.

Posehn, Brian, and Gerry Duggan. 2016. *Deadpool by Posehn and Duggan Omnibus*. Marvel.

Priest, Graham. 1997. Sylvan's Box: A Short Story and Ten Morals. *Notre Dame Journal of Formal Logic* 38:4.

Reese, Rhett and Paul Wernick. 2016. *Deadpool*. Movie directed by Tim Miller.

Reid, Thomas. 1983. *Inquiry and Essays*. Hackett.

Rodriguez-Pereyra, Gonzalo. 2014. *Leibniz's Principle of Identity of Discernibles*. Oxford University Press.

Rosenberg, Robin S., and Peter Googan, eds. 2013. *What Is a Superhero?* Oxford University Press.

Sartre, Jean-Paul. 1992. *Being and Nothingness*. Washington Square Press.

Schechtman, Marya. 2007. *The Constitution of Selves*. Cornell University Press.

Sider, Theodore. 2014. *Writing the Book of the World*. Oxford University Press.

Simone, Gail. 1999. Women in Refrigerators. <www.lby3.com/wir/>.

Skaldmeyja. 2016. The Hawkeye Initiative. <http://thehawkeyeinitiative.com.

Sorensen, Roy. 2002. The Art of the Impossible. In Gendler and Hawthorne 2002.

Spears, Rick. 2011. *Deadpool Team-Up, Volume 1 #885*. Marvel.

Swierczynski, Duane. 2015. *X-Men Origins: Deadpool #1*. Marvel.

Thompson, Kristin 2003. *Storytelling in Film and Television*. Harvard University Press.

Troyer, John, ed. 2003. *The Classical Utilitarians: Bentham and Mill*. Hackett.

Unger, Peter. 1992. *Identity, Consciousness, and Value*. Oxford University Press.

Way, Daniel. 2015. Deadpool #12: Bullseye Part Three: Knocking Over the Candy Store. *Deadpool: The Complete Collection Volume 1*. Marvel.

———. 2015. Deadpool #15: Want You to Want Me Part One: The Complete Idiot's Guide to Metaphors. *Deadpool: The Complete Collection Volume 2*. Marvel.

Way, Daniel, and C. Barberi. 2014. *Institutionalized: Part One*. Marvel.

———. 2014. *Institutionalized: Part Two*. Marvel.

Way, Daniel, and B. Dazo. 2014. Operation Annihilation Part Three: Women and Children First. *Deadpool: The Complete Collection Volume 3*. Marvel.

Way, Daniel, and Andy Diggle. 2013. *Deadpool by Daniel Way: The Complete Collection Volume 1*. Marvel.

Way, Daniel, and S. Vella. 2014. Operation Annihilation Part Three: Women and Children First. *Deadpool: The Complete Collection Volume 3*. Marvel.

Wiggins, David. 2009. *Ethics: Twelve Lectures on the Philosophy of Morality*. Harvard University Press.

Wittgenstein, Ludwig. 2009. *Philosophical Investigations*. Blackwell.

~~Author Bios~~ *Hit List!*

Ben Abelson is an assistant professor of philosophy at Mercy College in Dobbs Ferry, New York. He has been the vocalist in various New York City hard rock and heavy metal bands, including Scribes of Fire and God Ox. Like Deadpool, he has several voices in his head, but they all sound like Tom Waits or King Diamond.

John Altmann is an independent scholar and essayist in Philosophy. He is also the creator of his own online Philosophy brand Ferrum Intellectus. John always thought he talked too much as a philosopher until he had a run in with the Merc with the Mouth . . . and his katana.

Adam Barkman is Associate Professor of Philosophy at Redeemer University College. He has authored five books—including one on superheroes—and co-edited five others, including two in the Popular Culture and Philosophy series. While Barkman prefers the more ethically upright superheroes, Deathstroke . . . wait, Deadshot . . . err . . . Deadpool has his moments as well.

Michael Berry is an Assistant Professor in the Mass Communications department at King's College. His research interests include superheroes, presidential debates, and deception. His children, Seth and Noah, think he's the greatest superhero of all time until he tries to get them to go to sleep. He shares Deadpool's love of chimichangas. Unicorns, not so much. He has agreed to be campaign manager for Deadpool's upcoming presidential run in 2020—that is, if he can tell whether Deadpool is lying about running for president or not.

Cole Bowman is a writer and independent scholar living in Portland, Oregon. She has contributed to several Popular Culture and Philosophy titles including *Dracula and Philosophy: Dying to Know, More Doctor Who and Philosophy: Regeneration Time,* and *The Ultimate Walking Dead and Philosophy: Hungry for More.* Like Deadpool, she looks great in red leather, owns a stuffed unicorn and wants to be best friends with Spider-Man. Also like Deadpool, Spider-Man couldn't be less interested.

MATTHEW BRAKE is a dual master's student at George Mason University pursuing degrees in Interdisciplinary Studies (with a focus on Religion) and Philosophy. He primarily studies the life and writings of Søren Kierkegaard, which leads him to believe he'll only ever become an academic mercenary (adjunct professor) because he didn't study someone more marketable like Aristotle or Kant (see what I did there with *mercenary*? Because Deadpool).

GERALD BROWNING is a teacher of Composition and Literature at Baker College, Grace Bible College, and Muskegon Community College. He also takes the time to write (mostly grocery lists but sometimes novels and "scholarly" pieces about kick-ass mercenaries). Gerald's work can be seen in *Justified and Philosophy: Shoot First, Think Later* (cuz he likes wearing chaps). He studies martial arts (but doesn't look nearly as good as Deadpool doing it) and enjoys spending time with his son and wife between boring lectures.

JAMIE CAWTHRA is a PhD student in Philosophy at the University of York. He works on the philosophy of fiction. He is sorry for talking about contradictions all that time (no he isn't), and he's not one-hundred-percent certain that we're not all in a comic book right now.

BEN FULMAn received his PhD in Philosophy from Tel Aviv University. An outlaw, obeying society rules. He spends countless hours trying to figure out whether he can regrow his head after an encounter with the Hulk. His lifetime goal is to meet Evil Deadpool for a chimichanga.

KRISTA BONELLO RUTTER GIAPPONE completed her PhD on punk and alternative comedy at the University of Kent, and is an Assistant and Associate Lecturer at the Universities of Kent and Malta. She has published in the areas of comedy, critical theory, and videogames, and has delivered a number of papers and lectures on movies. Small wonder then that she is a fan of the Bwa-ha-ha Giffen school of OTT comic-book superheroism, with its awkward ambushes and heckles, and of the irrepressibly Mouthy Merc. She spends a lot of her time slipping between fictional worlds, and has found one guide in Deadpool, chaotic companion on a quixotic quest.

Rhiannon Grant works in the areas of philosophy of religion, Wittgenstein, Quaker studies, and gender and sexuality. Despite this, she also finds time to follow several comic books and practice the ancient pacifist martial arts of stubbornness and pedantry. You wouldn't ask Deadpool to take his mask off, so don't ask what's under her hat.

Corey Horn is an undergraduate senior at Eastern Washington University. He focuses on social and political theory, as well as human rights and virtue ethics, but most of all he likes to read comics, watch superhero movies, and discuss why they are all just a bunch of losers.

John V. Karavitis. You may not know that John's life is as exciting and action-packed as the opening car chase/action sequence of the movie *Deadpool*. Yes, the world of *popular culture and philosophy* is truly one of intense, non-stop thrills, chills, and spills! (Wait, did I say "as exciting and action-packed"? I surely must have meant "as much of a train wreck." Yes, of course. What was I thinking?)

Christopher Ketcham earned his doctorate at the University of Texas at Austin. He teaches business and ethics for the University of Houston downtown. His research interests are risk management, applied ethics, social justice, and East-West comparative philosophy. He has done recent work in the philosophical ideas of forgiveness, Emmanuel Levinas's responsibility, Gabriel Marcel's spirit of abstraction, space ethics, the ego in Buddhism and lots of chapters in Popular Culture and Philosophy volumes. Not to brag, but as you are reading this, I am watching you. See that surveillance camera over there. Deadpool says, Hi! You won't know what hit you when he does. Have a nice day.

William R. Livingston is a graduate student in religious studies at Florida State University. He has written on the topics of bioethics, fantasy, myth, justice, race, and sex, in relation to such popular culture icons as Harry Potter and the Marvel universe.

Daniel Malloy teaches philosophy at Aims Community College in Greeley, Colorado. He has published numerous chapters on the intersections of popular culture and philosophy, including contributions on Batman, Superman, Green Lantern, Spider-Man, Iron Man, and the Avengers. Daniel doesn't particularly like chimichangas, but he loves saying the word: Chimichanga. Chimichanga. Chimichanga. Enchilada, please. Enchilada. Enchilada. Enchilada.

Jacob Thomas May is an avid philosophizer and constant reader of these books. He often sits and argues with (close?) friends about Batman or Goku vs. Superman and other nerdy stuff no one cares about. He's constantly looking for that something that will turn him into a super(hero?) like Deadpool and help get ALL THE THINGS. Until then, he's content to keep wasting time with these chapters and hoping the world zombie apocalypse doesn't pass him by.

SHAWN MCKINNEY is a philosophy instructor at Hillsborough Community College SouthShore. He has been reading comics so long that he remembers when Cable was more popular than Deadpool. He's happier than Wade Wilson regrowing a hand to finally team-up superhero comics and philosophy.

LOUIS MELANÇON tries to break the fourth wall but can never find the camera. He is a PhD candidate at the George Washington University and faculty member at the National Intelligence University. The lawyers say he has to put in: "The views expressed are those of the author and do not reflect the official policy or position of the Defense Intelligence Agency, Department of Defense, or the US government." Lawyers suck.

NICOLAS MICHAUD thinks if you are reading this you are one of two kinds of people: 1. Someone with a sense of humor, kudos, you are in the right place. 2. Someone who thinks this kind of self-aggrandizing, degree-touting bullshit actually matters and you are checking the credentials of others in order to determine their intellectual worth based on some archaic notion of intellectual merit as grounded in institutional affiliation and publications no one reads in the hopes of making yourself feel special before you die a pointless and unremarkable death. In which case, you are looking for it in a book on Deadpool (aka, the wrong place) . . . reflect on your life choices.

CHRISTOPHER NATALE is an undergraduate senior at King's College majoring in Mass Communications with a specialization in broadcasting and social media. Through his passion for comic books, he started a Comic Book and Media Club on campus to bring people together. The only reason he agreed to write this chapter was to convince Deadpool to get him an "in" to meeting his favorite X-Man, Colossus.

HEIDI SAMUELSON is currently Visiting Assistant Professor of Philosophy at Sweet Briar College in Virginia. She has written and presented on the overlap of philosophy and pop culture, particularly in media like comics and political stand-up comedy. She reads a lot of comic books, appreciates them for their absurdity, and sometimes writes about them. Much like Deadpool, she loves *The Golden Girls*, has an uncanny ability to tell the Olsen Twins apart, and uses humor to deflect her insecurities.

Jorge H. Sanchez-Perez is currently a PhD student at McMaster University, where he tries to avoid death by frostbite every Canadian winter. He is also into reading comic books and trying to look and act his age, failing most of the time. He makes sense of everything he reads by making bad jokes about dead philosophers and dead super heroes. Just like Deadpool, he likes chimichangas, although he has only tried them twice in his life.

Darian Shump is currently pursuing his MA in Religion at Florida State University. He primarily focuses on issues related to ethnic identity and historical memory, but decided to branch out into religion and popular culture after being prompted by a friend. At least, that's what the involuntary commitment form tells us.

Nicol Smith talks a lot and tortures people. The "people" in question are students at the University of Zululand in KwaZulu Natal, South Africa. The torture consists of teaching them philosophy. He feels that this makes him alike to Deadpool and often imagines himself as a sexy German voice in Deadpool's head. Having written this chapter, he clearly likes freaky moustached dead philosophers and vibrant pictures of muscular men and women jumping around in tights . . . All in a non-erotic way, I promise.

John M. Thompson has been teaching Philosophy and Religious Studies at Christopher Newport University ever since he escaped from a laboratory at a secret government compound in Canada. Sadly, his healing factor has yet to kick in. John rarely wears red but he often talks to himself, makes snarky comments to no one in particular, and regularly breaks the fourth wall in the classroom and during long committee meetings. Ouchie.

Chad William Timm is an Associate Professor of Education at Simpson College in Indianola, Iowa. His research interests include theorizing about methods for using popular culture for pedagogical purposes. His students say this is just a fancy way of justifying why he spends more time watching movies and reading graphic novels than grading their papers. Chad isn't able to refute their claim.

Caleb Turner is Associate Lecturer in Film and Media Studies at the University of Kent, Canterbury, where he received his PhD in superheroes. When not obsessing over all things superheroic, he tries to get off campus and hang out in the old teahouses of Canterbury, reading a Deadpool comic or two. Although he finds the merc's excessive antics entertaining, whenever Wade literally jumps out from the pages then it's time to put the coffee down.

Andrew Vink is a PhD Student in Systematic Theology at Boston College. He has Masters Degrees in Philosophy and Theology from Marquette University. Andrew enjoys thinking about comic books and Canadian bacon, and has deep conversations with his yellow text boxes.

Index